DO THE BIRDS STILL SING IN HELL?

A powerful story of love and survival

HORACE GREASLEY

JOHN BLAKE

Published by John Blake Publishing,
The Plaza,
535 Kings Road,
Chelsea Harbour,
London SW10 0SZ

www.facebook.com/johnblakebooks
twitter.com/jblakebooks

First published in paperback in 2013
This edition published in 2019

Paperback ISBN: 978 1 78946 161 9
Ebook ISBN: 978 1 78219 641 9

British Library Cataloguing-in-Publication Data:

A catalogue record for this book is available
from the British Library.

Design by www.envydesign.co.uk

Printed and bound in Great Britain by Clays Ltd, Elcograf S.p.A.

3 5 7 9 10 8 6 4 2

MIX
Paper from
responsible sources
FSC
www.fsc.org   FSC® C018072

John Blake Publishing is an imprint of Bonnier Books UK
www.bonnierbooks.co.uk

For Brenda

ACKNOWLEDGEMENTS

For all the lads who never made it, and especially for Jock for his culinary skills with the little bit extra I was able to provide for the pot. And for Rose for making my life as a prisoner that little bit more bearable. But especially for my wife Brenda who urged me on to get this book written. For the unconditional care and attention she has given me throughout our marriage and especially in the last eight years when my health has failed me. Without her I wouldn't be here now to tell this tale.

Brenda, this book is for you.

Thanks to Ken Scott, without whom this book would never have been written, and to his wife Hayley, daughter Emily and son Callum. I thank them for taking such a keen interest; they have now become some of our closest friends.

CONTENTS

FOREWORD
BY THE AUTHOR KEN SCOTT

In the spring of 2008 I reluctantly agreed to meet up with an elderly gentleman. He was 89 years old. I was desperately trying to finish off my third book and had another two projects on the go, when I was notified that an ex-POW wanted to write his Second World War memoirs. 'Oh no,' I said to my wife, 'not another war story.'

It was a man called Filly Bullock who introduced the two of us in a small town called Alfaz del Pi on Spain's Costa Blanca, the White Coast, on an unusually hot March day. Filly had warned me I was about to stumble on the greatest World War Two story never told and that I would fall over myself to write it.

I secretly bet my bottom dollar that I wouldn't. This old boy just doesn't know how busy I am, I thought to myself, and anyway he's 89. Why the hell did he wait until now to think about getting his book written?

I sat in Horace Greasley's well-kept lounge while his wife Brenda ferried in the coffee. I'd talk to him for ten minutes I'd decided, let him down gently. Anyway what was I doing here? I'm a fiction writer. Sure I'd dabbled with the memoirs of a not so famous, not so exciting MP but the book had never made it to print. I'd had no experience whatsoever ghostwriting this type of book. I knew nothing about it, wouldn't even know where to start.

I sat with Horace for over two hours as he relayed his condensed story to me, first through numerous cups of coffee and then through the beers (Horace preferred gin). I sat with an open mouth as this old soldier took me through the dramatics of his unfortunate capture, the horrors of a death march and a train journey where Allied prisoners fell dead every few hours. The story was only just beginning.

I listened while Horace 'Jim' Greasley spoke.

Horace relayed his near-death experience in the first camp and then took me through his first meeting with Rosa, in Camp Two. There was an instant mutual attraction between the young German interpreter and the emaciated prisoner. Within a few weeks he would be having sex with her on a filthy bench top in the camp's drilling workshops, under the noses of the German guards. It wasn't love at first sight; that took the best part of a year. In fact at the exact point he discovered how much he felt about Rosa and how much he actually loved her, the Germans transferred him to yet another camp. He was devastated.

It was at this point that Horace told me that the good bit was only just beginning. He would relay his time in the third camp at Freiwaldau, in Polish Silesia, in dulcet whispered tones for nearly an hour.

I sat in silence. The book was formulating in my head as I desperately fought the urge to take my pen out and begin scribbling right there and then. I had questions. Why wait nearly 70 years before writing the book? Why me? How's his health? A book can take a year to write – is he going to hold out?

I never asked the questions as I didn't want to hear any

answers I might not like. I agreed to give it a go. For five months I sat with Horace while he relayed the greatest escape story ever. I thought back to my youth, the great Colditz stories and Steve McQueen in *The Great Escape*. Horace Greasley's account of his time in the POW camps blows those stories out of the water.

What makes it all the more amazing is that every bit of the book is true. I attempted to exaggerate at times with a little poetic licence. Horace wouldn't allow it; in reality I didn't need to. The words in this book are not those of Ken Scott, ghostwriter, they are the words of Horace Greasley, ex prisoner of war. Horace could not write or type because of severe arthritis. I take no credit for this book; I have merely acted as his fingers.

Horace's long-term memory and attention to detail was remarkable. At times reliving the brutality at the hands of his German captors would bring him to tears. I followed suit closely; it is one of my weaknesses. For me, tears are infectious.

I would like to think that telling his story brought a certain closure for Horace on the horrors he experienced during the war. He expressed on more than one occasion that this book is for his prisoner comrades – the men who suffered at the hands of their fellow man.

The experience of writing this book has made my life richer; meeting a man like Horace and hearing of his suffering has humbled me. I doubt whether my generation could have coped with the experiences these men went through. I relayed some of the stories to my children Callum, 9, and Emily, 12. They were fascinated, and listened at times in disbelief as I described the prisoners' suffering and the callous, barbaric acts committed by mankind. I think it is important that we never forget the suffering an ordinary individual goes through during war and remember that Horace was one of the lucky ones. He came home.

We must continue to teach our children about the futility and horrors of war. The politicians that instigate them must question their conscience. They never suffer; only the young men and women of their country and the countries they fight with.

My children met Horace. We socialised with him and his wife Brenda. I count myself fortunate to have met such a man as Horace Greasley and take it as a great honour that he approached me to write his book.

I only hope that I have done it justice.

Ken Scott
May 2013

This book is based on a true story, on information gathered from eyewitness accounts and over one hundred hours of interviews. It is a story about misery, genocide and enslavement... it is a story of one man's daring in the face of adversity.

PROLOGUE

It was early February 1945; the war was all but over. The Red Army had already liberated Auschwitz and other death camps and the shocking stories of what they had found there were relayed to an astonished world. At Belsen, the news reports sickened civilised people as images of dead and half-starved men, women and children were beamed around the world. Even the civilian German nation could not, or perhaps would not, believe what they were seeing and hearing. At Belsen the British liberators found over 30,000 inmates dead or dying. The skeletal figures who had survived the death camps gazed into the cameras with hardly the energy to stand or comprehend that they had been freed and their physical suffering was over. A few inmates talked of the unbelievable conditions they had been kept in, of the torture and brutality at the hands of their captors, and one man hung his head in shame as he explained that some of his fellow countryman had turned to cannibalism simply to be able to see the next day.

The camera crew focused on a sickening pile of dead, naked, emaciated women that had been located at the far end of the camp. Naked young girls, women, mothers and grandmothers – no one had been spared. The pile of decaying rotting flesh was 80 yards long, ten yards wide and four to five feet deep on average. The images were shown on cinema screens around the world. When the Supreme Commander of the Allied Forces, General Dwight Eisenhower, found the victims of the Nazi camps, he ordered all possible photographs to be taken, and for the German people from surrounding villages to be ushered through the camps and even made to bury the dead. He said. 'Get it all on record now – get the films – get the witnesses – because somewhere down the track of history some bastard will get up and say that this never happened.' His words were prophetic.

Two Russian soldiers of the 332nd Rifle Division sat in a makeshift camp ten miles from Posen on the German-Polish border in an area known as Silesia. Their comrades had entered Austria some weeks before and had also captured Danzig. The British and American forces had crossed the Rhein at Oppenheim. It was clear Germany was under attack from all sides.

The younger of the soldiers was named Ivan. A mere 19 years old, he had been thrown into the war as a 16-year-old conscript and was already battle-hardened beyond belief. Nevertheless, even he was horrified at the some of the tales he'd heard filtering through from the rescuing Allies and although he was looking forward to liberating the camps he had been assigned to, he was unsure as to what new horrors his young mind would encounter.

He had a phobia – one thing that shook him up more than anything else. What was it about a child's dead body? You'd think he'd be used to it by now. He remembered vividly the first child's body he had seen as his division had fought in the defence of Stalingrad. Why? he had asked himself. The young boy, no more than four years old, had clung to his mother's dead body until he simply froze to death in the bitter winter climate. His mother's skull had been torn apart by a piece of shrapnel from a German mortar shell as she'd made a desperate attempt to find sanctuary deep into the city. She'd died instantly. The sweet child would never know what it was like to pick up a book and read, never experience his first tender kiss from a girl, never know the joy of fatherhood.

Ivan's comrade sensed his fear and was trying to convince him it was the culmination of what they had fought for.

'Comrade, we will be seen as heroes. We are there to liberate our Allies who have spent many years at the hands of the Nazis. The poor prisoners have been brutalised for five years. We will give those German dogs a hell they will never forget.'

Ivan gazed into the flames of the fire. He should have felt warmth but all he could feel was a numbness of mind and body.

'Will we see children's dead bodies, Sergei?'

The older soldier shrugged his shoulders.

'Perhaps, comrade. Perhaps even worse.'

'Nothing could be worse, Sergei.' He shook his head and drank the dregs from the now cold cup of tea that had been freshly brewed a short while ago. Even in spring this part of Poland was deathly cold when the sun went down.

'The Nazis are capable of anything, comrade. They razed a French village to the ground. They rounded up and shot every man and boy then herded the women and children into the village church.'

Ivan wanted to cover his ears; he didn't want to hear what happened next.

'No, Sergei... no.'

'They set fire to the church, burned the women and children alive. The screams of the poor infants could be heard for miles around.'

DO THE BIRDS STILL SING IN HELL?

Ivan wiped a tear from his eye. His comrade grasped at the sleeve jacket of his ill-fitting uniform.

'We must avenge those women and children, comrade. We must do what we have to do, we must avenge the deaths at Kharkov and Kiev and Sevastopol, and we must remember every Russian man, women and child slaughtered at the hands of the German filth, murdered in the huge death factories.

At Stalingrad they cut off our lines of supplies, deliberately starved our people to death because they couldn't defeat us by fair means. We ate dogs and cats and even raw rats, we ate the glue from book bindings and industrial leather. It was whispered in certain places that our countrymen ate the flesh of our brothers and sisters.'

A few minutes' silence ensued while Ivan took in the magnitude of Sergei's statement.

'They are truly inhumane, comrade Sergei?'

The older soldier sighed and nodded his head.

'They are, comrade, they are.'

'But they will flee, Sergei, no? They know we are coming. Surely they will run?'

Sergei smiled.

'They will run, comrade, but we will run faster and harder and for longer. We will hunt them down and catch them like rats and we will have our fun with them.'

Sergei reached across suddenly and gripped roughly between his comrade's legs, taking his testicles in a vice-like grip.

'These will be emptied of their stagnant milk by tomorrow evening, comrade. I can guarantee it.'

Ivan struggled with his friend's firm wrist, tears in his eyes and a puzzled look on his face.

'We will fuck their *Fraüleins* while their fathers and brothers watch, then we'll kill them one by one. They'd better run, comrade; they'd better run like the wind, run into the hands of those soft Americans.' He sighed again. 'But those Americans haven't experienced what we have, comrade, those Yanks came into the war too late.'

The young soldier looked at his comrade, his mentor, the man who had looked after him like a father since their paths had crossed what seemed like years ago. He looked at the man who had saved his life on the battlefield on more than one occasion. He looked at a man whom he loved and respected as much as his father and was now advocating behaviour no different from the filthy Hun, the Nazi.

Young Ivan was confused. The fire before them crackled and spat out its tune. The embers were dying but still glowing brightly. Ivan reached across to the stockpiled wood and threw two large logs into the heart of the fire. The glow seemed to dull for a moment but Ivan and Sergei watched as slowly but surely a gentle flame began licking at the bottom of the new wood. The heat was instant. Ivan felt nothing.

'Tell me, Sergei...'

'Speak, child of the Union.'

'These camps of death, do the birds still sing in these terrible places?'

Sergei frowned, unable to give an answer.

'I mean... the birds, Sergei... surely they have witnessed every-thing? Do they still sing?'

Sergei let out a sigh.

'You are becoming soft like the Americans, comrade. You'll be writing poems next.'

'I will wake early tomorrow and if the birds are singing everything will be fine. The birds Sergei... the birds... they will tell us.'

'Be quiet!' a voice cried out a few yards away. 'Let us get

some fucking sleep before tomorrow; we need to save our energy for the German bitches.'

Sergei smiled. His teeth shone in the pale moonlight, and Ivan wondered how he had managed to keep them in such good condition given their diet and vitamin intake over the last few years. Hell, there was a time when they were battered down by the Germans without a crust of bread passing their lips for days.

'You see, comrade, it is to be expected of you. Tomorrow you must do your duty. We must eradicate the Nazis off the face of the earth and keep going until we reach Berlin.'

'Yes, the Nazis, Sergei, I agree, but all Germans can't be monsters. Our comrades are acting like animals now; they are turning on defenceless villagers and old men and women.'

'Revenge, comrade. Who can blame them? Who can blame us? The German civilians, those old men and women sat back and let it happen. The Russian people revolted when we were unhappy with our leaders; why didn't the Germans?'

Ivan had heard enough. He had a feeling he wouldn't sleep well that evening. He pulled his sleeping bag tight around his head, nestled a little closer to the fire. He was exhausted after the relentless march and just beginning to doze off when Sergei leaned over and whispered in his ear.

'Tomorrow, comrade… and for many days and weeks after, we will show the German nation, the soldier, the civilian and the man, woman and child in the street what bad really is. The German will wish he'd never been born.'

To live on in the hearts and minds of readers is truly not to die

CHAPTER ONE

J oseph Horace Greasley had enjoyed life on his parents' Leicestershire smallholding for as long as he could remember. He'd enjoyed milking the half dozen cows, tending to the hens and feeding the pigs, and he'd especially enjoyed looking after his father's Welsh ponies.

Although the elegant animals had towered over him as a small boy when he'd replaced their salt licks in the stables, turned their hay and mucked them out almost every day, he had never ever been afraid of them. In turn they seemed more than happy to have the young boy messing about under their feet, feeding them daily and replenishing their water supplies. Joseph Horace Greasley was always known as Horace; his mum had seen to that from quite an early age. No way were people going to call him Joe like his father. She couldn't comprehend why anybody would want to shorten people's names.

Horace enjoyed the backbreaking manual ploughing of the fields, sowing the seeds and generally keeping the place ticking over so the whole family could reap the rewards of the 30 or so acres left to them by their grandfather many years before. Home was number 101 at the end of a row of miners' cottages in Pretoria Road, Ibstock.

Horace, his twin brother Harold, older sister Daisy, young sister Sybil and baby Derick were luckier than most pre-second world war families at the time. Although rationing was yet to be introduced, times were still hard and even though Horace's father was employed full time at the local pit, money was tight, to say the least. No matter. Horace and his father would see that the family was well looked after.

Joseph Greasley senior was a miner, a hardworking coalface worker who would get out of bed at 3.30 each morning to milk his cows before completing a ten-hour shift at the nearby Bagworth Colliery. As he set off for work a few hours later he would give young Horace a shake and though extremely tired and bleary-eyed, Horace would continue to pick up the chores where his father had left off. The animals trusted him; he was comfortable in their company, they in his. He was their regular feed master, the person who cleaned their beds and tended to their injuries, and they seemed to sense it. They were his animals; he was the luckiest boy in the school. Including the chickens and the ponies he had nearly 50 pets. The pigs were his favourite – so ugly, so dirty. Life had dealt them a raw deal but they were his favourites, no doubt about that.

John Forster who lived at number 49 on the same street had once boasted in class that he had seven pets: three goldfish, a dog, two cats and a mouse. Pah! Horace had put him in his place when he'd begun reeling off the names of the Welsh ponies, the cows, pigs and even the hens. Twenty-two hens at the last count and each one had a name.

Only they weren't pets, Horace knew that, not really. Each November would end in an accepted sadness when his father killed a pig to supplement the family's diet. The meat took them right through to Christmas and sometimes beyond. Horace understood, at least he did when he enjoyed the regular weekend bacon sandwich or a ham joint on a Sunday afternoon complete with roasted potatoes from the fields and quite often an egg or two collected that morning.

It was the food chain, the law of the jungle, survival of the fittest. Man needed meat and it just so happened the Greasley family had plenty of it walking around their fields. Horace would sit for hours after the pig kill (not through choice, but because it was kind of expected), rubbing salt into the meat to cure it. Hour after hour his father would come into the big open scullery where young Horace sat working on the body of his dead friend. His father would look at the meat, press into the flesh, occasionally take a slice off and after tasting it would announce, 'More salt!'

Horace's shoulders would drop, his fingers already red raw, swollen and stinging, but not once did he argue or complain. The pig that only a few days earlier had a name would be unceremoniously turned so that its arse pointed into the air, and another pound of salt would be expended into the body.

When the salting was complete his father would come into the scullery with a large boning knife and expertly take the pig apart. The hams would be removed and stored in a cool pantry just off the hallway and the sides of bacon would be hung up the flight of stairs that led to the family's bedrooms on the first floor. It was a strange sight but that was the best place in the house to hang them, his father had often argued with his mother. It gets the through draught of the house, a constant flow of oxygen preserving the meat by many weeks, he'd explained.

Mabel didn't argue for very long. She knew her husband was right and no other family in the street had meat on their table in such a plentiful supply. It just looked so unsightly, especially when she opened the door to the local vicar. The shame of it!

A week after one kill the priest, Gerald O'Connor, came calling. Mabel asked him in and as he walked into the hall he gave a disapproving look while following her through to the lounge. He seemed happier though after his cup of tea, though, after she'd sent him away with a 3lb joint of bacon that he swore he would turn into a huge pan of bacon broth at the forthcoming Christmas fundraising fair.

'Hot winter broth,' he announced gleefully. 'Tuppence a cup.'

Mabel attended that fair several weeks later but try as she might, she couldn't find the stall serving the bacon broth.

On Horace's 14th birthday – Christmas Day 1932 – his father presented him with his first gun: a 410 Parker Hale single-shot shotgun. It was his reward for his long hours toiling on the farm, his father's way of saying thanks. Harold got a couple of books, an apple, an orange and some nuts, and Sybil, the oldest sister, got nothing. She was too old, his mother had explained. Daisy and Derick fared slightly better: a little wooden train for Derick and a dolly – or was it a dolls' house? – for Daisy. Horace only had eyes for one thing... his hands trembled with excitement as he handled the gun.

It had been torture waiting to fire the first shot. His father had made the family sit down to a Christmas breakfast of bacon and eggs, hot buttered rolls and steaming hot tea with the obligatory teaspoon of whisky that was a Greasley family tradition each Christmas morning. The Parker Hale sat atop the Welsh dresser, almost taunting him. Between each bite of bacon or a mouthful of hot bread he looked at his father, then the gun, then back to his father again.

'Remember, it's not a toy,' his father told him as they walked up to the small copse at the far end of the farm, each footfall crunching on the frozen earth. A dusting of snow like icing sugar covered the ground and the trees.

'You must treat the gun with respect. It's a killing machine – rabbits, ducks, hares, even humans.' He pointed to the weapon Horace held tightly in two hands while trying to ignore the penetrating cold of the steel and wishing he'd run back for his woollen gloves. But even if he'd been marooned in outer Siberia at −40 degrees, there was no way he was going back.

'That gun will kill a man, remember that, and watch where the hell you point it. I catch you pointing it at me and I'll crown you with it.'

Over the coming weeks his father taught Horace all about his new acquisition. He taught him how to take the gun apart, how to clean it and what size cartridge to use when hunting different sizes of animal. But most of all, his father taught him to shoot. They spent hours shooting at targets pinned to the trees and tin cans sitting on tree branches and fence posts. Horace shot his first rabbit after only four days and his father took it back and showed him how to skin and clean the animal ready for the pot. The family ate rabbit pie that evening and more than once Joseph senior advised the family that the food they were eating was down to Horace. Father and son's chests had swelled with pride.

His father explained how important it was to kill only for meat and how wrong it was to kill just for the sake of it. Horace grew to be an expert shot and could take out a starling or a wren from 50 yards. But each time he did, and he did so only occasionally, he suffered from guilt. He'd taken a pot shot at a young robin one day, never believing he would hit something so small. The robin's feathers exploded as the lead shot tore into its tender flesh and it fell from the telegraph cable onto the grass below. Horace whooped with joy as he ran over to examine his kill. His joy turned to anguish as he picked the small bird up in his hand, felt its warmth. Why? he thought to himself as a trickle of blood oozed onto the palm of his hand and the robin breathed its last breath. Why did I do that? What was the point?

From that day onwards, he vowed, he would never to shoot at a living creature unless it could be cooked and eaten. He would break that vow in 1940 in the fields and hedgerows of northern France.

The following year Horace left school, along with his twin brother Harold, the two H's as they were affectionately known. They were not inseparable as some twins. The simple truth was that they were different. Academically, Harold was brighter than Horace, always at the top of the class or thereabouts, and loved books and study. Horace hovered about the middle of the same class and longed for the end of each school day so he could hunt on the farm, tend to the animals or cast a roving eye towards the pretty girls on the short walk home.

Jobs were at a premium in 1933, the year a certain Adolf Hitler became Chancellor of Germany, but within days of leaving school Harold's academic achievements secured a much sought-after position in the ironmongery department of the local Co-Operative. There he joined his older sister Sybil in gainful employment, adding most of his wages to the family budget. The Greasley family now had three wages coming into the house. Mabel made fresh bread, baked cakes and almost overnight, a fruit bowl appeared in the middle of the kitchen table with exotic fruits such as bananas and oranges from hot countries overseas.

Horace had just returned from yet another hunting expedition. He couldn't wait to tell his father he'd dropped a running hare from 90 yards. Number four shot, he was about to explain, when his father announced he'd found Horace a job.

'An apprentice barber?' Horace whispered in astonishment.

'A three-year apprenticeship, Horace, 12 months as an improver…'

'But…'

'Twelve months semi-qualified and one more year fine-tuning thereafter.'

'But… but…' Horace objected, but somehow his father didn't listen.

'You start next week. Norman Dunnicliffe's in the High Street.'

The following week four wages went into the Greasley household and Horace's involuntary career as a gentlemen's barber was under way. The two years' training soon passed and as he honed his skills in the third, his wages rose to ten shillings a week. 1936 was going to be a good year, Horace thought, as his newfound confidence gave him the nerve to ask a pretty young girl called Eva Bell to the pictures. While they wrestled with each other in the back row of the local Roxy on Saturday night, a Pathé newsreel showed footage from the Berlin Olympics with Adolf Hitler and Benito Mussolini parading in their finery for the world to see. Horace did not see them; his hand was up the jumper and down the skirt of his new girlfriend.

Eva was a year older than Horace but a hundred years wiser. Several weeks into their courtship she suggested he bring to their next date a packet of French letters sold at the gentlemen's hairdressers where he worked. Being a barber definitely had its compensations.

Eva persuaded her mother to let Horace stay over in the spare room one Saturday night as the dance they were attending in her village of Coalville came out after midnight, far too late for Horace to catch the bus home. Mrs Bell liked Horace so she and Eva convinced Mr Bell that no shenanigans would occur. Nothing was further from the truth. Eva liked Horace; it was time to make a man of him.

About six o'clock on that special Sunday morning Horace lost his virginity. Eva's father was a miner and had left for his Sunday morning shift at 5.30. Twenty minutes later Eva crept through to the spare room. Before she had even slipped out of her nightie Horace was standing proud and as he fiddled with the rubber sheath, Eva gave him her undivided attention, so to speak. Once the rubber was firmly in place, Eva took over, straddled him like a jockey, gently easing him inside her. Horace looked on bewildered as Eva groaned and moaned and pushed herself to a climax. Each thrust and grunt convinced Horace that it was only a matter of time before the girl's mother would hear and make an unwelcome appearance, so he kept one eye on the door and the other gazed at Eva's beautiful heaving breasts inches from his face. But her mother slept on and Horace achieved his own orgasm in double quick time. No matter. They would practise this wonderful act of nature wherever, whenever and as often as they could. The Saturday night stopover at Eva's house would become a regular event.

Horace stayed with Norman Dunnicliffe until 1938 when he was persuaded to jump ship to Charles Beard, Gentlemen's Hairdresser. What a great name for a barber, Horace thought, and the money was better too. Of course he would still have an unlimited supply of 'dobbers' as they were comically known, and without the cost and embarrassment his friends had to endure. There were worse jobs, he thought to himself.

Although the money was good, Horace had to face an unenviable 28-mile round trip to Leicester every day. Even though his bike was equipped with the latest technology – an AW Sturmey-Archer three-speed gear hub – the old bike was heavy and on some days strong head winds made for impossibly slow progress. Horace didn't mind; his young body coped and developed well, and his added strength and stamina pleased Eva in the bedroom.

Towards the end of 1938 Horace was transferred to Charles Beard's shop in Torquay, the first time he'd ever left home. A little overawed at first, he settled in quickly and enjoyed life to the full. He missed Eva, sure, but there were plenty of pretty distractions to take his mind off his girlfriend in Leicestershire. He was also keeping an eye on events across the Channel.

The country breathed a sigh of relief, for a while at least, when Prime Minister Neville Chamberlain returned from Munich after meeting Adolf Hitler and announced in a speech at Heston aerodrome that there would be 'Peace for our time'. Hitler had signed the agreement containing the resolution to commit to peaceful methods. Horace heard Chamberlain's statement on a radio in the backroom of Charles Beard's shop. Somehow he wasn't convinced.

He was to be proved right. The fun on the English Riviera lasted only six months for Horace and he was recalled to Leicestershire as the government announced conscription for all 20- and 21-year-olds. It was only a matter of time before Horace and Harold would be called upon to do their duty. War, it seemed, was looming.

Horace resumed work in Charles Beard's Leicester shop and sure enough, within two weeks the letter lay waiting on the kitchen table, unopened, as he returned from work on a wet Wednesday evening. The letter informed both brothers they had to report to a church hall in King Street, Leicester in seven days, where the 2nd/5th Battalion Leicestershire Regiment were handling recruitment. Harold had returned from work somewhat earlier in the day and sat at the table looking distraught. Horace's first thought was for his twin. He would not cope. In all the years they'd played and grown together on the farm Harold have never once attempted to fire the gun, skinned a rabbit or pulled the neck of a hen, or picked up a catapult or a slingshot and fired a stone in anger. He couldn't bear to knock a fly from a bread roll, his father had once commented. Harold was visibly shaking at the prospect of picking up a rifle and pointing it at a fellow human being.

By this time Harold had found God. He was deeply involved in the church, something Horace – as an atheist – couldn't relate to. Horace couldn't figure out how an intelligent man could simply believe that an omniscient supreme being sat on a cloud up there somewhere, seeing and hearing everything every person in the entire world said and did. It was just too preposterous for words, almost laughable.

Harold didn't drink or smoke and Horace was damn sure he had nowhere near the kind of fun he'd been having in Torquay with the ladies. While each weekend Horace had made sure he carried his 'pack of three' – sometimes two packets – his brother had reached for the Bible. Harold was now a practising lay preacher and every Sunday he pontificated to the converted masses at the local Wesleyan chapel. Harold's religious convictions preached goodwill to all men... even Germans. Horace preferred a few beers with his pals and an afternoon out with Eva.

At that moment in the kitchen all Horace wanted to do was take his twin brother out, get him dead drunk and convince him things weren't as bad as they seemed. He couldn't. Harold was teetotal. Drink was the scourge of the working man, the root of all evil. Horace couldn't quite understand his attitude but never looked to challenge or change his brother's beliefs, even though Harold had tried to preach the gospel to him on more than one occasion.

'You realise he's bloody shitting himself, Horace, don't you?' his father said when Harold eventually went to bed.

Horace nodded. 'We'll be together, Dad. I'll take care of him.'

Joseph reached across and squeezed his son's hand.

'I know you will, son. I know you will.'

They made a pact. Or rather Horace made a commitment. The following evening he sat down with Harold and told him they were in this together. They would join the same unit, bash the same square, shoot at the same targets – and if it were possible to get through this damned war unscathed, they were just the two to do it. Horace gave the greatest speech of his life, far more sincere than Chamberlain at Heston aerodrome, and at the end of a long night, having downed half a dozen whiskies to Harold's cups of tea, Horace was pleased with his performance. He went to bed happy, determined to do what was right for his country and in particular, his family and his twin brother Harold.

Harold seemed to appreciate his brother's commitment, glad of his protection. Or so it seemed...

Two days later Horace was finishing off one of his clients in the salon of Charles Beard.

'You don't seem with it today, young Horace,' the customer commented.

He was right. Horace was miles away from his scissors. He was with Harold, and in the head of his mother, his sisters. He was wondering how his father would cope on the farm and what it would be like to shoot a gun at a German.

Horace explained to Mr Maguire in the chair that he'd been called up, had to report to 2nd/5th Battalion Leicesters next week and how he was convinced that a major war was just round the corner.

'I thought that might be what it was, Horace. I saw the article in the *Leicester Mercury*. "Ibstock twins for Militia Army," it said in the headlines.' He grinned at Horace in the mirror. 'You're quite famous, Horace, one of the first lot round here to get called up.'

'I'd rather not be, Mr Maguire. I'm 21 years of age and about to be shipped off for some basic training, then to the war. I like my life here – I've a good job and a nice girlfriend. Why can't the politicians sort it out?'

He wanted to say how concerned he was about Harold, how he thought his brother just wasn't up to it. He bit his tongue. He was lost in his thoughts when Mr Maguire reminded him of his occupation as a chief inspector in the fire service. He informed Horace that a fireman was a reserved occupation and stayed home in the event of war, and that the selection process to recruit firemen was taking place at his station that week.

'You could always apply, Horace. We're taking in the new applicants on Wednesday, a 30-minute exam, a little fitness training, then seeing how hard the buggers shake up a 30ft ladder.'

Horace caught the gentleman's gaze in the mirror. Scissors poised, he pulled at a strand of hair ready to be clipped. Mr Maguire winked at Horace.

It was a wink that turned his blood to ice. Horace was aware of a trembling sensation in his legs. He pulled the scissors away from the gentleman's scalp, afraid his shaking fingers might do some damage. He knew exactly what that wink meant. Mr Maguire was throwing him a lifeline, a get out of jail free card. Mr Maguire had the power to prevent Horace from going to war, to protect him from the horrors he would no doubt encounter.

'Are you saying you're giving me a chance to be a fireman?'

Maguire shook his head, looked up into the mirror and smiled.

'You're a good lad, Horace. I've known you for some time, you come from a good family and you're fit and intelligent too. What I'm saying is that if you can climb a ladder you'd make a great fireman.'

Horace stuttered. 'So I'd stand a good chance.'

Maguire shook his head again, confusing young Horace. The next few words John Edward Maguire released from his lips couldn't have been any clearer. They were to turn Horace's world upside down.

'The job's yours, Horace. I'll make sure you're selected, it's my decision.'

Maguire left soon after. His hair hadn't been cut to the normal high standard. Horace sat in shock.

No war, no guns and a £2 increase in wages. He'd still be fighting for his country, still with a risk of injury or worse, but he'd be at home, not in some far-flung field in France or Belgium or Germany. He'd still have the farm, see his parents, and continue with his nocturnal activities with Eva. Perhaps the French letters would be a little bit more difficult to get a hold of but no matter, he'd cope. And he'd asked Mr Maguire if there would be a similar position for Harold. Mr Maguire had shaken his head, explained that people may suspect some favouritism. It wouldn't look good; the answer was no.

A day later Horace walked into the fire station in Leicester city centre. By coincidence John Maguire was walking through the front office. He looked up, a frown on his face.

'Horace,' he said, then took his hand and shook it warmly. 'You're a day early: selection isn't until tomorrow evening.'

Horace shook his head as the £5 weekly wage, the moments of passion with Eva, the Sunday morning breakfasts with his family and the precious moments on the farm with his father flashed before him.

'No, sir. No, Mr Maguire, I'm not early. I've just come to thank you and say I won't be applying.'

'B... but...' Maguire stammered in disbelief.

Horace left the man speechless, turned his coat collar up and walked into the fog-dimmed light to the muffled chime of a church bell somewhere in the distance. A light rain had started falling and a shiver ran the length of his spine. All he could think of was Harold and that pact and how he had made the right decision.

The following Friday evening Horace was strangely subdued as he walked through the front gate of the only home he'd ever known. The scullery light shone brightly against the dark of the night. He peered through the window. Strange, he thought as he made out the figures of his parents and Harold sitting around the table. Dad doesn't usually sit down at this time of night; Mum is usually by the kitchen stove preparing the evening meal. Why are they all sitting down as if... as if in a conference?

As Horace entered the room his father stood. His mother reached for a handkerchief and dabbed at the corner of her eye. Any other time Horace would have expected news of the death of a relative. Not this time.

Horace knew... just knew... and the look in Harold's eye confirmed his suspicions.

CHAPTER
TWO

Harold had gone, with his Wesleyan minister for moral support, to a specially convened panel set up for conscientious objectors. Horace had never even heard the word conscientious until Harold had almost whispered it across the table that ill-fated Friday evening.

By all accounts Harold and the man of God had presented a most convincing case and the panel had agreed that Harold would not have to fight on the front line, point a gun at a human being nor attend the enlistment procedure. Instead Harold had agreed to take up a non-combat role and had been put forward to join the Royal Army Medical Corps. The RAMC did not carry a regimental colour nor did it have any battle honours. It was not a fighting unit and under the Geneva Convention, its members could only use their weapons in self-defence.

So Horace stood in the enlistment line at King Street, Leicester on his own... the loneliest man in the world, waiting his turn. He wanted to say he wasn't angry, wanted to say he wasn't bitter, but the truth of the matter was that he was. He had stood open-mouthed, staring in disbelief as his father explained they'd been working on Harold's case for over a week. Even the minister had called at the house. It was a combined effort that Horace knew nothing about.

Horace had seethed as Harold explained that his great friend and mentor Father John Rendall had drunk several cups of tea around the pine kitchen table of 101 Pretoria Road, on the very evening that Horace had gone to the fire station to turn down the opportunity of a lifetime in order to watch the back of his twin brother.

'It was a combined bloody effort alright,' Horace mumbled to himself as he remembered the stand-up row he'd had with his brother that evening. He'd wanted to hit him. Not because of what he'd done but because he'd done it behind his back. It turned out everyone knew – Mum and Dad, Daisy and Sybil and of course, Father Fucking High Almighty God-fearing Rendall.

'What was that you said, soldier?' A voice bellowed out, bringing Horace back to the present. A sergeant major with a waxed handlebar moustache stood upright, as if to attention, directly in front of Horace. Horace noticed the crowns on his uniform and thought it best to address him correctly.

'Nothing, sir, I just wondered if I was in the right building.'

Horace stretched out a hand and offered the papers to the sergeant major, who took a quick look and without lowering his voice said, 'Correct, soldier. 2nd/5th Battalion Leicesters, one of the finest regiments in the King's Army.' He took a step forward. 'You don't know how lucky you are to be joining us.'

Horace was confused. He was still angry and perhaps he hadn't been thinking straight, but the letter definitely said he would have the choice of the Army, the Navy or indeed the Air Force. He felt intimidated, a little under pressure; he looked at the rest of the young men in the queue and they all seemed happy that the attention was focused on someone else – some other poor bastard, he thought to himself and cursed under his breath. Horace cleared his throat; he wasn't about to be frightened by this man. What chance did he have with the Germans if he bowed down to one sergeant major?

'Actually, sir, I haven't quite made my mind up who it is I'll be choosing to join.'

The sergeant major took a step forward. Horace could smell his breath – stale tobacco and tea. His teeth were stained. He raised his voice and Horace was aware of a gun holster he'd pushed round to the front of his trousers. The officer flicked open the top cover. 'Do you want to be bloody shot?' he bellowed and a slither of spit hit Horace in the eye.

Horace was tough but he was also taken aback. He kept quiet, sort of nodded his head then shook it quickly.

'Then get back in the fucking line and don't you even think about insulting my regiment again.'

'No, sir... sorry, sir,' he whispered, so quietly that the rest of the queue hardly heard him.

Within 20 minutes he'd signed up for the 2nd/5th Battalion Leicesters and had been given a 48-hour pass with instructions to report to Leicester County Cricket Ground for seven weeks' basic training.

Forty-eight hours. What could a man do in 48 hours? Actually... Horace called on Eva Bell on the way back from the church hall in King Street and in 48 hours he'd used up three packs of three. It was the height of a hot summer and their love-making sessions took place in the corn fields, wheat fields and meadows of Leicestershire.

The first person to greet Horace at Leicester County Cricket Ground was Sergeant Major Aberfield, the man who had browbeaten him into joining the battalion. Aberfield gave the new recruits an hour-long lecture about what it meant to fight for king and country, the honour of the regiment and how a certain Austrian with one testicle, a cowlick hairstyle and a pathetic little moustache needed his arse well and truly kicked. Horace was quite happy to go along with that and if the truth were told couldn't wait to join in the action.

Horace settled in to the seven weeks' training surprisingly well. On his first day he was renamed Jim. 'Ain't no fucker called Horace coming into my billet,' joked a young corporal as half a dozen recruits looked on and laughed. From then on he was simply Jim – a name plucked from the air. Even his friend from Ibstock, Arthur Newbold, with whom he was bunking up, started calling him Jim, and he'd known Horace as Horace for as long as he could remember.

Horace knuckled down to the task in hand and realised almost immediately that there was little point in harbouring any grudges against his brother, the British Government or even the sergeant major who had forced him into a battalion of infantrymen. He'd save his hostility for the men with the square helmets running amok across the other side of the English Channel. Horace had a job to do... end of story.

Once a week the new recruits would be transported by bus to a firing range on the Leicestershire and Northants border. Horace loved it. It was his territory, his domain. There was something about the Enfield 303 rifle with its basic 'V' sights he adored, and the hairs on the back of his neck never failed to rise as he snuggled the butt of the weapon into his shoulder and took aim at the target 80 yards away. Horace's shooting was exemplary; he was beginning to be talked about and he came to the attention of the staff sergeant in charge of the range. Staff Sergeant Caswell pulled him aside one day after he'd fired ten rounds into the target. Ten rounds grouped in a circle no bigger than a tennis ball – he had his sights on the battalion trophy that would be awarded at the end of the seven weeks.

'You're bloody good, Greasley, maybe one of the best I've seen.'

'Thanks, Sergeant.'

'The thing is, Greasley, Sergeant Major Aberfield is good too, holds the record for the battalion. He practises at least an hour every day.'

The NCO paused. A sickly feeling welled up in Horace's stomach.

'And, Sergeant?'

'Look, Greasley, I don't really want to knock you back, but believe me your life won't be worth living if you beat that bastard. He'll make your life a merry hell.'

Horace could just imagine that he would. Aberfield was a bully who never spoke, always shouted, and never ever raised a smile.

The following week Horace pulled half a dozen shots wide. One missed the target altogether and Sergeant Major Aberfield took the battalion trophy by two points. Private Horace 'Jim' Greasley finished second.

Half way through their basic training, on 3 September 1939, Arthur and Horace sat in the mess hall as an address by Neville Chamberlain, the British Prime Minister, was relayed on loudspeaker across the hushed dining hall. Chamberlain stated that an ultimatum for Germany to withdraw their troops from Poland had expired and 'consequently this nation is at war with Germany.'

The troops were strangely subdued. A few were full of tales and bravado, relaying to any companions who would listen what they were going to do to the Germans when the action started. Most just sat and stared into space. Horace thought of his family and in particular, his twin brother.

Horace made the most of another 48-hour pass and Eva returned to her village rather pleasantly sore between the legs.

'Don't you think of anything else, Horace Greasley?' she'd asked as they'd exchanged a tender kiss in a deserted barn about two miles from the camp while Horace worked his fingers into her knickers.

Horace thought about her question and when he came to analyse it, thought it rather stupid. Of course he thought about other things. It just so happened that the touch and the taste of Eva Bell's beautiful young body occupied his brain most waking hours. Come to think of it, he dreamed about it quite a lot too. His sexual appetite was insatiable, and Eva's matched his. Although he wasn't to know it just yet, it was a sexual craving that would place him under an almost weekly death sentence in the years ahead.

Rather disappointingly for Horace, the 2nd/5th Battalion Leicesters didn't head for the war immediately. September, October, November and most of December was spent at the barracks practising drill, polishing boots, performing mundane tasks around the camp, listening to the BBC World Service and making an occasional visit to the rifle range. It was as if the Army didn't have anything for them to do.

Suddenly, at noon on 23 December 1939, all leave was officially cancelled. A letter had been sent to the next of kin. They were due to leave for France on Boxing Day. Horace was devastated. He was due to leave for home that evening and spend Christmas Day – his birthday – with his family. Jesus Christ, he thought, surely a couple of days wouldn't have made any difference to the war? Didn't these colonels and politicians realise how important this day was to people? He imagined his mother sitting at the kitchen table with the letter, the tears streaming down her face. Horace felt bitter and angry.

He awoke at five minutes to six on Christmas morning. He had no intention of going AWOL – it just sort of happened.

He took a trip to the toilet, completed his morning ablutions in double quick time, and passed his sleeping comrades in the huge dormitory. Some snored, or let loose an occasional fart on account of the copious amounts of beer they'd consumed the night before at a hastily arranged Christmas party. He walked through the billet in darkness and wondered how many of these young men would ever return to the shores of England. How many would die, how many would end up languishing in a prisoner of war camp, how many would be maimed or crippled? He would be fine, of course; the thought that he might not make it back home never even crossed his mind. It would never happen to Joseph Horace Greasley.

He changed into his combats, picked up his coat and fastened it up to the collar. The bitterly cold December morning air took his breath away when he stepped outside. The ground was frozen; a thick white rind of frost covered the grass, the windscreens of vehicles were frozen solid. A thin plume of smoke drifted from the chimney of the gatehouse as he walked over towards it. John Gilbert and Charlie Jackson had been on duty that evening; the poor bastards had missed out on the Christmas party. Horace would tell them all about it over a hot cup of tea.

But John Gilbert and Charlie Jackson were fast asleep. One of the boys had sneaked a bottle of whisky over to them around midnight, and they had been greedy.

Horace ducked under the barrier and began walking home.

Just over an hour into the walk the sun made an appearance and the perspiration started building on Horace's back as he was bathed in a golden light. The birds that hadn't flown south for the winter chimed out their sweet dawn chorus and as Horace climbed a five bar gate four miles from the camp he saw his first robin. It sat on a fencepost, cocking its tiny head in the direction of the stranger walking towards it. Horace stopped. He marvelled at the beauty of the tiny, perfectly formed creature, captured as if in a photograph frame with a brilliant white frosted background behind it. And he thought back to the day he had pointed a gun at its brother.

Nothing else mattered. Being AWOL didn't matter, nor did the war. This moment was worth anything his battalion military police would throw at him when they eventually caught up with him.

Horace walked into the kitchen of 101 Pretoria Road just after 9.30. His mother dropped the teacup she'd been holding and it shattered into a hundred pieces as the dregs spilled across the linoleum floor. She managed to squeeze out 'Happy birthday, Horace,' before collapsing into his arms in a fit of tears. Harold just sat at the table looking dumbfounded. The commotion from the kitchen attracted Horace's father and his other siblings from the lounge where they were sitting by the open fire. It was the Christmas Day that shouldn't have been, and that made it all the sweeter for Horace.

His father ushered him through to the lounge and pushed him in the direction of the chair by the fire. 'You must be frozen, son. Sit there, get thawed out.'

Horace looked at the chair. It had seen better days; the leather was worn and scratched and in more than one place the horsehair interior had made an unwanted appearance. The chair was strategically placed a few feet from the fire; it was placed in such a way that the person sitting in it could view the whole room and everyone in it. It was in the prime location, it was the master chair, father's chair, and no one ever dared to sit in it. It was respected... expected.

'But Dad... it's your...'

'Sit,' his father commanded as he smiled and handed him a cup of tea with the familiar faint aroma of Scotch whisky.

It could have been the best Christmas Day ever. It could also have been his last.

Horace left home around 11 that evening and arrived back at the camp just after one in the morning. The sentries weren't sleeping this time and challenged him at the gatehouse.

'Where the fuck you been then, Jim? Nobody's seen you all fucking day. You missed your Christmas dinner.'

Horace smiled. 'I've been for a walk, Bob, that's all. A long walk.'

He ducked under the barrier and started walking in the direction of his billet. The other sentry called after him, but Horace never heard a word he said.

Horace was expecting something to happen that morning – a visit from the commanding officer at least, maybe a charge. He got neither. What could they do, throw him in jail as the regiment left for France? That's what they'd been told; they were heading for France to start work as labourers on a French railway a little south of Cherbourg. They'd been told little else, but Horace knew from radio and newspaper reports – not to mention the squaddie grapevine – that France was about to be overrun by the army of the Third Reich.

The troop train seemed to crawl its way to Waterloo station in London. It was familiar to Horace; he had passed through on his way to Torquay. Thousands of soldiers lined the platform, young men the same age as Horace looking bewildered, dazed, some absolutely terrified. Horace had never seen such a huge concentration of men in one place. He scoured the platform looking for just a glimpse of a pretty face, a young nurse perhaps, even a female ticket inspector. Nothing. As if reading his mind Arthur Newbold, sitting opposite, smiled and spoke.

'No shagging for a while, eh, Jim?'

'No, I suppose not, Arthur.'

'My girlfriend Jane's a pal of Eva's, didn't you know?'

'No, I didn't.'

'Eva tells Jane everything. She reckons you're a bit of a lad, an unlimited supply of dobbers – and boy do you put them to the test.'

Horace smiled. He couldn't quite believe that Eva had shared so much information with her friend.

'How long do you think it'll last, Jim? How long before you're back home rattling Eva's bones again?'

Horace shrugged his shoulders and gazed out of the window as the train pulled out of the station. 'That all depends on Mr Hitler, Arthur. He wants peace with us, of that there's no doubt, but Chamberlain won't have it.'

'Rumour has it there are 200,000 British troops in France now. Surely the dozy bastard will call it a day and pull his squareheads back home?'

'I hope so, Arthur. I hope so. Then I can get back to Eva and give her a good seeing to.'

The two soldiers laughed but despite their vocal optimism both feared the worst. The French Premier, Edouard Daladier, had rejected Hitler's offer of peace, and earlier that month Hitler had orchestrated the first air attack on Britain when the Luftwaffe had bombed ships in the Firth of Forth. Just a few days ago, the British government had released information about the Nazis building concentration camps for the Jews. Horace wasn't daft; he knew that in modern warfare the battle of propaganda needed to be worked on too. But building camps to exterminate an entire race? That was just plain daft. It was like something out of the dark ages, Genghis Khan reincarnated. Surely Hitler wasn't that evil?

The train eventually arrived at Folkestone under the cover of darkness and the regiment of the 2nd/5th Battalion

Leicesters waited patiently on the dockside to be loaded onto the huge cross-channel ferry. As the ship set sail for France, Horace cast his eye on the fast-disappearing silhouette of the English coastline as a cramp gnawed away in the pit of his stomach. He couldn't explain it and couldn't understand the feeling that he was experiencing. Something in his head told him this was his last look at England for a long time.

The regiment arrived in the early hours of the morning at the small town of Carentan, 30 miles south of Cherbourg. The following morning they were set to work on the railway. It was backbreaking work and the men moaned constantly.

'Fuck me, Jim, it isn't what I expected,' shouted Arthur Newbold from across the other side of the track as he shovelled another spade full of stones onto the already huge pile. They moved to one side, glad of the two-minute break as a steamroller followed in their wake to compact the stones into the earth, ready for the next sleeper to be laid.

'Nor me. Give me a few Germans to shoot at any day of the week.'

Mile after mile they laid the stones and the sleepers for the new railway line that would run from Cherbourg to Bayeux and eventually on to Paris. They worked ten hours a day, but were fed and watered well and spent their evenings reading and listening to the war reports on the radio in a huge, stone-fronted building on the outskirts of the village. It was two weeks before they were given a night out in Carentan.

Two lorries dropped the troops off in the centre of town and strict instructions were given to be in the same place to be picked up three hours later. Horace and Arthur had an amble around the town before making their way into what looked like a dated, run-down old hotel. The paint flaked off the blue-fronted shutters, their hinges and clasps worn and rusted.

The English troops were greeted warmly as they ordered a few beers and sauntered over to a table. The bar was almost deserted but for a few more Allied troops from a different regiment and two old men conversing in French. The bar smelled musty and damp and the wallpaper peeled from the walls at the corners. Not like a good old traditional English bar, Horace thought to himself. He tasted the beer. Not bad, but not as good as a nice dark bitter.

A lady in her mid-forties approached the table and spoke in broken but good English.

'Gentlemen, I have some entertainment lined up for you.'

Oh well, thought Horace, it's getting a little better. The lady pointed up to the top of a rickety old staircase. Pictures of scenes from Paris and Versailles lined the stairs and a huge dusty chandelier hung from the ceiling where the staircase turned and led to a red-carpeted landing. Three young ladies stood in their frilly finery, hands on hips, smiling down at the soldiers below.

'Oh well,' said Arthur cheerfully, 'looks like we're going to get a few dancers.'

'Possibly singers,' commented Horace innocently.

Sergeant Thompson, a regular soldier in his late thirties, who'd just taken a mouthful of French ale, sprayed his beer across the table, unable to control his laugh.

'You dozy bastards,' he guffawed with a huge grin. 'They're prostitutes... French fucking whores. The only thing they'll be singing to is your dicks.'

As the truth dawned on the two young men from Ibstock, their mouths gaped open. It all fell into place, the red carpet, the madame with too much makeup and a hard face standing next to the table and the oh, so expensive French beer. There were no prostitutes in Ibstock. Horace didn't think he'd even heard the word mentioned in 21 years at 101 Pretoria Road. A woman spreading her legs for any man on earth as long as he had a pocket full of money. It was simply unthinkable... quite disgusting.

By now Arthur had turned a ghostly shade of white. His beer glass trembled nervously in his hand as he held it in front of his face in a vain attempt to look unruffled. Sergeant Thompson answered the madame.

'No thanks, luv,' he said in a rough Derbyshire accent that surely the madame couldn't make out. 'I've got everything I need back home.'

She turned her attention to Horace who sat in a stunned silence. Sergeant Thompson and Arthur looked across the table too. Arthur gave a nervous laugh and shook his head. 'Who could do such a thing?' he asked his companions.

Horace grinned, bundled a fistful of French francs into the madame's hands and took the stairs two at a time. He had no time to make a choice – he was simply grabbed unceremoniously by the oldest-looking of the three girls, a slim, large-breasted redhead named Collette, no more than 25 years of age. She led him to a room at the far end of the corridor, opened the door and pushed him inside. She stood with her back to the door and defrocked, revealing a red basque with matching stockings and suspenders.

'And now, Englishman,' she said with a seductive smile, 'it's time for you to find out what a lady's tongue is for.'

As she moved forward she untied the basque and it fell to the floor, exposing her breasts. Her hand reached out instinctively for Horace's groin and with an expert twist of her wrist his flies were unbuttoned and his trousers at his ankles. Her small delicate hand squeezed at his already erect penis as she lowered herself to her knees. She pushed at him gently with her free hand as Horace's knees buckled against the bed. As he fell backwards and felt the girl's wet mouth on him he lay back and thought of England.

Back in the camp dormitory as they prepared for lights out, Arthur and Sergeant Thompson ridiculed and teased him relentlessly. Horace didn't care. Collette had taught him things he didn't think possible in the two hours he'd spent in her company and she'd made good her promise about finding out what exactly a girl's tongue was for.

Exactly two weeks later the first letter arrived from Eva. Horace was excited and settled down on his bunk to savour each word. He was not to know that Arthur had written to his girlfriend the week before, or that Jane Butler had a mouth bigger than the Humber estuary.

The letter started off nicely, asked how the accommodation and food was and when he was likely to see any action. He was already formulating his replies to her questions in his mind, thinking he might start the letter that evening, when he went on to the second page.

> *I know all about your indiscretions with the French prostitute and quite frankly Horace I am disgusted. I hope she was worth it. I cannot understand how you could have stooped so low, especially after I gave myself so freely to you. Your words seem so empty now; your actions so false and insincere and I wonder if I have it in my heart to ever forgive you. I do not think it possible at this stage to take you into my arms again.*

Eva went on to say that when Horace returned home he would get a piece of her mind. Horace would not be looking forward to that day. But neither Horace Greasley nor Eva Bell knew at the time just how many years it would be before that meeting took place.

CHAPTER
THREE

It was mid-May 1940 when the 2nd/5th Battalion Leicesters got the call for action. Germany had invaded France, Belgium and the Netherlands. Neville Chamberlain had resigned and Winston Churchill became Prime Minister of the United Kingdom.

The Third Reich was on the march. Luxembourg had been occupied and General Guderian's Panzer Corps had broken through into Sedan in France, a strategic disaster for the Allies. Churchill tried to rally the country with his 'blood, toil, tears and sweat' speech. Rotterdam had been carpet-bombed by the Luftwaffe, causing thousands of civilian deaths, and the Dutch army had capitulated. Churchill had made a surprise visit to Paris and to his dismay found that French resistance was all but over. Effectively the United Kingdom stood alone in Europe.

Only the rumbling of the slow, four-ton troop-carrier could be heard; the lorry's occupants were silent. There were unsubstantiated rumours that the Maginot Line had been breached by the Germans and they were advancing through France. The Maginot Line – made up of concrete fortifications, tank obstacles, artillery casemates and machine gun posts – had been established during the First World

War. It was designed to repel any attack by the Germans and thought to be impregnable.

Sergeant Major Aberfield had denied the rumour and said the line had held firm. He'd also said the battalion was on its way to Belgium to welcome the Hun. Horace had asked his sergeant, a high-ranking lieutenant and then Sergeant Major Aberfield how the war was going and where exactly they were heading. Each time he received a different answer. He got the impression that nobody really knew.

Horace held a roughly drawn diagram he'd sketched from the one map of northern France his section of 29 men had in their possession. It belonged to Sergeant Major Aberfield, who'd left it unattended while eating dinner the previous evening. Horace had sketched it in pencil and had filled in the towns of Lille and Lorraine, and several little villages in the Alsace region. He'd carefully shaded the borders of Belgium and Luxembourg, and plotted his section's progress as they passed through the villages and towns en route.

So now he was more than a little puzzled. Only a little while ago they'd passed through Caudry and, he supposed, on to Hirson in the direction of the Belgian border. To his surprise they'd turned and headed north and now, in the town of Hautmont just 25 miles from the border, the convoy had stopped and the men told to disembark for a quick fag and a pee. Several officers had assembled and were chatting over a large map spread on the ground. Sergeant Major Aberfield was pointing a stick at the map, but Horace couldn't quite hear what he was saying.

They all returned to the truck and the driver now turned west in the direction of Cambrai. Horace held his drawing on his knees, and his hands began to tremble as the awful truth dawned on him. The battalion had about turned... they were on the retreat.

An hour later the lorry stopped and the troops were told to disembark again. It was if the whole section heard it at the same time, just a split second after the engine of the lorry had spluttered to a halt. Gunfire. There was no mistake.

Gunfire and artillery shells – the sound wafted in on the wind from the east. It was hard to tell exactly how far away the sound was: maybe two, three miles. Horace smiled as a burst of adrenaline caused a shiver up the entire length of his spine, and he was ready. He'd never felt so sure about anything in his life. At last it seemed he was going to see some action.

They had stopped by the side of the road near a wooded area. The lorry Horace had been travelling in pulled into a firebreak in the forest and drove in about half a kilometre. The rest of the convoy left. Horace's group were on their own, ready for some sort of scrap, though in what form he didn't know. Horace sensed it and so too did some of the other troops, who were strangely subdued. Aberfield stood under the cover of the trees pulling on a cigarette with trembling fingers. He was a deathly shade of white, a walking corpse.

Horace was instructed to climb up onto the canvas roof of the lorry with a Bren gun. The rest of the men stood around the lorry, Lee Enfield 303 single-shot rifles at the ready. He was told by the corporal that a German reconnaissance plane was close by and it was Horace's job to bring it down with a continuous burst of fire from the machine gun. 'You're the best shot, Greasley,' the corporal said by way of explanation as Horace climbed up and was handed the Bren gun. Horace didn't need any justification... he was ready. In fact he couldn't have been more excited.

Horace lay on his back on top of the tight tarpaulin for nearly two hours. The safety catch on the Bren gun had been disengaged, his finger poised on the trigger as he held the gun pointing to the sky. A couple of times he thought he heard the drone of an aeroplane engine in the distance, but to his disappointment it had faded away.

'Down you come, Greasley,' the corporal shouted up to him. 'You've been up there long enough.'

'I'm fine, Corporal, never felt better. I'm...'

'Get your arse down here when I tell you, Greasley! Two hours up there is enough for anyone's concentration. Come on, we haven't got all day.'

'But Corporal, I...'

'Now, for fuck's sake! That's an order!'

Another youthful squaddie was making his way up onto the roof looking none too pleased. Horace smiled as he held out a hand to pull him up.

'Looks like you're going to get all the fun, Cloughie.'

The young squaddie didn't reply; he looked absolutely terrified.

Private Clough had been on the roof no more than ten minutes when they heard the unmistakeable noise of an aircraft swooping in from the west. The Messerschmitt ME 210 had been on a reconnaissance patrol, viewing and reporting back on the Allied troop movements. Nevertheless it was equipped with four 20mm cannons and a rear gunner in the tail with fully armed MG 131 machine guns. The pilot radioed through to the rear gunner: they were about to have some fun.

The plane banked steeply as the pilot held both thumbs on the buttons of the cannons high up on the joystick. He dropped the aircraft down another hundred feet or so and lined it up with the firebreak in the forest as if approaching a huge, long runway ready to land. This was going to be easy; take out a few of the English pigs and return home in time for supper.

Horace had to admit it was a frightening sight as the aircraft roared towards them no more than 80 feet from the ground. The noise was deafening as the aircraft sped towards the exposed lorry. Most of the section had taken cover in the forest; a few were discharging their weapons but couldn't possibly hope to hit anything firing through the branches of the trees. Horace stood alone in the clearing, the 303 rifle butt tight into his shoulder, firing into the propellers of the plane through gritted teeth. At any second the Bren gun would open up a volley of shots and the plane would be brought down. And then it came; it was music to his ears, round after round from a machine gun. A beautiful sound, thought Horace, and he wished he'd been the man on top of the four-tonner.

Even closer now, Horace expected to see a plume of smoke, an explosion in the sky. But in a split second he realised to his horror that the gunfire was not coming from the Bren gun on the lorry but from the aircraft. Twenty metres ahead in the dust of the forest floor the bullets penetrated the ground with a dull thud. Horace stood directly in their path as they pounded the ground. Nearer and nearer they came, as if in a slow death motion.

He didn't have time to think. The adrenaline urged him forward and his rifle kicked into his shoulder so much it began to ache. The two lines of bullets ripped into the roof of the four-tonner and ricocheted around his ears. And then.... blackness, as a searing pain in his skull sent Horace into unconsciousness.

Horace didn't feel any better when he came round a few seconds later and found out what had happened. A medic had applied a bandage to a deep gash in his forehead and he had a bump on his head the size of an egg. At the last second a raw survival instinct had propelled him under the vehicle and he'd caught his head on the iron support bar that held the spare wheel. He'd been so close to being killed: one bullet had gone straight through the khaki of his trousers, missing his leg by a fraction of a millimetre.

He'd stared death in the face. In fact, he'd given it one almighty slap in the chops. He had every right to feel shocked, numb even. He deserved to feel elated that he'd escaped with his life and pleased with the praise his colleagues were doling out. Even Aberfield had slapped him on the back and mumbled a few words of congratulations.

But he felt none of that, only disappointment. The one man he'd relied on had been Private Clough on top of the lorry. Two hundred rounds a minute that Bren gun could release and he hadn't fired one shot. As Horace Greasley had stood alone in the clearing, firing shots at the Messerschmitt almost as soon as it had come into view, Bill Clough had shat himself, leapt the ten feet to the ground in one fluid motion and scampered like a frightened rabbit deep into the forest. Horace had faced the awesome firepower of the Messerschmitt alone, with only a single-shot repeating rifle against a fully armed aircraft with a rear gunner capable of ripping a man to shreds in a few seconds.

Horace had been lucky, of that there was no doubt. But he'd only stood there because he thought he was being protected by his mate. He told the sergeant to keep Bill Clough out of his way for a few days.

The whole section was loaded back onto the lorry and Horace was allowed to travel up front in the cab. Aberfield thought it wouldn't be good for troop morale if Horace had suddenly started laying into one of his comrades.

Horace caught snippets of Aberfield's conversation with the driver, but most of the time he just stared into the fields. Swathes of yellow corn were dancing to a tune on the wind. Occasionally he took note of another road sign that told him they were retreating even further. It wasn't supposed to be like this, he thought, as he remembered the stirring lectures he'd listened to in the old clubhouse at the cricket ground in Leicester. The good old 2nd/5th Battalion Leicesters weren't supposed to run and hide; that wasn't what he'd heard from the officer as he'd described the glorious history of the regiment. And there wasn't supposed to be a coward in the ranks – for that's what Bill Clough was. How could he do that?

Horace rubbed the bandage on his head. The medic had been right; the swelling had gone down but Jesus Christ how it hurt. After an hour they stopped by a river and Aberfield ordered the troops to disembark. They were just outside the town of Hautmont on the river Sambre. An old stone bridge crossed the river there and as the troops stood on the west side they received their orders from Aberfield.

'The bridge is of strategic importance, men, and we have good information that Jerry will be trying to cross it very soon.' Aberfield was wearing his white mask again; his words almost faltered as he spoke. 'There's a German patrol headed this way. We have a good few hours by all accounts, so dig in and get camouflaged up.'

Horace and his comrades dug in for two days and two nights. They took turns to catch a few hours' sleep but their rifles lay primed at the ready. The Bren guns were positioned on a small grassy knoll and manned by two of the older boys from the section. Aberfield was conspicuous by his absence, choosing to take up a position on the perimeter of the town with the radio operator. Halfway through the second day Aberfield and a sergeant returned with a dozen French loaves and an urn of warm milk. The men ate and drank voraciously; these were the first things that had crossed their throats for nearly three days. The battalion mess kitchen had been split from the company, its location unknown.

It was six in the evening on the second day when the mood of the commanding officers suddenly changed. The tension in the air rose to an unprecedented level as they were informed that a German patrol was minutes away from the bridge. Horace arranged his camouflage tight around his head and pulled the rifle butt into his shoulder. He controlled his breathing and listened to the sergeant explaining that they were only to open fire on his first shot.

Horace lay as still as he dared. He was aware of an eerie silence. The guns that had sounded in the distance, the lull of the traffic from the village that could be heard occasionally drifting in on the breeze seemed to have been frozen in a bizarre silent time warp. Even the birds had stopped singing as if somehow they knew.

Horace spotted the first German cautiously approaching the bridge a mere ten minutes later. The information had been good – at last, it seemed, someone on the Allied side was getting something right. His finger hovered over the trigger as he slowly lined up the V sight into the chest of the enemy soldier taking his first tentative steps on the bridge. Another five or six Germans came into view. Horace felt beads of perspiration forming on his forehead. He was about to kill a fellow human being, of that there was no doubt. He'd gone past the point of no return.

The first German soldier was now about half way across the bridge with at least a dozen of his compatriots treading nervously behind. Without warning a shot rang out behind him and the lead soldier's head exploded like an orange, a fine red mist seeming to linger eerily above him as he fell to the ground. A volley of shots pounded into the patrol as Horace switched his sights to the second soldier. He squeezed the trigger, the rifle cannoned into his shoulder as the round discharged and the man dropped like a sack of potatoes onto the parapet of the bridge. Instinct took over. He didn't have time to contemplate the absurdity of war or the young man's family back in Berlin or Munich, how they would react when told their father, son, brother had been killed in defence of the Fatherland. Horace took out at least another two and pumped two more rounds into a dying body on the bridge decking as the unfortunate man made a last-gasp effort for his rifle. The Bren guns completed a job well done. The German patrol had been massacred. Horace felt strangely elated... he had done his bit without hesitation. A few cheers broke out among the men. Horace remained quiet.

The sergeant major instructed Horace and three more members of the section to make safe the bridge – Army talk for ensuring that the Germans were in fact dead. Horace led the team of four – Ernie Mountain, Fred Bryson and section leader Charlie Smith – onto the bridge. His heart was pumping viciously now, a mixture of adrenaline and a little fear. He was sure the men following him could hear it. It was not unusual for a wounded or dying man to be clutching a live grenade, determined to commit suicide by blowing himself up along with any enemy in the vicinity. Horace had heard tales of dead Germans miraculously coming alive and taking out half a dozen careless Allied soldiers. He was determined to follow the job through and wouldn't relax until every one of the soldiers lying bloody and still on the bridge was confirmed as dead.

He looked back over his shoulder. The rest of his section had retained their positions, rifles trained on the bridge. He hoped they were as accurate a shot as he was, as he became acutely aware that his own body now stood in their line of fire. As he and his three colleagues now took up their positions, rifles trained on the German corporal's head. Horace propped his rifle up against the bridge wall, knelt down and studied the German's breathing – or rather the lack of it. He had watched the first body the whole time during the slow-paced walk over the bridge. Nobody could hold their breath that long, thought Horace. He took hold of the soldier's uniform, one hand on the shoulder and one on the lapel of the tunic. Slowly but with a forced action he fell backwards and the German soldier exposed his body and face to the three men's rifles. The shout went up.

'Clean.'

Horace breathed a sigh of relief. They took it in turns as they made their way over the bridge, carefully examining each body. They'd shot well. Not one German was alive. His colleagues were smiling now, visibly relaxing as one by one the enemy soldiers were pronounced dead. Young men – 18, 19 years of age. Boys.

At the far end of the bridge something extraordinary happened. It was Horace's turn again to approach the body, the last one, and the men adopted their now familiar positions, rifles at the ready. The German soldier lay in a pool of crimson. Fragments of skull bone, tissue and brain had splattered the wall of the bridge. Horace did not even take the time to gauge the breathing of the man. He was clearly dead and his body lay grotesquely twisted in an unnatural position face down in his own blood. Horace knelt, trying to avoid the steaming, sticky pool. He went through the motions.

'Clean,' came the cry.

'What's that?' The section leader was pointing at the dead man's midriff.

'It's a belt with writing on.'

The soldier bent down to take a closer look as the rest of the men lowered their rifles. He studied the writing.

'*Gott ist mit uns*,' he spelled out slowly.

'What does that mean?' Horace asked. He looked over to

Ernie Mountain, who spoke a little German. Ernie removed his tin helmet and scratched at his forehead.

'Well, fuck me... unless I'm mistaken it means "God is with us".'

'What God do they worship then?' asked the section leader.

'They're Christian,' replied Ernie.

'Fuck off, they can't be. They're evil bastards.'

Horace sat on the small parapet of the bridge as the conversation continued. The men were genuinely amazed as it was eventually agreed that the Germans – the Nazis, the Huns – actually worshipped the same God as good old Tommy.

Horace shook his head. It had never crossed his mind before. They'd read the reports, listened to the radio and watched the Pathé newsreels in cinemas up and down the country. This nation, these men, the soldiers and the SS seemed determined on world domination, intent on ethnic cleansing and eradicating anything that didn't meet their ideology. They seemed to go against everything that the good book preached, yet here was proof they worshipped the same Lord – Jesus Christ, God, the big fellow – as the men, women and children in England.

Horace stared into the faces of his stunned comrades. They weren't religious men, far from it. But they'd been brought up in decent family homes and schools, with morning worship and prayers at night as they settled down to sleep and, no doubt, Sunday school too.

'God understands German?' Ernie asked.

Horace nearly collapsed with laughter.

'Apparently so. And French and Russian and Polish too.'

'But he's on our side, not theirs,' said Fred Bryson as his brow furrowed. He looked around at his comrades as if expecting one of them to solve the puzzle right there and then. Four men. Four men who until that day hadn't ever believed, hadn't ever imagined that a Nazi could possibly worship Our Father, couldn't believe that they'd find hard evidence such as the belt they had just stumbled across.

Horace pointed to the body. 'Hasn't done that poor fucker any good, has he? Probably thought he was invincible with that belt on, probably thought he was afforded a little extra protection.'

Fred spoke. 'But the padre, he said we...'

'Don't go there, Fred,' interrupted Horace. 'It's all a pile of shite and now you know it for sure. Just think about it. Think about it when you say your prayers tonight.'

The men turned around and trudged back across the bridge towards their section. Fred Bryson lingered for a moment then removed the soldier's belt. As he walked back to join his colleagues he threw the belt over the bridge wall and down into the swollen river below. He didn't know why, it just seemed the right thing to do. This man didn't deserve to be buried with such a fine Christian inscription... let alone one in German.

An hour later the section holding the bridge was relieved and driven about a mile to the far side of town. The first thing Horace thought about was the hunger gnawing away at his stomach, and the second was sleep. The sergeant pointed across the field to an old dilapidated-looking farmhouse three hundred yards away.

'You can kip in there, lads. It's been checked out, not too clean but plenty of beds and running water. I think the present owners fucked off a few weeks ago when Jerry started flexing his muscles.'

'Any grub?' asked Horace.

The sergeant smiled. 'I'm sure you'll find something, Jim. There's a few tins lying around the cupboards and vegetables in the fields. I've even seen a few hens scraping about if you're fast on your feet.'

Fred rubbed at his stomach while his tongue caressed and moistened his lips. 'Chicken and roast potatoes, lads. Sounds good to me.'

'A little wine perhaps to wash it down with...' Horace smiled. It was a nice thought; there could be a small wine cellar and an oil stove to cook on, maybe a few pots and pans. As they set off along the tree-lined, pot-holed track leading up to their sanctuary, he listened to the artillery shells in the distance. Perhaps he was mistaken but they seemed to be getting a little louder.

The first shell exploded without warning. It had been fired from the west by the French Allies. The blast, no more than 30 yards away, knocked the men off their feet. Horace groaned as he was slammed into a tree. He lay still, shouted at the rest of his section and asked if everyone was OK.

Fred rose to his knees. 'Everyone's fine, I think. No damage done.'

'Get down, you idiot,' Horace screamed as the second shell whistled overhead. It exploded harmlessly behind the farmhouse. For the next 20 minutes the forward section of the 2nd/5th Battalion Leicesters lay face down in the French dirt as artillery shells rained down around them. Aberfield confirmed the shells were coming from the French lines. Friendly fire. The phrase had been coined in the First World War. Grossly incompetent generals directing fire into an area where their own troops were. Lack of communication, trigger happy, friendly fire. Wouldn't it be ironic if the section were wiped out by the very country they were there to protect?

The men could do nothing; their fate was in their allies' hands. Trees were flattened, the fields and forests all around pounded relentlessly. The noise was unbearable and Horace stiffened up as he heard every whistle from every shell overhead and wondered if one of them had the name Joseph

Horace Greasley etched into its casing. It was the nearest he had ever come to death, and the sheer destructive powers of the big guns frightened him. He had never witnessed it close at hand before. He had seen an occasional destroyed vehicle and of course the pictures on Pathé News, but nothing had prepared him for the immense power of destruction he was witnessing first hand. Aberfield lay just in front of him, his hands covering his head. Horace sought a tree trunk for protection, figuring out that the hundred-year-old tree would absorb most of the blast of any shell landing on the opposite side of the field. To a man the whole section curled up in balls as tightly as they could or pressed themselves deeper into the contours of the land and prayed that it would all be over soon.

And then it came. The shell with Greasley on it.

Horace heard the faint whoosh in the distance; his mouth was dry in an instant and as the whoosh turned into a whistle it was louder than anything he had heard previously. The other men sensed it too. This shell was heading their way. 'Take cover!' screamed someone behind him as it came ever closer. The noise was unbearable; the shell was coming straight for them. Horace covered his head and cursed for mercy as it exploded in the middle of the track. He remembered the noise as a huge fireball plumed 30 feet into the air and then a split second later – darkness.

Horace heard the groans at first. He had no idea how long he'd been out. It was silent now apart from a few birds singing. Those birds again, thought Horace. How do they know when to start singing? How do they know when to stop?

Most of the men were on their feet. Some attended to their stricken comrades and applied bandages to head wounds and an odd broken bone. No one lay motionless that he could see. Miraculously they had all survived. They had made it.

Horace tried to get to his feet. He couldn't. He tried again lifting his body from his hips, aware of a hot sensation in the small of his back as he attempted to push his backside up into the air. Nothing. He couldn't move. His back was stuck fast as if a huge weight was pressing down from above; his ammunition pouches bit into his chest. His worst nightmare, a broken back, life confined to a wheelchair. But somehow he sensed that was not the case. His back felt fine. He wiggled his toes. Fine. He bent his left leg from the knee so his heel pressed into one of his buttocks. It worked perfectly. The brain had sent the signal all the way down the spinal column and the leg had obeyed the order. Nevertheless he was still scared.

'Help me, Fred! I can't move.'

His comrade walked over to where Horace lay and his mouth fell open in amazement.

'Fuck me, Jim, you've been lucky.'

'Lucky? I... what?'

Fred held out a hand, which Horace reached for and Fred dragged him out from beneath the stricken tree. A piece of artillery casing an inch thick, the size of a car tyre, had almost split the tree in two, embedding itself seven or eight inches deep into the trunk. The protruding bit of smouldering red hot metal had entered the tree parallel with Horace's back, a fraction of an inch above it. It was this piece of French shrapnel that had temporarily disabled Horace. Fred shook his head in disbelief.

'Two inches lower, Jim, and it would have cut you in half.'

The enormity of just how close Horace had come to death sank in and his breathing became laboured. He sat for a few minutes in silence, staring at the broken tree and the shell casing. He removed his webbing belt and his hands instinctively massaged his kidney area. He'd had a close shave, of that there was no doubt. He took a deep breath and eased himself to his feet. The drama was over, time to put it to the back of his mind and think of more important matters, like food.

Twenty-nine men were grateful for an almost uninterrupted night's sleep under a sturdy roof for the first time in a week, and each fell asleep on a full belly. They'd managed to catch two hens that that they'd cooked and shared between them. There had been eggs in abundance and their feast had started with a makeshift egg mayonnaise minus the mayonnaise but with onions and chopped tomatoes from the fields. The main course was a type of chicken stew. Several tins of unlabelled green beans went into a huge pan along with the chicken, salt, pepper and sweet corn. An unlimited supply of boiled potatoes filled the men's stomachs to capacity and although they didn't manage to find a wine cellar, the fresh water from a well at the rear of the house tasted as good as anything they could have imagined. Horace fell asleep content. It was amazing the effect a full belly had on morale. He remembered an expression by a French general from long ago, 'An army marches on its stomach.'

It was around six in the morning when Horace awoke. He didn't know what had woken him first: thoughts of more food, Eva's lithe body or the sound of more artillery fire less than a few miles away. Outside, Sergeant Major Aberfield stood with a corporal and two or three men studying the sweeping corn fields to the east. Plumes of smoke rose to accompany the dull thud of the gunfire in the distance. The stems of the corn swayed gently in the breeze, a wallowing sea of yellow and green dancing to the tune of the wind.

But then something strange. The cornfield was moving but the timing was wrong. No longer did it flow back and forth like a wave, it, well... sort of jerked. A flash of grey. Aberfield had spotted it too and pointed open-mouthed as the helmets came into view. The men froze for a second as now the torsos of at least a dozen Germans became visible. They marched in a straight line, making no attempt to conceal themselves.

'Fuck me!' shouted Corporal Graham as he made a sprint to the farmhouse for his rifle. Horace didn't panic; he knew exactly what to do. The Bren gun stood poised, unmanned, at the door of a small barn 20 yards away, and by sheer coincidence primed and pointing in the right direction. Just what were the Germans playing at? He'd take most of them out before they even knew what was happening. He covered the 20 yards like an Olympic sprinter, Aberfield following in his wake. He reached for the tripod of the gun.

'Take your hands off the gun,' Aberfield said, pointing his revolver at Horace's temple.

It wasn't happening... it couldn't be happening.

'Hands off the gun!' he repeated.

'What are you doing, sir, for Christ's sake? They're lined up like sitting ducks!' Horace screamed, shaking his head, unsure what exactly was beginning to unfold. The sergeant major's pistol trembled in his right hand and Horace had no doubts whatsoever that he would pull the trigger. Aberfield's left hand went into his pocket and slowly withdrew a white handkerchief.

'No!' Horace howled out. 'No...'

The handkerchief fluttered in the breeze as Sergeant Major Aberfield held it up high and not one shot was exchanged between the section of the 2nd/5th Battalion Leicesters and the advance party of the German 154th Infantry Regiment.

As Horace marched into Cambrai he had never felt at such low ebb. His feet ached, his stomach groaned and he thought of his family back home. He thought of that Christmas Day and the robin, he thought of birdsong and long hot summers and the smell of fresh bread and wet summer grass. He was lost in his thoughts, desperately trying to project his mind away from the living hell he was looking at.

At least ten thousand Allied prisoners of war were packed into the medieval town square, surrounded by German guards. Night was just drawing in; the day was grey and bleak. The prisoners' faces portrayed sadness – all hope had gone, they were united in misery. Some were bloodied and broken, some clearly dying on their feet. French citizens stood among them, persuaded by the occupying forces to surrender without resistance, and for that they would be rewarded with jobs in munitions factories in Germany.

They had given up their country with barely a shot fired.

Horace was overawed by the sheer scale of the German presence, of their sleek, well maintained vehicles, far superior to those in which his section had travelled the breadth of France. They were better equipped, their uniforms of better quality, and a field kitchen had been set up in the entrance to the square as sausages, bread and steaming hot cups of coffee were handed out to their smiling, well fed faces. They were organised, battle hardened and more experienced.

They were also brutal and desensitised. The POWs were instructed to lie down where they stood in preparation for the night ahead. No tents, no huts, not even a blanket, just the uniforms they stood up in. A German soldier lunged at a poor unfortunate who was just a little slow obeying the order. He was dragged out of the main body of prisoners and attacked with rifle butts by half a dozen guards. The furious assault lasted no more than half a minute as the sickening thud of the rifles split his skull open and poured his blood onto the already damp cobbles of the square. The dazed man, barely conscious, looked up at the officer standing over him, pleading with terror-filled eyes. He knew what fate awaited him. The German officer smiled as he withdrew his pistol from the leather holster at his hip and pointed the gun at the head of the prisoner. In an act of unbridled cruelty the officer delayed the inevitable execution. The man begged and pleaded and shook his head and the tears poured down his cheeks for half a minute as he lay pained and bloodied on the ground. Then the officer's smile disappeared as he moved a step closer. Horace closed his eyes a split second before the shot rang out and when he opened them the man lay motionless, his eye socket a bloody empty hole.

Just after the town clock struck midnight the rain started. As if it couldn't get any worse, Horace thought. Within an hour he lay shivering in the cold night air, completely saturated. Incredibly Horace actually slept through the night but awoke the next morning to find himself lying in a channel of water running down from the streets that led into the square.

The clock struck seven and a volley of shots burst from an officer's pistol. Collectively the whole square understood them as a command to rise. Some never made it; they'd died from their untreated injuries. Incredibly a few slept through the noise, from sheer physical exhaustion. They were unceremoniously executed by enthusiastic guards, as if taking part in a bizarre sport.

An SS officer stood on the steps of the town hall.

'For you the war is over,' he shouted. 'You are prisoners of war, prisoners of the glorious German nation.'

He rambled on for another ten minutes, enjoying the power he yielded over the assembled masses, but whatever he said Horace didn't hear; he was thinking about crispy bacon and fried bread, an egg lightly cooked and hot, oversweet tea. The unmistakable aroma of cooking sausages wafted around the square as at least 50 guards stood patiently in line for their morning rations. They smoked, laughed and talked as if they had not a care in the world.

Ernie Mountain had slept alongside his friend for warmth and the two boys from Ibstock stood talking as the early morning sun, combined with their body heat, began to thaw their bones. A little later steam started to rise from the uniforms of ten thousand wretched souls, making a bizarre viewing spectacle. The German guards stood in shop doorways and on the town hall stairs, grinning and pointing at the thousands of smoking, smouldering prisoners as if they were about to burst on fire at any moment.

'Look at those fuckers,' Ernie said, tugging at Horace's damp uniform sleeve. He was pointing to a group of French prisoners feeding from what looked like a small leather suitcase. They sat on a small embankment on the outskirts of the square.

'Hungry cunts, eh?'

Horace nodded.

The French prisoners had had time to prepare for their incarceration and had stocked up on the bare necessities of life. They ate baguettes filled with meat and cheese; one man chewed on a bar of chocolate.

'Think they'll share it out, Ernie?'

'Not a fucking hope in hell. They're huddled around like a pack of wolves.'

A plan formulated in Horace's mind. For the first time in his life he was going to become a thief. He placed a hand on his pal's shoulder.

'Ernie, my friend, we are about to partake in a little breakfast.'

'What?'

'I'm going shoplifting. Your job, Mr Mountain, is to stop

any froggies coming after me. I'll disappear into the crowd with my ill-gotten gains and catch up with you later.'

'No, you crazy cunt! You'll be shot.'

Horace pointed over to the field kitchen.

'They're all having breakfast, mate. I've made my mind up. Now get ready, I need some bloody food.'

Before Ernie could protest, Horace had sauntered through the mass of bodies in front of him and stood on top of the embankment less than two yards from the Frenchmen. He didn't have to wait long, and what a result! Half a baguette was being handed across the circle. Without thinking, Horace covered the short distance as quick as lightning and grabbed the prize from the startled Frenchman's hand. He was down the embankment like a whippet as the Frenchman scrambled after him. Horace dropped his shoulders, picked out the unmistakeable bulk of Ernie and ran for him. As he passed Ernie the Frenchman seemed to be gaining on him. The rest of his friends had risen to their feet and were shouting, attracting the attention of a few guards.

'*Voleur!*' they cried. Thief!

Ernie gritted his teeth and aimed for the bridge of the Frenchman's nose. He didn't even swing a punch, just a stiff outstretched arm and a huge balled fist. The runner's momentum did the rest. There was a sickening crunch as bone met bone and the pursuer's legs kept going as his head remained motionless. At one point his body wavered vertically for a fraction of a second as he crumpled unconscious to the floor. Ernie about turned, looking innocently skywards as two German guards forced their way into the mêlée with their rifle butts.

The Frenchman's friends were picking up their unconscious, bloodied friend from the ground. '*Au voleur! Voleur!*' they cried, pointing through the crowd. Ernie cursed them under his breath and prayed that Horace hadn't been caught. Thankfully the German guards didn't appear to be interested in justice among prisoners. It didn't exist, and they cuffed a few of the French for the hell of it before returning to their breakfast. Horace found his friend and took great pride in tearing the baguette in half.

The two soldiers smiled as they bit into the delicious bread and savoured the taste. Ernie spoke between chews.

'You dozy cunt. You've pinched a fucking sandwich with fuck all sandwich in it!'

Horace opened up the bread and sure enough it was empty. It didn't matter; their stomachs appreciated it none the less.

Two hours later they began marching eastwards out of the village. The prisoner grapevine that would yield so much information in the coming years said they were embarking on a two or three-day march to the train station at Brussels in German-occupied Belgium. The grapevine got it dramatically wrong. The march would last for what would feel like an eternity and take Horace to hell and back.

CHAPTER
FOUR

The prisoners were a nuisance. They were nobodies and life was cheap. Horace sensed this almost as soon as the column of prisoners left Cambrai. For the first four or five miles the Allied prisoners marched along the main road out of the town, the line stretching as far as the eye could see. At one point the road dipped and straightened and Horace could see the front of the march shimmering in the rising heat of the day. Horace gasped at the sheer numbers; the line of sorry souls stretched at least three miles.

German trucks and convoys passed every few minutes and the hordes of prisoners were herded with rifle butts into the ditches by the side of the road to allow them to pass. The convoys of German troops, tank operators and drivers jeered and goaded and spat at the poor helpless unfortunates. A shaven-headed German thug hung from the roll bar of a truck with one hand. His trousers were at his ankles, his other hand on his penis as he sprayed urine onto the prisoners below. His friends on the back of the truck bent double with laughter, pointing and gesticulating. Horace thought back to his time on the farm and wondered how his fellow being could stoop so low. An animal wouldn't behave like that. Horace was beginning to build up a hatred he'd never felt before.

Later that day the line of tired, hungry and dejected men was made to march across the fields because they were causing congestion on the roads, slowing up the masses of the Third Reich heading west. As night approached, the blue sky faded into a darker hue. A light wind brought a chill to the evening air and Horace felt a desperate hunger. Surely the Germans had made provision to feed the march?

An hour later several large trucks rumbled into the field where they'd halted. Horace breathed a sigh of relief as the trucks turned and he spotted boxes of food and water containers and a huge pile of French loaves in the rear of one lorry. As expected the German guards took turns and lined up patiently as the starving and thirsty throng looked on. Hope turned to anxiety and then to disappointment and despair as the trucks were made secure and one by one, left under the cover of darkness. Horace settled down for the long night ahead.

The march left again at daybreak but not before they had watched yet another torturing German feast. The steam rose from the cups of coffee the guards held as they chewed on boiled eggs and bread baguettes.

For three days and three nights there followed the same routine. The men alongside Horace were now desperate. What were the Germans playing at? They'd been told in the town square in Cambrai they were being sent to work in camps and factories, but what sort of condition would they be in when they got there?

The men ate anything they could along the way, their eyes continuously scouring the ground for long-forgotten potatoes or turnips left to rot from last year's winter harvest. They stole the berries from the hedgerows and chewed on the shoots of any plant they could find, including recently planted root vegetables. It was dog eat dog; arguments broke out between two men over an ear of discarded corn or even a field beetle unlucky enough to cross the path of the march.

On the fourth day they passed through the small village of Cousoire. A signpost in the middle told the marchers they were 20 kilometres from Belgium.

A few villagers, mostly elderly ladies, lined the street, their eyes unable to take in yard after yard of stumbling, weary, desperately hungry men. As Horace passed a group of three old women his eyes caught the swift movement of a hand. The youngest of the group, around the same age as his own mother, held out an apple and her eyes made contact with his as she smiled. An apple. A sweet-tasting apple. Horace raised a half-hearted smile and reached out to take the offering. He'd made his mind up to divide it into three for the days ahead. Before it even touched his hand he could taste the sweet juice inside; he could feel the taste exploding in his mouth and the texture of the fruit as he chewed voraciously.

Horace never got to savour the experience. A young German soldier had spotted the incident and dragged the old woman into the middle of the road by her collar. His rifle butt had smashed the gift from Horace's hand and it rolled deep into the crowd. A dozen hands clawed for the prize, pulling and punching at each other as three German guards waded into the mêlée with their rifles flailing and feet kicking at any head they could connect with. Horace lay helpless, clutching at his wrist as the woman squealed and screeched like a pig being led to the slaughter.

'*Bâtard allemand!*' she screamed as the soldier took her by the hair. '*Bâtard allemand!*' she shouted again, and a few of the prisoners laughed at the spectacle unfolding in front of them, impressed by the lady's defiance and colourful language.

Horace's knowledge of French was basic to say the least but he knew exactly what the old lady meant.

The German threw her to the floor and pointed his rifle at her face. A threat, thought Horace, why? She had given him an apple, for Christ's sake. What had she done to offend the man, to upset the German nation? And then the unimaginable happened. The old lady seemed to freeze, a look of horror on her face as she made eye contact with her aggressor. The action slowed down as if in a bizarre slow motion as the soldier pulled the trigger.

The old lady lay motionless on the ground as a pool of blood spread like a crimson lake around her head. A young prisoner ran at the soldier, his eyes filled with hatred as two of his mates rugby-tackled him to the floor.

'You fucking bastard!' he screamed as a life-saving hand clamped his mouth shut. A tear ran down Horace's cheek as he lay motionless, unable to understand the cowardly act he'd just witnessed. It was simply incomprehensible. He wanted to kill the soldier, to tear out his eyes with his bare hands. He recalled how he'd likened the Germans to animals a few nights before. They weren't like animals; he'd insulted the good name of an animal. These men were worse.

The condition of the men deteriorated over the next few days but thankfully the Germans seemed to turn a blind eye to villagers handing out whatever scraps they could spare. Horace was positioned towards the back of the queue and managed to get very little. He ate the skin of an orange one day and a cup full of milk, crumbs of bread and some grain. The march swept into the villages like a swarm of starving locusts.

Nothing survived, anything that could be eaten was. Hens, dogs, cats... anything. They were eaten raw, the warm blood of the freshly killed animal savoured by those lucky enough to catch it. There were regular altercations between prisoners fighting over a piece of stale bread or a fat insect, even stagnant water. The Germans looked on as full fist-fights developed. It was a little light entertainment for them on the long monotonous journey.

When allowed their one rest each day, a dinner time break without the dinner, the men would sit around in groups and speak of their families back home. It kept them going, and some would talk full of hope that it would all be over soon and they'd be back with their families within weeks or months. Horace worried more that England would be overrun by the Germans and his family's lives would be as wretched as his had become.

Then the dysentery started with a vengeance. Every few minutes somebody left the line and walked a few feet to a ditch by the side of the road, squatted, and without a shred of human dignity left, emptied the watery contents of his insides in full view of everyone. Some had time to grab at a handful of grass and clean themselves best they could. Others didn't bother; they were past caring and simply pulled up their shit-covered trousers.

The stench was permanent, the flies constant. Some men collapsed, too weak to go on. They were left by the side of the road and executed by the section of Germans following up the rear. The executions were regular and could be heard by the chain of human misery. They followed a pattern. Horace could see the signs – men staggering, stumbling as if in a drunken stupor, then buckling at the knees. Occasionally a rifle butt in the back, an order to continue. The men would be helped by their friends and comrades and urged to press on, and some would do that, glad of the support. But some would just shrug off the assistance, resigned to the fact that wherever it was they were being taken, they would never get there. They would be left where they fell, prepared to meet their maker. And a long two, three minutes later... that awful sound.

The days turned to weeks. How many Horace didn't know, but the men grew weaker and the executions increased. Horace held a bizarre secret that he only divulged to a few of his companions. As a child, his mother had scattered the family's summer salads with dandelion leaves. They were full of moisture and nutrition and tasted strangely sweet. Every opportunity he had he picked the tiny leaves at the side of the road and chewed at the succulent gift of life every few hours. His mouth was constantly refreshed, stopping him from drinking the rainwater at the side of the road, the same water that had been polluted earlier by the dysentery-ridden souls at the front of the march. He'd wait... he'd survive, praying for a water fountain or a recently filled rain butt in the next village when he'd drink till his belly was full to bursting.

Horace passed weaker soldiers almost every hour in an attempt to survive by getting to the front of the line, figuring that those at the front got the first option on any food that happened to be available. He hadn't seen his old mucker Ernie Mountain for at least two weeks now and thought about him constantly. He thought about Sergeant Major Aberfield too, the bastard of a coward that had surrendered the entire section without as much as one bullet being fired. Horace took a bizarre comfort in the fact that he'd never surrendered. He would take that comfort right through the war.

'I never surrendered,' he'd tell anyone who'd listen. 'I didn't get the choice; some bastard took the choice from me. I was surrendered by a coward.'

Night after night he'd wonder what might have happened if he could turn the clock back. He'd lie on his back looking up at the clear night sky as the stars from a distant galaxy twinkled through the haze. He took a strange comfort in watching them for hours on end.

But before long the man who had sealed his fate would creep back into his head and he would tremble with rage. He'd rerun the events again and again. He'd been in no doubt that Aberfield would pull the trigger. Aberfield had tried to explain he'd saved their lives. Horace didn't buy that. There had been more fit men in the section of 2nd/5th Leicesters than the Germans who'd captured them. They'd had a chance, a very good chance: an opportunity to take out the patrol and regroup. Nobody knew how many Germans were behind that initial patrol but Horace didn't care. They'd had a chance to fight, to survive, a chance to escape and run to fight another day. Aberfield had made the decision for each and every one of them and he didn't have that right.

Horace had read accounts of soldiers in the First World War being shot for disobeying orders. He'd read reports of working-class infantrymen turning on the officers in charge. Now he could understand just what it was that had driven them to do so.

They were now deep in the heart of Belgium. It was rumoured they were heading for Holland where they were to be placed on barges and sent down the Rhein to the prison camps in Germany. This time the grapevine had got it right. Unfortunately those plans would be scuppered by the RAF a few days later when they sank every barge.

Horace's feet had broken down; he felt he couldn't go on any longer as they settled down in a wet field on the outskirts of Sprimont, less than 30 miles from the border between Belgium and Luxembourg. He'd struck up a friendship with a man from London, Flapper Garwood. A giant of a man weighing some 16 stones prior to the march, Flapper reckoned he was losing six or seven pounds a day.

In the few short weeks they'd been on the road he'd lost over two stones.

Horace watched as the big man dropped to his knees.

'So how come they call you Flapper? I've never asked.'

Garwood shrugged his shoulders. 'Nothing very exotic, Jim. The lads reckon my arms flap around like windmills when I play football, that's all.'

'You play a lot then?'

Garwood looked at the column of prisoners, the German guards, and raised his eyebrows.

'Not had many games lately, Jim. They must have been cancelled for some reason.'

The two men laughed at the irony of the statement.

'But yeah, I used to play a fair bit, signed professional forms with Spurs before Hitler started flexing his muscles.'

'Flapper, eh? What a bloody name to be lumbered with,' Horace said.

'You can call me by my full name if you like.'

'Which is?'

'Herbert Charles Garnett Garwood.'

Horace shook his head. 'Flapper it is, then.'

Flapper held onto Horace's calf muscle, gently tugging at the heel of his boot. Horace cried out in pain as Flapper eased the boot free. Flapper held up the foot as he inspected it.

'Fuck me, country boy – I can see the white of your bone through this one.'

Flapper pointed to the blister.

'You're kidding me, right?'

He wasn't.

Flapper walked off and returned a little later with clump of soaking wet grass that he applied to the worst affected spot. Neither man knew the medical benefits of this treatment or whether it would do more harm than good. Horace didn't care

58

– it felt like heaven. It would feel like hell the next morning as he struggled to his feet, his heavy boots biting into his bloody, pus-filled feet. He hung on to Flapper for the first few miles, the big man uncomplaining and seemingly happy to carry the burden of a friend he'd only known for a few days. After a couple of miles the boots eased and Horace was able to hobble along unaided, his feet now so numb the pain didn't register.

Then he saw him. A few yards ahead Horace registered the crowns on the lapels, that familiar stoop, the short, stocky unmistakeable shape of Sergeant Major Aberfield.

Horace's pace picked up. Flapper sensed the urgency in his steps and wondered what was going on as he raced after his friend. Horace tapped Aberfield on the shoulder and he turned round. He smiled. He actually fucking smiled, thought Horace afterwards.

'Morning, Greasley. Bearing up, old chap?'

Horace's hand grabbed the sergeant major's groin and located two testicles. He gritted his teeth, snarled, squeezed hard and twisted with all his rapidly draining strength. The officer's mouth fell open and the blood drained from his face as he stood on tiptoes in a vain attempt to minimise the excruciating pain.

Horace had never head butted anyone before. He couldn't even recall heading a football at school: he'd had no interest in that sort of thing. It was not something he'd planned to do; it just came naturally. But boy, was it effective. He released Aberfield's balls and leaned back a few inches. The relief on his sergeant major's face was instantaneous, bordering on the orgasmic. As a brief smile flicked across the officer's face Horace powered his forehead into the bridge of his nose. The soft bone and cartilage collapsed on impact and a spray of blood flew through the air. As Aberfield collapsed, squealing like a wounded pig, a rifle butt struck Horace in the back and he fell to the ground. He jumped up immediately, ready to take issue with the attacker, to slam a fist into the Hun's face and sign his own death warrant. Right now he was beyond caring, ready to die.

But Garwood intervened, wrapping his friend in a bear hug and dragging him away deep into the crowd. Flapper wouldn't release him for a good five minutes, no matter how hard Horace struggled and protested. As his breathing returned to normal he thanked a god he didn't believe in for his newly formed friendship.

For Horace, the weeks of continuous marching across France, through Belgium and into Luxembourg were a living, starving, leg-breaking, strength-sapping nightmare. He watched his comrades die in front of him without being able to lift a finger. That was the worst – the mental torture of being useless, being controlled, dominated, herded like animals. No choice of when to eat or when to piss and shit. Nothing in life could be as bad again. Or so he thought.

The next three days on a train to Poland would make the march seem almost luxurious. They didn't climb aboard the train, just inside the Luxembourg border at Clervaux, they were herded and kicked and punched. Once again the end of a rifle was the German soldiers' favourite assault weapon. Flapper Garwood took the full force of one of them as his skin split wide open under his uniform. Untreated and unstitched, the scar would be with him forever.

The platform of the station was strewn with about 20 dead bodies – the Allied prisoners who'd been just a little slow in obeying the orders of their captors. They were made to run a gauntlet made up of about 20 Germans on each side. The Allied prisoners were literally running onto the trucks of the train, herded like cattle. A quick sprint meant less chance of getting struck. Garwood took Horace by the sleeve.

'Are you ready for a run, Jim?'

'Ready as ever, Flapper. At least the fucking hike is over.'

'And at least they'll have to feed us properly if they want some work out of us.'

'Right enough, Flapper. Let's go.'

The two men ran as fast as they could, covering their heads with their hands. Horace took a glancing blow from a fist and Flapper another rifle butt in the back in exactly the same spot as the first wound. He winced with pain as a sick, nauseous feeling welled up in his empty stomach. But others inside the truck fared much worse.

'Looks like we got off lightly,' said Flapper, pointing to one prisoner with blood pouring out of a head wound. Other unconscious bodies were dragged onto the train.

By the time the Germans bolted the door the men were packed in like sardines, perhaps three hundred to a wagon. Some men were panicking and screaming as claustrophobia kicked in. Horace couldn't even lift his hands above his head. His feet ached and all he wanted to do was sit or lie down, but it was impossible.

An hour into the journey Horace had to take a shit. He was luckier than most: he could control the moment, unlike those with dysentery.

'I need a shit, Flapper,' he said in a whisper that only his pal could hear.

'Awwww... Jesus Christ, you don't, do you?'

''Fraid so, mate.'

Flapper decided to attract the attention of the men discreetly, spare some dignity for his friend.

'Make some space... man here needs a shit,' he shouted.

A collective groan reverberated around the truck as men jostled and pushed Horace over into the far corner.

'Station approaching,' someone shouted, leaning from the

open window of the truck, and suddenly Horace had an idea. He muscled his way over to where the shouter was standing. By this time the pain in his bowel was excruciating. He clutched at the cheeks of his arse.

'Any Germans on the platform?' he shouted up to the man leaning from the small opening.

'Dozens of the square-headed cunts, mate.'

'Then get out the way quickly, will you?'

As the rest of the truck looked on in amazement Horace dropped his trousers and emptied his bowels into the open flap of his Glengarry hat. The smell was overbearing but Horace managed to scramble up to the opening, taking care not to spill any of the shit from the hat. He studied the motion of the train. It wasn't slowing down, wasn't stopping as it trundled along at about 20 miles an hour. A wide grin spread across his face as he spied a line of six German soldiers a mere foot or two from the platform edge. He positioned the Glengarry so he could hold it with the two flaps in one hand. By now the rest of the men realised what he was up to and whooped and howled messages of encouragement.

Horace timed the action to perfection. With a flick of the wrist he released one of the flaps two or three feet from the line of Germans. The shit sailed through the air at face level like a flock of disoriented starlings, the momentum of the train propelling it onwards. The first German managed to turn his head away as he realised what was happening but his five friends were not as quick. It was a direct hit as the foul-smelling excrement exploded onto their heads and shoulders and Horace's arm rose in triumph as the cheers of the carriage rang in his ears. He'd scored the winning goal in a cup final, the winning runs in a Test match.

All too soon the moment of euphoria ended. But it was soon repeated over and over again. It was the only weapon they had to fight against the Germans but it mattered not. It was a protest, a talking point, two fingers up to the enemy, and the sport continued. A corner of the truck was designated 'crap corner'. Prisoners would shuffle and twist and turn to allow the next poor unfortunate soul the space to drop his trousers and his 'bomb' into a helmet, a hat or a container, ready to be flung at any Germans manning the next station. Occasionally they had to step over dead bodies, the heat and starvation and thirst having taken their toll, but they threw shit at Darmstadt and Hammelburg and Kronach. Each time a soldier bared his arse and the smell of shit rose from the floor of the wagon muffled cheers rang out from the tightly packed masses.

But still men died.

At night the prisoners slept standing up, propped against each other as the swaying motion of the train rocked a few hours' rest inside them. Horace had run out of dandelion leaves, his meagre rations shared with his best friend from London. His mouth was bitterly dry, and a giant rat gnawed at the lining of his stomach, crying out for food. He could survive no more than a few hours, he wanted to lie down and sleep. He wanted to surrender to the inevitable.

Daylight now, but still he wanted to sleep. His eyes closed and he leaned into the body of the man next to him. The man was stiff – board stiff – and as Horace looked into the face of the wretched soul, he looked like he'd been painted a deathly grey.

His thoughts drifted away... He was in a meadow with his father shooting at rabbits, a good day, at least three kills and a short trek home through the wet grass. The smell... the smell of wet grass, and later the rabbits baked in a pie as Mum lifted the dish from the oven. And the family sat down at the kitchen table one by one – Mum, Dad, Daisy, Sybil and Harold... with baby Derick in his wooden high chair grinning and gurgling, banging a spoon on the arm like a drumstick. Happy faces, everyone ready to share the food, drink the cool lemonade Mum had bought as a special treat from the mobile shop that drove up Pretoria Road twice a week. And the taste of the tender flesh, the gravy and the pie crust that only Mum could make... But then someone was looking through the window, pointing a torch. A scowling stranger, then a command in an unfamiliar language. And another man bursting through the door, a rifle in his hand, and Horace jumping between his mother and the brute of a man covered in swastikas from head to toe, dealing a backhander to his face....

Flapper slapped at his cheek.

'Don't you be quitting on me, you cunt of a country boy. We're going to get through this together.'

Flapper pushed a few dandelion leaves into his mouth.

'Eat. I kept a few back, found a good supply just before we got into Luxembourg.'

Horace hardly had the willpower to chew, the energy and the juice of the leaves barely kicked in. They had lost their goodness in his mate's pocket. He did not want to chew, did not have the strength, but Flapper took his jaw between his huge hands and forced his teeth to grind together with a circular movement.

'Chew them. We're in this together.'

Horace nodded, whispering quietly, 'A pact, Flapper... me and you together. No surrender.' And with that he lapsed into unconsciousness and no amount of coaxing, cajoling or slapping was going to wake him.

When Horace came round he was sitting on the platform of a station and the aroma of some sort of soup permeated the air. Flapper knelt in front of him doling out tender slaps to his cheeks.

'Wake up, Jim. We're going to get some grub.'

Horace was not dreaming – he had smelt soup. He looked over as a line of prisoners collected their meagre rations in whatever it was they could get a hold of.

'Hot fucking soup, Jim – hot loop the loop!'

Helped by Flapper, Horace scrambled to his feet and they almost ran to join the queue. He wondered where his sudden burst of energy had come from. The prisoners of war were given one half-ladle of the liquid and a lump of heavy dark brown German bread. Horace gratefully took the bread, took a large mouthful and stuffed the rest into his pocket.

'No bowls!' shouted Flapper as they neared the front of the queue. Horace looked up ahead. Some men were lucky enough to still have an army issue helmet, but most accepted the hot soup in their filthy bare hands.

Those that swallowed too quickly paid the penalty as the hot soup hit stomachs that had shrunk beyond belief. The liquid nourishment was spewed back up almost as soon as it was swallowed. Despite the hot soup stinging their hands Flapper and Horace sipped slowly, savouring each mouthful. The soup had been provided by the Red Cross, which had somehow found out about the death train making its way across Germany. They also provided the fresh clean water the men drank afterwards.

The dead bodies were removed from each truck and piled high at the far end of the station. Then the prisoners were herded back onto the train and Horace felt guilty about the extra room it gave him on the truck. They were still unable to sit down but his belly was full and he had quenched his thirst. He had survived another day.

Early the following morning the train stopped with a jolt.

Three or four of the prisoners leaned from the windows. One of them read from the sign in the middle of the platform.

'P. O. S. E. N.' someone spelled out.

'Where the fuck's that, then?'

Flapper Garwood looked across to Horace. 'Poland, Jim. We're in Poland.'

They had finally arrived at their destination. Joseph Horace Greasley had arrived in German-occupied Poland, where he would spend the next five years of his life.

CHAPTER FIVE

The early months of the war did not go well for the Allies. In August 1940 Hitler prepared an invasion of Great Britain, scheduled to take place on 15 September in an operation named Sealion. He was confident of an early victory. His troops and air force were ready and primed and the military hardware in place, and the Allied troops were seemingly in disarray. Only the force of Mother Nature's weather prevented him from going ahead with the operation.

The RAF offered a glimmer of hope, proving more than a match for the German Luftwaffe in wide-ranging flights along the east coast. However, the Germans still managed to bomb London and continued shelling Dover with long-range artillery. Towards the middle of September Hitler, who had now ordered all Jews to start wearing yellow stars for identification, sent waves of aircraft to bomb British cities but most were driven off. The Luftwaffe failed to make significant inroads into British defences. The RAF was beginning to claim victory in the Battle of Britain.

Horace Greasley was unaware of any of this. He and his fellow prisoners had spent some weeks at a large holding camp at Lamsdorf and then about three hundred were transferred during darkness to another facility a few miles away. The prisoners were updated on the progress of the war, but only from a German perspective. Although Horace realised that the Germans would stretch the truth in the war of propaganda, his thoughts drifted back to his capture and how easily France and the other Allies had capitulated. He thought back to the German troops at Cambrai and their weaponry, and how well organised and motivated their whole war machine seemed to be. And he feared the worst. Horace was in a depression he had never experienced before.

It was early in the morning when Horace would awake on his bed of straw on concrete. Even though the summer sun still retained a little heat, the concrete below him had already begun to cool significantly in the few short weeks since they had arrived. Winter would be with them soon enough, a thought Horace dreaded.

He awoke each morning thinking only of food. Gone were the days when his first thoughts were of a particular girl back home, a pair of pert breasts or the soft downy pubic hair of Eva Bell. Now, instead, his early morning dreams were of bread and meat, his mother's homemade pies and scones and fruit cakes. And as the awful realisation hit him every morning when he awoke and realised where he was, his first thoughts were of death and torture, of control and brutality, and how his fellow man could commit the acts he was witnessing first hand. And then came thoughts of home and his family and just how long it would be before the Third Reich would sweep up through England and into his home town.

Horace turned over. It was not yet time to get up and face the bleak day ahead. For that's what it was: he was in Charles Dickens' *Bleak House*. He recalled reading the book as a teenager, but this *Bleak House* was a hundred times worse.

For everyone is lonely in *Bleak House*. Everyone in *Bleak House* is lost.

Horace closed his eyes. Perhaps he could put off the horror of the day ahead for another hour. His feet ached; he had not removed his boots since the night in the field in Belgium. He'd tried several days afterwards but it was as if his boots, what was left of them, were glued to his feet. As each day passed the glue strengthened and his reluctance to discover just what sort of condition his feet were in grew.

Fort Eight Posen had been an old First World War cavalry barracks. The prisoners slept in what were once the stables. There were no bunks, no blankets. The buildings and the filthy, broken-down straw were alive with mice and cockroaches and lice. The conditions inside Fort Eight at Posen were a living paradise for body lice, which lived in the seams and folds of clothing – the dirtier the better – and were transmitted by infected clothing and bedding as well as direct contact with an infected person.

Horace was luckier than most as he'd managed to conceal an old nail file in the breast pocket of his uniform. He kept his nails short and clean, a barber's tradition and a habit he found difficult to break. Horace didn't scratch, he rubbed. The men with nails – filthy dirty nails – clawed at their bodies where the lice were biting, compounding and spreading the problem.

Every prisoner dreaded that first initial sign. The men would wake in the morning and minute, dark brown specks of louse excreta would clearly be visible on the skin. Several days later the biting would start. There was no escape, no hot water to wash in, no soap, no earthly chance of keeping clean. The lice fed on human blood, and after their feast would lay eggs on skin and in the creases of clothing. The infection caused intense itching, demoralising and degrading the men who could do little about it.

The itching was irritating beyond belief and scratching was unavoidable. Even when the skin had broken, the poor men still couldn't help themselves and huge sores grew into large ulcers as each day passed. And then the flies, part of nature's food chain, moved in. It was common for a man to awaken with hundreds of tiny maggots feeding on the exposed pink and yellow pus-infected mess.

Horace lay on urine-soaked straw. The strong smell of ammonia always lingered in the air, as some men were too weak to stand and answer the call of nature. Horace was barely able to move. It was as if the life had been sucked from him. His feet throbbed every few minutes from the exposed flesh on his heels rubbing against his boots. It had been weeks since he had removed them, memories of the pain when he had put the boots back on in a field in Belgium too intense to tempt him to take them off again. He longed for the wet grass poultice his friend had applied.

The rat still gnawed away at his stomach lining and lice ran across his skin, torturing him each minute of every day. At times, even though he knew they were biting into his flesh, he let them. Let them have their fill of my blood, he said to himself, perhaps then they'll leave me alone.

Worse lay in store every couple of days when nature called and he was forced to defecate. The prisoners would put it off as long as they could but inevitably after two or three day's cabbage soup, their bowels would need to move.

It was called the toilet block. Horace didn't know why. He was generally about 30 yards away when the smell kicked in. As he reluctantly got closer the smell intensified and it was all he could do to prevent himself throwing up. He needed to keep the food in his stomach as long as he could. Some of the men couldn't manage it and grew weaker by the day.

The block itself was crude. A floor made of wooden planks

had been nailed onto a huge frame over an exposed tank. Two 3ft by 20ft gaps had been left exposed and at waist level, on a separate framework, two long planks had been nailed loosely into place. The prisoner would sit between the two planks and shit through the gap into the tank below. No privacy, no sinks, no running water, no toilet paper. The prisoners cleaned themselves on whatever they could get a hold of, normally a handful of grass. Some didn't bother.

At ground level an eight-inch diameter waste pipe poked out. Every few weeks a tanker arrived, connected a powerful suction pipe to the valve and literally sucked out two tons of human excreta. As the pipe sat four feet above the base of the tank, the tank was never emptied completely. Always four feet of shit for the flies to feed on. In the summer months it was simply unbearable – a fly and cockroach paradise.

Horace was physically weak, but far worse was his mental state. His mind was near to breaking and he dreamed and hallucinated by the hour. Still the nightmares continued: of Germans in his village, Germans in his home, Germans terrorising his mother and sisters. And the dreams continued long after he awoke. Jackboots everywhere. Skeletal bodies littered the floor, some snoring, some moaning and one man on his knees sobbing a prayer to his Almighty.

'Oh Lord, why have you forsaken me? Why do you do this to me? Why do you make me suffer so much?'

Tom Fenwick's father had been in the Church of England ministry and Tom was brought up in the way of the church.

'Shut the fuck up, Fenwick,' a voice shouted close by. 'He ain't fucking listening now. Get some kip.'

'Why, Lord? I'm a good man. I pray every day. If this is a test of my faith let it end now. Surely I have passed? Give me a sign, Father.'

The last few words were said between tears, barely a whimper. He turned to Horace.

'He doesn't hear, Jim, does he?'

Horace looked into Tom Fenwick's eyes. He was beaten: all hope had gone. As a small boy he had followed the Ten Commandments to the letter. He'd believed that good would always triumph over evil, that the man in the clouds would always listen and answer his prayers.

'Thou shalt not kill, Jim. That's what the good Lord tells us, and yet these men are breaking his commandments every day and he lets them get away with it. Why isn't he stopping them?'

Horace shook his head.

The tears were streaming down Tom Fenwick's face now as his voice rose.

'Why doesn't he do anything, Jim? Why doesn't he stop them like he stopped the tribes that plotted against Israel?'

Horace opened his mouth to speak, ready to tell Tom Fenwick that his God didn't exist. Horace always had his doubts, wondered how his brother could have been sucked in so easily. Harold had wanted his twin brother involved. He had wanted him to attend at least one or two services he preached at. Horace had refused, wondering why so many grown men and women wasted so many hours of their lives preaching and praying to someone or something they had never met, never touched, never even seen. He could understand the ancients worshipping the sun, the giver and taker of life in times of darkness and bad summers. Yes, he could understand the man who would pray for a good harvest, pray for the sun to shine...

Yet he'd always kept an open mind. He'd admired the teachings of the Christian church. He'd respected the man Jesus Christ and his ideals, respected and somehow believed, or rather hoped, that good would always triumph over evil. Until now.

There was no God. There couldn't be.

At that very moment it was he who wanted to stand up in the pulpit and preach to this man and tell him how ridiculous his belief was. But there was no need. At that same moment Tom Fenwick lost his faith, lost the God he'd believed in for as long as he could remember – and Horace saw it in his eyes. The young man buried his face in his hands and sobbed like a baby.

After the roll call the prisoners were marched over to the far side of the camp to the kitchen. Their daily ration was one bowl of cabbage water soup and a third of a tin loaf of stodgy, heavy, dark brown bread, an hour or two after they were woken around seven. It was the highlight of each day. Horace broke his ration of bread into three for the long day ahead, as did most of the men. Horace sat with Tom Fenwick who, unusually, wolfed down his bread ration in one. It was the action of a man taking his last meal, though Horace didn't know it at the time.

The fort was surrounded by a huge moat, though empty of water. The only way to exit the fort was across a drawbridge patrolled on either side of the wall by German guards. To set foot on this bridge without permission was tantamount to suicide.

Tom Fenwick smiled at Horace and mumbled something about being reunited with his father again. Before Horace had realised what was happening, Tom Fenwick sprinted towards the bridge, screaming something undecipherable at the top of his voice. As was intended, it drew the attention of every German soldier on duty and as he leapt onto the wooden gantry he was cut down in a hail of bullets before his feet touched the ground. Still the Germans pumped more bullets into the body lying on the wooden surface and Thomas Albert Fenwick breathed his last.

Horace looked into the faces of the soldiers who had ended the life of the young man without hesitation. They were smiling, congratulating each other... not unlike the praise Horace had received from his father all those years ago as a teenager when he had taken down a fast-running hare or rabbit at long distance. It seemed the Nazis had enjoyed their early morning sport.

The Waffen SS ran Fort Eight at Posen with an iron fist and near hatred for the incarcerated men. There was a total lack of respect for the soldier who had ended up there. The SS were indoctrinated that the honourable man died on the battlefield and only the lowest surrendered or were captured. The beating of a prisoner was a common occurrence; a man just had to look at a guard the wrong way and the shit would be kicked out of him.

Within a week the prisoners fit enough to stand on parade were asked by an SS officer if any of their civilian occupations could help with the glorious German war effort. It was the wrong approach. The men kept quiet – except one.

'I will help the marvellous German war effort with my civilian work skills.'

It was Frank Talbot, an airman from Worcester. The prisoners were dumbfounded. Some sneered and hissed.

'My skills were made for the wonderful German soldiers.'

The SS officer smiled as he spoke. 'Excellent... and what was your profession back in England, prisoner?'

Talbot looked back at the mass of prisoners and then back to the SS man.

'I am an undertaker, sir.'

A huge cheer rang out from the ranks of astonished and laughing men. After the beating that followed, Frank Talbot spent two weeks in the sick bay with a fractured skull and a broken tibia. He would tell the men afterwards that the pain he suffered was worth it.

The men were ordered to reveal their civilian roles. Incredible though it seemed, a gentleman's barber would be spared the normal duties. By this time every man in the camp had lice and keeping prisoners' heads shaved was the only way to control the spread.

Horace was shown into a small room adjacent to the offices of the camp and a queue of POWs made to line up outside. It was there that Horace shaved the lice-ridden heads from dawn until dusk with no running water or electricity. As the day went on his feet swelled inside his battered boots until they cried out for mercy, but by sitting the prisoners on an old shoebox and distributing his weight from one leg to the other every few minutes, he managed to give each foot a break. And he thanked his lucky stars that he could manage cutting hair, for nothing could be worse than the work the outside parties were being made to undertake.

The first workers returned after day one looking more pale and gaunt then their starving malnourished comrades inside the camp. Flapper had been one of those assigned to the work party. He said that at first that the men were glad of the change of scenery, happy about the fresh air and a little exercise as they'd been marched the short distance just outside the village of Mankowice.

They had been carrying shovels, picks and spades and some assumed they were about to start work on a building project, perhaps digging the foundations for a new factory or maybe another camp. They had stopped outside a graveyard and one by one were ushered through the gates of the elegant, well-kept cemetery.

At first Flapper believed they were simply there to tidy things up, a gardener's working party. Then he noticed the names on the gravestones. Isaac and Goldberg, Abraham and Spielberg. And the Star of David carved or painted into each stone. A Jewish cemetery. Given the rumours that flew around the camp there was no way the Germans would want to trim the bushes and control the weeds. Instead the prisoners were instructed to dig a hole six feet deep.

'This grave is for anyone who disobeys my orders,' an English-speaking sergeant explained.

The full horror of their task became clear as he rambled on. They were to exhume the dead bodies of the Jews and rob them of everything they had taken with them in death. Gold rings, watches... even the gold fillings from their rotting teeth were pulled out with pliers. The SS stood watch as the crumbling skeletons were abused, robbed of everything. Afterwards the remains of the bodies were taken to a huge pit dug by a previous party and thrown in without ceremony. Garwood cried as he relayed the details to his friend: the bodies of small children and women dressed up in what were once their finest clothes – mere rags now, soiled rags – and how the prisoners had been made to strip the skeletons bare, just to make sure nothing was missed.

'Is nothing sacred to these bastards, Jim?' he asked between tears.

It had been a bad day, possibly the worst so far. As each day, week and indeed month passed since he had been captured, Horace had drifted off to sleep at night thinking things couldn't get any worse. But they did.

As unpleasant as conditions were, Horace could not complain about the task he had been allocated inside Fort Eight at Posen. The men were glad of the respite and a pleasant conversation as they sat in the makeshift barber's chair. It was as if an air of normality had returned to their wretched lives in the few short minutes it took to take off their hair with a cut-throat razor, cold dirty water and a lather stick.

Both barber and client transported themselves back several years and a kind of make-believe act took place for a few precious moments before reality kicked in again and the men were back to face the brutality of the SS soldiers and the ruthless conditions outside of the room.

'Off to the dance on Saturday night, sir?'

'Why yes, Jim... and you?'

'Wouldn't miss it for the world, sir. Got myself a pretty little thing to take along too, her name's Eva.'

'Fantastic, Jim, you're a lucky man. I noticed her too, figure like an hour glass and well built up top.'

'I'll say, sir.'

Another filthy creature crawled down the gleaming blade of the razor. Horace squashed it as it settled on the nail of his thumb, leaving a bloody imprint as the blood sucked out of its host exploded from its miniscule body.

'Managed to get your hands on them yet, Jim?'

Horace smiled, pursed his lips and smiled at his client.

'I'll say, sir... Finest pair of tits this side of Leicester, nipples like bloody organ stops,' he laughed.

And so it went on, and at times Horace felt he was actually back in his old employer's shop in Leicester. That was all he could do, play with his mind: imagine and play tricks on it. He would get through the war; he had to.

A few weeks into the operation two German SS officers walked in to the shop. Three prisoners waited patiently on shoeboxes by the door. They were told to leave, their place in the queue had been taken, and one of the SS soldiers sat down. The other walked over to where Horace was shaving a prisoner and cuffed the man across the back of his head. Horace recognised the guard instantly. He was a towering man of six foot three with a noticeable stoop and a craving for unnecessary violence against the prisoners. The men had nicknamed him Big Stoop and he was to be avoided at all costs. There were strong though unsubstantiated claims that he had beaten to death more than half a dozen prisoners in his previous camps.

'*Hinaus, dies ist jetzt mein Platz.*' 'Out, it's my seat now.'

The prisoner scuttled across the floor, his head half shaved. As he got to the doorway the other guard kicked him in the seat of the pants.

'*Hinaus!*' he screamed.

Horace was stunned and a little wary that he was now alone with two German SS men. As he stood there with a cut-throat razor in his hand the hatred inside him welled up. The German lowered himself onto the shoebox and pointed to his face.

'Shave good,' he instructed.

No, he wanted to say. I don't want to shave you. But he knew what the consequences would be if he refused.

Horace made a point of washing his razor as best he could and as he lathered up his customer his hands trembled gently. As Horace prepared to begin, the German made a point of unbuckling his holster belt with his heavy Luger 9mm pistol encased inside. He placed it on his knee and said something Horace did not understand. He pointed to his throat and traced a finger down his neck then took the Luger from the holster and pointed it at Horace. All of a sudden Horace knew exactly what he meant as the German replaced the gun in the holster.

Horace looked the German straight in the eye and smiled reassuringly.

'Listen here you ugly bastard, if I do spill any of your blood you can rest assured you'll be in no fucking state to pull the trigger of a gun.'

The German's colleague by the door jumped up and

shouted something to the man in the seat. He kicked the shoebox away and shouted at Horace. Horace groaned as he realised the waiting German spoke perfect English and had relayed the remark to his friend.

The brutal assault lasted a full five minutes.

The German used nothing but his holster. He battered Horace to the floor around the head and face and continued relentlessly with the assault as Horace lay in a pool of blood, desperately attempting to cover his head with his hands. Blow after blow was landed with the heavy leather holster and the steel grip of the gun. The attacker was breathing heavily now and seemed to take a break from his exertions. He studied the bloody mess of the prisoner before him. Horace was unrecognisable and on the brink of unconsciousness. The SS officer seemed happy with the mess he had made of Horace's head and face. Then he started on his body. The back first, then around the kidneys and the shoulders. Horace winced as the Luger connected with his collarbone and he felt a crack.

The German finished off with his legs, battering Horace's thighs, hips and shins and eventually after the prolonged assault, too tired to go on, he relented and it was over. Before he left he bent over and spat in Horace's face, stood up and aimed a final kick to his stomach.

Horace lay breathless on the floor, too sore to move. His whole body ached; his eye socket, his nose, collarbone and four fingers were broken, several of his teeth lay on the floor swimming in his blood. But inwardly he smiled... he had won. The German would not be getting his shave. Despite his injuries he could not have been happier as he lay in his own blood, his body a broken mess. Eventually he drifted off into a strange, satisfied unconsciousness.

After five minutes the door opened. Horace had not moved; he was unable to move.

'Jesus fucking Christ – the cunts have killed him.'

It was Flapper Garwood. He, John Knight and Daniel Staines tended their badly injured comrade as he lay still on the floor.

'I can't feel a pulse,' Staines said, 'he's pretty fucked up.'

Horace was breathing – barely – and at the third attempt Dan Staines managed to find a faint trace of a pulse. They decided against moving him and instead treated his injuries on the floor of the makeshift barber's shop. They bathed his wounds with cold water and managed to splint his broken fingers with bits of wood pulled from the doors of the hut.

Flapper was nearly in tears. 'I'll get that big cunt back, mark my words.'

John Knight looked up. 'You and whose army, Flapper? Remember where you are, no weapons, no guns. Nice thought mate, but it ain't ever going to happen.'

Flapper looked over to Horace's cut-throat razor lying open on the floor and started to think.

After two days Horace regained consciousness and the men gave up a little of their own rations in order to build up his strength. In a bizarre way it was the best thing that could have happened to him. He lay in what was labelled the sick bay: a room no more than six feet by six with a bed made from discarded ammunition boxes. But it had a mattress of sorts and Horace's wounds had been washed and disinfected and treated with paper bandages. But best of all, his boots had been removed when he had been too weak to argue. His blackened flesh had been pulled away like the skin of a peach with the lining of the boot but the medic had bathed them and disinfected them and the oxygen did the rest as he lay for many days, his feet bare and exposed to the cool, moist air.

Horace grew stronger by the day, but the medic argued with the camp commandant that he was not to be moved and reminded him of the terms of the Geneva Convention. He had complained vociferously about the attack but the commandant had merely shrugged his shoulders and said what did he expect – he had threatened to cut a guard's throat.

Horace lay there for a further six days, thinking about life and his family and atheism and girlfriends and poor Tom Fenwick, but above all how against all odds, no matter how small the victory, how he could make a difference. He thought about the shit he had thrown from the train and about the great friends he had around him and about the working party in the Jewish cemetery – about Flapper Garwood and how the toughest man he had ever met broke down and cried like a baby as he relayed the horrors of what was to become his normal daily routine.

To the consternation of the medic, Horace insisted on resuming his duties only hours after he had been granted another 48-hour spell in the sick bay. His old boots had been discarded and he now stood in wooden clogs, his feet wrapped in flannelette, protecting him against the cold and the hard wood of his new shoes. He would not see another pair of socks for over four years. The clogs felt strangely comfortable, the MOD telling him they would keep out the wet weather and at the same time allow his battered feet to breathe.

The POWs stood and applauded him as he made the short journey to his workstation early that morning and the German guards looked on uncomfortably as he shuffled into the room. Big Stoop, who had inflicted the beating, would not return to the barber shop. Horace knew he would not, nor any German in a Nazi uniform.

Horace had his victory. Horace Greasley, on his own against Big Stoop and the might of Third Reich, had won. He had turned a corner. He had his pride back again.

CHAPTER SIX

Come winter, Mother Nature showed no sympathy to those interned in an unheated German prison camp. Horace thought he had experienced some harsh winters back in Ibstock but nothing had prepared him for the mind-numbing temperatures he faced that in first winter of 1940/41.

He remembered a BBC radio presenter announcing temperatures of ten below when he was about 14, as Horace, Mum and Dad, Sybil, Daisy and Harold had sat huddled around a roaring fire just a few days before Christmas. He remembered being sent out into the frozen back yard for another scuttle of coal as the falling snow found its way down the back of his neck, and how the cold metal of the scuttle had drawn the heat from his fingers. That winter in Poland, the temperatures would touch nearly 40 below.

The former cavalry barracks had been designed to be camouflaged from the air. Two thirds of the living quarters were underground and the roof of the huge complex was turfed with rough grass. It was like an enormous fridge.

The horses had been stabled on the lowest floor, now the sleeping quarters of the Allied POWs. The next level up, still underground, had been the sleeping quarters and the offices of the cavalry, and now housed the German guards. They had their home comforts: decent bunks, a kitchen and an area to relax with a huge open fire constantly burning from September onwards, and even a library and snooker table. The level above ground was a series of individual outbuildings, offices and private dormitories for the officers. Again, each room appeared to have a log-burning stove or fire grate constantly burning. The logs were well stockpiled under cover near the entrance to the fort. The camp was surrounded by forest so firewood was not a problem, and the guards ensured the prisoners kept up a constant supply as the winter grew harsher.

The sleeping quarters of the prisoners never saw any sun, never felt the warmth of an oil-fired stove or a burning log. It had been badly designed; Horace sympathised with the poor horses that had once been stabled there. The temperature in that basement hell rarely crept a few degrees above the temperature outside. The only heat generated in there was the body temperature of the men who slept there.

To a man they dreaded the hours of darkness as the temperatures plummeted in January. The basement slept five prisoners to a stable stall, a space given over to one horse when the barracks were in use. The men huddled together for warmth, but snatching a few hours' sleep was nigh on impossible. They shivered collectively, changing positions through the night so that the man on the end of the stable stall would not freeze to death. Inevitably, some still did.

Horace described the cold in a small diary he wrote during his captivity. He asked for some paper to keep the records of the prisoners' conditions with body lice, and the camp commandant supplied him with a small notebook and two pencils. He wrote:

One could not imagine how cold it was down there. Take the coldest you have ever been back home in England and double your discomfort. Imagine the coldest, most severe winter's day you had ever the misfortune to be out in. I cast my mind back to a walk home from school in early February 1929. We had all been caught out by the severity of a winter blizzard as we made the two mile trek back home. That morning had been relatively mild, none of us had bothered with hats or gloves, but temperatures had plummeted as the day went on. By the time we left the school gates the snow had begun to fall gently and we all thought it a great wheeze. A mile into the journey home a full scale blizzard had developed and I don't know yet how we all made it home. I sat in the kitchen propped up against the black lead stove like a block of ice as Mum thawed me out with warm sweet tea.

I remembered that day. I remembered that day well as I lay shivering in my icy tomb in Poland, my warm breath freezing instantly as it left my mouth. I would have gladly traded ten of those days against one night in this stinking, shivering, frozen shit hole. But the worst of it was that it went on night after night, week after week, month after month. There was no respite from the cold.

The endurance of the men holed up in that basement was staggering. They were walking, talking zombies. In the morning they were simply glad they had survived another night and prayed that their daily ration of cabbage soup served a few hours later would be hot. Some days it was not. Occasionally the German guards whose job it was to keep the fire going under the huge cauldron had simply let the fire go out as they could not be bothered to make the short journey to the log pile. They did not care; they had had their daily breakfast of ham and eggs and hot coffee, and within an hour would be back in front of an open fire toasting their feet. Horace could not believe the pure selfishness and the mental torture these brutal SS soldiers doled out.

Every day, no matter what the weather, they would be forced to complete the formalities of a roll call, and the worse the conditions the longer some guards would make it last. During a snowstorm the guards would often take a heat break, as the prisoners called it, and would reappear after 20 minutes, their faces reddened by the fire they had been sitting in front of. They would grin and laugh among themselves as they looked at the poor emaciated souls covered in a thin layer of snow as the icy wind whipped through the camp.

Why? thought Horace. He tried to put himself in their shoes, wondered what his reaction would be towards German prisoners of war if he had been on the other side. As much as he hated the men now smiling at him he could not imagine in his wildest dreams that he would treat a fellow human being this way.

None of it made any sense. They wanted the men to work yet they kept them in conditions worse than a dog's. They kept them in such a malnourished state that a day's work was nigh on impossible. They beat the prisoners, tortured them both physically and mentally. Horace wondered if they had ever thought about what would happen to them if they lost the war. He looked out for a kind soul in his time in that first camp. Perhaps just one SS man who would not kick out at the prisoners, would not be so handy with a rifle butt. Perhaps just one soldier with an ounce of compassion who would give an extra ladle of soup on a specially cold day or keep the cauldron fire burning an extra hour or two to give the prisoners some relief from the biting cold. He looked to the officers giving the commands, looked into their eyes for just a glimmer of concern as one of their number doled out a beating to a prisoner who had not moved quickly enough or who had dared to question an order.

Horace looked, but found nothing.

It was mid-March 1941 before the weather started to turn. At least a dozen men had died simply from the cold during that awful winter. The snow turned to rain, the droplets carrying the smell of death, of hopelessness.

Big Stoop had beaten another three men to death and had raped two more of the younger prisoners from the outside working party in the forest beyond the camp. He had chosen them himself, unable to control his homosexual desires. Homosexuality was not to be tolerated in German-occupied territory in 1941. The two young men were raped then beaten to within an inch of their lives, and left under no illusion as to what would happen to them if they dared breathe a word about the sexual attack. Big Stoop had loaded them, battered and broken, into a cart pulled by two prisoners and claimed to the commandant he'd caught them attempting to escape. Horace could not help noticing the look of sheer hatred on Garwood's face every time Big Stoop's name was mentioned. If Big Stoop was anywhere near, Flapper positively trembled with rage.

Mercifully, the temperature seemed to increase as each day passed. The men resumed their duties in the Jewish graveyards now that the frozen earth had thawed out, some work parties continued to stockpile wood and Horace went on cutting lice-ridden infected scalps.

Horace sensed the change of regime in the camp almost overnight. Their daily ration of soup had been increased and incredibly, an odd fleck of meat had made a most welcome appearance in it. The camp commandant had begun to address the prisoners once a week, informing them that they were being treated well and that he had adhered to the Geneva Convention when it came to the treatment of prisoners. A cup of sweet tea had been introduced in the afternoons and the SS guards no longer seemed intent on physical confrontations for the slightest of reasons.

At last, the broken down, lice-infested straw in the sleeping quarters was removed and the urine, dried excreta and dead cockroaches hosed away. When the basement was dry, fresh straw was moved in and the prisoners ordered to spread it out in their individual stalls. Candles were issued to the prisoners, so not only did they have the luxury of light in their stables at night but they were able to burn the lice from their bodies and clothes. Things, it seemed, were beginning to look up.

A day or two later a German guard appeared in Horace's barbershop with new scissors and a new cut-throat razor, and a small gas stove was made available so Horace could heat up the water, giving the prisoners the luxury of a warm shave. In the yard adjacent to the front gates a crudely constructed wooden outside shower was built, with rubber piping leading from the main water supply. The men were ordered to strip and file, 20 at a time, into the showers. The water was icy cold, but still Horace enjoyed what was his first real wash in nearly a year. He was freezing but he did not want to leave. The Germans supplied scrubbing brushes and soap and the men grasped the opportunity to rid their bodies of the filth and grime, of the caked-on shit, the lice and the eggs that had poisoned their bodies for so long. Some scrubbed so hard they bled.

As Horace and his pals lined up to be given fresh underwear, clean flannelette and the stolen but clean uniforms of Polish, French and Czechoslovakian soldiers long since gone, he noticed that a few of his fellow prisoners were actually smiling. It was a sight that had been so alien to him. They were smiling; his comrades were bloody smiling. At last, Horace thought, the Germans were beginning to show a little compassion for their fellow man.

It was not the case. Two days later an inspection delegation from Geneva in Switzerland turned up at the camp. It had been a charade; the Germans wanted to show how they had complied with the terms and conditions under the convention. Horace and his fellow prisoners looked on in disgust as they were lined up for roll call in their pristine new clothes. Most of the men had gained a few pounds, their bodies clean, free from lice – not yet back on them, but they would return. The camp commandant smiled as he showed off the new showers, and gloated as he pointed out the fresh dry straw that made up the prisoners' beds in the stable.

The men were asked if they had been mistreated in any way. Several SS guards stood menacingly behind the delegation, rubbing at their rifle butts, one of them drawing a finger across his throat. The prisoners almost in unison shook their heads.

Except one man.

Charlie Cavendish took a step forward and said that he wanted to speak privately to the delegation. The prisoners looked on in disbelief, as did the guards. The man was shaking, trembling with fear. He had not gained any weight and he looked sick. A German guard tried to persuade him otherwise and voices were raised. The delegation did not look happy and one member was quoting from a pamphlet held in his hands. The man was taken away and returned to the ranks after an hour. By this time the delegation was shouting and remonstrating with the commandant.

The man who had made his point was smiling through the

tears that ran down his face. Horace looked at him. 'What are you so happy about, Charlie?'

'They're closing this shithole down, Jim. You lot are on your way out of here. I spilled the beans on just what these cunts have been doing.' He pointed to a man with a military-type hat. 'That's the gaffer. He said they've broken every rule in the book; he's absolutely livid and told the commandant that the camp would be closed by the end of the week. I've shopped Big Stoop too, told them how many he's killed, told them he's a rapist.'

As Charlie wiped at the tears drying on his cheeks, Horace stood with a puzzled look on his face. 'Then if we're on our way out, why are you crying?'

The man cocked his head with a frown. 'You didn't listen to me, Jim, did you? I said you are leaving – not me, not us. You don't think these bastards will let me live after what I've just done, do you?'

The following morning Charlie Cavendish was conspicuous by his absence at the roll call. Nobody had seen him leave; he'd simply disappeared during the night. He was never seen again. He had given his life voluntarily to save his friends and comrades.

Flapper Garwood had planned the operation meticulously. For many weeks he'd studied Big Stoop's movements and patterns of work. He'd counted the guards on duty and timed their work patterns and meal breaks to the second. And over the last few weeks he'd thrown an occasional smile in the direction of Big Stoop. He'd flirted with the big German.

Garwood had almost thrown up when Big Stoop had winked at him earlier in the day. He'd bitten his tongue and smiled back. The German's face had softened noticeably at his response. Garwood was not normally his type – he preferred the younger, slightly effeminate prisoners – but this man seemed eager to please. The rapes were stimulating but it would be a pleasant change to have a willing participant. Big Stoop came over to Garwood as he stood in line awaiting his cabbage soup.

'You, prisoner, come with me. I have a job for you.'

Garwood did as he was told. When they were out of earshot, Big Stoop spoke in a whisper.

'You want a little fun, prisoner, is that right?'

Garwood nodded his head, tried to smile and wondered if the officer would see through the pretence. 'Tonight,' he replied. 'At 9.45 when everyone is locked up.'

The German looked puzzled. 'Why such a strange time, prisoner?'

Garwood stepped forward, pushed his hand into the German's groin and squeezed.

'Because we will not be disturbed. The prisoners will be locked up and your comrades will be in the mess hall.'

As the blood flow in his groin increased Big Stoop grinned. 'You have planned our rendezvous well, prisoner. I will make sure I lock you in tonight but I will leave the main stable door open. No one will think to try it, no one ever does and we Germans do not make mistakes. We will meet at the door of the main office. No one will be there.'

The German leaned forward, his mouth open. Garwood could smell his sour breath and wondered how anyone could kiss such a monster. He almost ran for the door.

'You must be patient...if we are caught now no one will get any pleasure.'

Big Stoop grinned and let out a grotesque, almost animal-like laugh. He watched the shape of the prisoner as he walked out of the door and shouted after him. 'I only hope you don't disappoint me, pretty arse.'

Flapper Garwood turned around. 'I won't disappoint you, my friend... Don't you worry about that.'

Flapper took two steps into the fresh air, steadied himself and emptied what little contents he had in his stomach onto the parched earth.

At exactly nine o'clock Big Stoop walked into the filthy stable block and ordered the prisoners onto their straw beds. Horace was puzzled. Normally they only heard the key turn in the main door, anytime between nine and ten.

Big Stoop had washed; a distinct smell of cheap gentlemen's scent permeated the air. Must be away out on the town, Horace thought to himself. As the German monster retired to the other side of the door he seemed to take a little longer with the intricacies of turning the key in the antique brass lock.

The German arrived a good five minutes early. He had anticipated his moment of sexual release most of the day, planning the acts he would perform on the prisoner. He paced around the building like a caged animal for what seemed like an eternity. Finally he picked out the unmistakeable figure of the big English prisoner. Unknown to him, Garwood had earlier located Horace's cut-throat razor in the drawer of the officer's desk where it was returned each night.

'Not before time,' Big Stoop smiled, as the shape of the nervous Garwood appeared in the light from the office window. He opened the door and beckoned the prisoner inside.

Flapper was breathing hard now, his face flushed. 'Not here. Someone will come.'

The German stepped forward and took him by the throat. 'You do as I say, prisoner... inside.'

'No please, not here. We'll be caught. I'll be shot, and you'll be shot too.'

Big Stoop released his grip and Flapper took a deep breath of cool evening air. 'Over there,' he pointed, 'in the forest by the toilets. I have a rug hidden there. It will be more comfortable.'

The German chuckled. 'You have planned this well, haven't you? You want it outside like the animals.' He purred, turned Garwood around and slapped him on the backside. 'Then move quickly.'

Flapper gagged but managed to maintain his charade. He walked the dozen or so steps until he stood adjacent to the toilet block as the guard followed.

'Keep walking, handsome, it fucking stinks here.'

Flapper stood motionless, with a look on his face that puzzled Big Stoop.

The German took a step forward, went to push the prisoner in the chest. 'Move, you pig dog. It stinks here, didn't you hear...'

Garwood pulled hard on the arm of the guard and spun him round so his back was to Garwood. Before Big Stoop could realise what was happening, Flapper brought the cut-throat razor up and across the man's throat in one well-executed motion. The sharp blade sliced effortlessly through skin, sinew, tissue and windpipe, only coming to a stop against Big Stoop's vertebrae. Garwood removed the weapon and held it by his side.

The German's mouth fell open as he tried to scream. Blood cascaded down his body like a waterfall and he managed nothing more than a gurgle from the new entrance carved into his body. As the German tottered on the brink of collapse, Flapper sliced through his belt and pulled his trousers to the ground. The last thing Big Stoop saw as he breathed his last breath was his own bloodstained penis inches from his face.

Garwood dragged the heavy body into the toilet block and filled the dead man's pockets with stones. He was breathing heavily, and the smell of the shit seemed a hundred times worse than he could ever remember. Positioning the body under the wooden frame, he took a hold of the plank with both hands. He placed one foot on the German's thighs, the other in the small of his back, and with one final surge of effort pushed the body over the edge six feet into the excrement-filled tank below. He watched as the body floated for a moment. Then, as pockets of air hissed and gurgled their final release, the body tipped like a stricken ship and sank into the depths below.

The executioner spent the best part of the next hour cleaning himself and rearranging the sand and dirt of the compound in an attempt to cover the blood stains. Thankfully most of the blood had been soaked up by the dead man's uniform but a few telltale signs remained. He used dead pine needles in the toilet block to wipe away the trail of blood on the floor. Sweating but satisfied with his night's work, he cleaned the blade and returned it to where he had found it. Then he walked slowly back to the stable block, confident that the night creatures and early morning flies would complete his task.

Big Stoop was officially pronounced missing at noon the following day. The camp commandant sent a guard to his home in the village and found the small cottage deserted. The commandant made a few tentative enquiries and interrogated some of the prisoners but nothing was discovered. It was assumed that Big Stoop had deserted. It happened. In fact it was quite a regular occurrence.

Meanwhile, the normal 'one ladle, no meat' ration had resumed and the afternoon tea had disappeared from the menu. The makeshift showers had been dismantled and the wood chopped into kindling. But the sun was still shining and an air of optimism hung around the camp as the Germans made arrangements to leave. Forty-eight hours later a convoy of lorries rumbled into the camp and the prisoners were ordered on board.

Horace was more than happy as the lorries pulled out across the bridge over the moat. The prisoners had not been told where they were going, nor for what reason. But nothing could be worse than what they had been through at Fort Eight in Posen. Horace and his comrades were on the move. They had survived a living hell on earth.

CHAPTER
SEVEN

Horace sat in the back of the open truck as the camp that had claimed so many of his comrades disappeared from view. The men were strangely subdued, quiet, as they laid to rest the ghosts and memories of that awful place.

Horace remembered the beating that had nearly killed him, and poor Tom Fenwick, and the bitter cold of the winter, how the snow kept falling day after day, week after week. He recalled the smiling faces of Big Stoop and the SS guards as they dished out beatings, and he remembered the tears of joy and despair rolling down the cheeks of Charlie Cavendish as he'd returned to the ranks after telling the delegation from Geneva all about the camp.

Horace wondered whether Charlie had died naturally or whether the SS had helped him on his way. Charlie had been in a bad way, as if already resigned to death, and he knew as the guards argued with the men from Switzerland that he would never see another day dawn. Horace had seen the signs, seen the same relaxed, seemingly carefree attitude in Tom Fenwick as he'd munched greedily on his last loaf of bread. It was as if they were at peace with the world. They knew their time had come and in a comforting sort of way, knew their suffering at the hands of these monsters was drawing to an end.

For hours his head was filled with the horrors from the camp. Flapper sat opposite and a kind of mutual understanding allowed each man to sit in silence with his own private thoughts. An hour into the journey Horace posed the question.

'Where did you hide his body?'

'Who?'

'Big Stoop.'

'I don't know what you're talking about.'

Horace looked for telltale signs. There were none.

After a minute or two Garwood spoke.

'Did you take a shit this morning, Jim?'

Horace thought for a second then nodded. 'Yeah, Flapper, I did.'

'Good, Jim. Good. Better out than in, eh?'

As each hour passed and the truck put mile after mile between the camp and the tortured souls on board, remarkably, their spirits lifted. They'd been on the road for six hours when the convoy came to a stop. They had pulled into what looked like a huge factory compound. The walls were whitewashed and sterile looking and could have easily been mistaken for a hospital. It wasn't. Hospitals didn't need barbed wire and high fences to keep their patients from absconding.

It was another camp, but as Horace and his fellow prisoners were herded inside and made to stand in an orderly queue, a feeling washed over him that he wouldn't be there for long. Suddenly he was nervous, frightened even. The Germans had told them nothing and one or two prisoners were beginning to get edgy. To a man they all harboured their private thoughts; some even discussed what would happen if the POWs became a nuisance to the Germans. Had that day arrived? Nobody knew. Nobody asked the question.

The prisoners were ordered to strip naked, pushed and prodded into distinctive groups of twenty-five. Although it was early summer a cool wind whipped through the camp. They stood shivering for over an hour before being marched through an open compound in full view of a dozen civilians working on what looked like piles of clean laundry and uniforms. Two girls aged around 16 giggled nervously as the naked men walked within a few yards of them. The prisoners did their best to cover their modesty as the girls diverted their gaze.

As they approached the large tiled building at the far side of the compound Horace heard what sounded like running water and unless he was mistaken the cheers of a few men.

'What the fuck's that, Jim?' asked Garwood.

'Seems to me like a shower block, Flapper,' Horace said as he pointed to a grate above the building. Steam was rising from the roof. 'And if I'm not mistaken I do believe they have a little hot water.'

Horace stood under the jet of water. He had forgotten what hot water felt like. It had been a year since he had felt hot water on his body. He thought about his last hot shower; he thought back to his indiscretion with the French prostitute and how he'd showered afterwards in Carenten, as if the hot water would somehow cleanse him, wash off the smell of the girl just in case he was back home in England in double quick time and in the arms of Eva Bell.

Daniel Staines looked across to his pal as the hot water cascaded down his face and body and he smiled and moaned out loud.

'Better than sex this, Jim, eh?'

Horace grinned and shook his head. 'You're doing something wrong, Dan. It's good, but not that good.'

But it was good. It was luxury. The Germans had provided cakes of soap and scrubbing brushes and the men scoured their lice-ridden bodies. The white stone floor of the shower block was a swimming carpet of the tiny creatures. After the shower the prisoners were deloused with a white powder and assured by the Germans they'd be completely free of the blood sucking parasites.

Next they were issued with clean clothing. This time Horace collected the uniform of a soldier of the Polish 16th Pomeranian Infantry Division complete with a small bullet hole in the left breast pocket. The larger exit wound in the back had been patched and stitched with a crude black thread. It didn't matter. Flapper, Horace, Dan and a few others laughed and joked with one another about their ill-fitting uniforms as the German guards looked on, puzzled.

A little while later, in the early evening sun, they were ordered back on the lorries for the remaining part of the journey, to the prisoner of war camp at Saubsdorf in Czechoslovakia, near the Polish border. It was dark when they arrived but as they made their way through the gates they were handed a bowl of hot stew. Not soup… stew. Meat, potato, a little boiled carrot – it was stew, real food. In the space of a few hours Horace had sampled two things that had been denied to him for so long. Two things, the basics of life, hot water and food. Surely it wasn't much to ask?

Compared with the previous camp Horace and his pals had just entered the foyer of The Ritz. Little did he realise it would be the one meal a day the POWs would be given. But Horace thought he'd died and gone to heaven when they were led to a large dormitory with a shower block, double bunks and real mattresses. The men were like children at a scout camp as they clambered eagerly into bed. The lights were switched off and despite their best efforts to stay awake, within five minutes the entire room reverberated with the sound of snoring. For the first time in captivity Horace managed to sleep the whole night through.

He awoke around seven the next morning and experienced another pleasure denied to him for so long. He woke with an erection. In a moment of unbridled hi-jinks he leapt from his top bunk and dropped his underpants to his ankles. 'Look, lads!' he shouted. 'Look at this beauty!'

John Knight opened his eyes. He lay on the bottom bunk and Horace's swollen penis hovered at eye level. 'For fuck's sake, Jim, what are you playing at?' he shouted as he pulled a blanket over his head to escape from Horace's pride and glory.

Horace had his two hands around it now and was more than happy to show it to anyone whose eyes were open. 'But I've got a hard on!'

'So fuck,' Dan shouted from the other side of the room.

'But I haven't had a hard on for months. Look at it, man, it's a beauty.'

Flapper peeked out from under his blanket. 'Fucking hell, Jim, watch where you're waving that thing! You'll have some cunt's eye out.'

Ernie Mountain sat up and laughed. 'You could hang six pairs of boots on that fucker, Jim. You weren't at the back of the cock queue when they were dished out, were you?'

'No good to you though, mate,' Dan muttered, 'Nowhere in here you can stick it.'

Horace didn't care. Things were looking up for him and his mates. A warm bed, a hot shower, food, and now a hard on. All Horace wanted now was a nice young lady. Ah well, he thought, Rome wasn't built in a day, as he wandered off for his shower wondering if it were at all possible to get three or four minutes' privacy.

Later that morning the men were assembled and detailed

their work schedules by the guards. To Horace's immense relief the guards did not wear the uniforms of the dreaded SS. In comparison, these older looking men, 40 to 50 years of age, looked positively angelic.

The camp was situated close to a huge marble quarry and the prisoners were given pickaxes and sledgehammers on arrival. A German civilian, Herr Rauchbach, addressed the men in his native tongue but although the majority of the men didn't understand a word, it was plainly obvious what sort of work they'd be doing. John Knight smiled as his party walked the short distance to the quarry face and the German guards pointed to the huge slabs of marble. No more digging up Jewish skeletons. The work might be tough, but at least he'd sleep at nights.

And so the backbreaking ten-hour shift began. Horace worked with Flapper, splitting the marble into manageable sections and loading the stone onto trucks by hand. Half a dozen civilian women swept up around the men, gathering the smaller marble chips into large buckets and stacking them by the door of a large wooden workshop. It was clear the women were terrified and forbidden to speak to the prisoners and they worked in silence whenever the German guards were around.

But the German guards were few and far between and Horace at first was a little puzzled. Escape was always at the forefront of his mind but at the first camp it had been impossible. Here, though, it seemed a distinct possibility. The camp wasn't fenced in; he would later find out that Rauchbach had forbidden any fencing. They were simply locked in their huts at nights. To prevent escape, four or five guards routinely patrolled the area. During the day it was as if they were almost being casual in their disregard for security.

Horace would learn that it was possible to escape – but then where could the escapee go? The camp was situated on the edge of a huge forest. Perfect cover, thought Horace. But there were no maps, no compasses. They were surrounded by German-occupied countries for at least four hundred miles in every direction. In which direction would he run? West into Germany wasn't an option and his knowledge of Czechoslovakia and Poland was sketchy to say the least. Oh, how he'd wished he'd taken more notice in geography lessons at school. The Germans weren't stupid; that's why the camps were situated there.

Every night, in the dark, Horace wrestled with his conscience. Surely he owed it to his family, his country, to at least try to escape? The prisoners formed escape committees; they talked hour after hour about their chances, made plans and fantasised about what lay beyond the forest. But that's all it was... fantasy. They were stranded in the middle of nowhere, with no papers, no grasp of the Polish or Czech languages, no money, no food, no weapons, nothing.

Horace knew escape was impossible and the Germans did too, that's why the guards were few and far between. But it gave the men a chance to talk with the women from the camp. The women were from the local villages on the border of Poland and Czechoslovakia. Middle-aged and hard-faced, their stocky muscle-bound bodies bore testament to years of hard work, their faces etched with lines and scars. The border towns had a turbulent history and had changed hands many times over the centuries. Although some of the villages were in Czechoslovakia, many of the residents classed themselves as Poles and were fiercely patriotic, despising the Germans just as much as the POWs did. The women were paid wages and allowed back to their villages each night but were no more than slave labourers and treated as such by the Germans.

The ladies told of a girl who had worked there, fraternised with a French POW and ended up pregnant by him. Somehow the Germans had found out and neither the girl nor the POW were ever seen again. The Frenchman was shot by firing squad the next morning and the girl sent to prison. The ladies crossed their chests with their hands each time they mentioned her name, a clear reference to what they thought had happened to her.

As the days passed, a few of the female workers smuggled food in for some of the prisoners – a stale bread sandwich, mouldy cheese or a scrap of ham. No one cared how fresh or otherwise it was; it supplemented their meagre rations and tasted like heaven.

Horace had been in German captivity for over a year and had managed to pick up a basic understanding of the German language. Herr Rauchbach, the quarry camp owner, singled him out and they managed to hold a conversation of sorts. Rauchbach seemed different from the other Germans, especially when the guards weren't around. He was almost sympathetic to the plight of the prisoners, and on more than one occasion Horace noticed a certain hostility towards the guards. He asked Horace about the food and the general conditions back at the camp. He promised to get the POWs' rations increased and sure enough, as the prisoners finished their day's work one evening, an argument of sorts took place between the camp commandant and Herr Rauchbach. The commandant had raised his voice, stating the prisoners were getting sufficient quantities of food. Rauchbach argued that more food meant more work, and said that several men had fainted during the morning shift on account of empty stomachs.

Later that week the prisoners were given a cup of lukewarm water and one tasteless biscuit at breakfast time, and a few more potato pieces made an appearance in the stew. Production in the quarry increased and the camp commandant was happy. The increase, however, was not on account of the extra rations, but because Rauchbach had told the men the marble was needed for headstones on German war graves.

One morning Rauchbach announced to Horace that the following week he would be bringing his daughter to work as an interpreter at the quarry. He had cleared it with the camp commandant, who allowed her to attend once a fortnight as she was keen to practise her English.

Rauchbach walked over to where Dan Staines and Horace were working on a warm but wet August morning. 'Jim!' he shouted and Horace looked up.

She stood like a goddess.

Horace drank in inch by glorious inch as Rauchbach introduced his daughter Rosa. She nodded her head shyly and blushed. Horace felt a nervous tremor well up inside him and realised just how long it had been since he'd seen anything so appealing. There were no magazines or newspapers in the camps, no pictures or Pathé news footage. He didn't even possess a photograph of Eva. His memory of a pretty girl had been wiped clean... until now.

Horace nodded back and greeted her politely in German. Rosa smiled and looked to the ground. Eventually she looked up and spoke nervously.

'I speak English. Father wants me to translate. I need to practise more.'

Her voice was soft and delicate. Accentuated by her broken English, it was sensual and mysterious. This isn't healthy, Horace thought to himself. He looked across at Flapper Garwood who stood as if frozen to the spot. Flapper spoke quietly.

'I'd give her one, Jim, wouldn't you?'

'Two or three, Flapper,' he whispered quietly.

'Sorry,' she said, 'I did not hear that.'

Horace stuttered and dropped the sledgehammer. 'I said your English is good.'

Rauchbach spoke in German. 'Yes, but it needs to be better. We need to prepare for after the war.' He turned to Horace and grinned, 'You will give instruction to Rosa?'

'Yes, yes, certainly, Herr Rauchbach.'

'And now we must see the commandant and thank him, Rosa.'

Rauchbach and his beautiful daughter left the two men staring in amazement as they walked back towards the workshops. The rear end of the 17-year-old dressed in tight black riding britches was the sole focus of their attention. A whole division of Waffen SS wouldn't have been able to alter the direction of their stare.

'Look at that arse, Jim. Look at the way it moves.'

'I can't take my eyes off it,' replied Horace.

'Imagine it bouncing up and down...'

'Don't even go there,' Horace interrupted. 'You think I had a big horn the other morning? It will be twice that size tomorrow thinking of that pretty little backside.'

As Horace watched the most perfectly formed rear he'd ever set eyes on slowly disappear from view, he cursed the German nation yet again for denying him another basic human right. But he was right; the visit of the lovely Rosa wasn't healthy. He simply had to get out of that camp. He needed his family, he needed food, he needed to be able to choose when to come and go, he needed a beer and he wanted sex.

For the next week Horace was in a deep depression. Rosa's visit had brought back memories of home and of life as a free man. He began to resent the guards as the key was turned in the lock each evening. He was on a short fuse and the rest of the prisoners seemed to sense it and kept out of his way. He took his aggression out on the slabs of marble and for every lump smashed out of the slab he envisaged a dead German. Oh, how he hated them. He returned each evening physically and mentally exhausted and no matter how many times Garwood or John Knight told him to slow down he just wouldn't listen.

But as he counted the days until Rosa's next visit his mood lightened. He counted the days off on a scrap of paper and kept a secret diary – one that if discovered would almost certainly result in an appearance before the firing squad. In it he fantasised about sex. Sex with a German girl. Sex with the young daughter of the owner of the quarry camp. It was a chance he was prepared to take. Another two fingers up to Jerry, another little victory.

CHAPTER
EIGHT

On her next visit two weeks later Rosa looked even prettier. It was a sunny day and she'd dressed accordingly. Gone was the heavy waterproof coat. Instead, she was dressed in a tight-fitting, plain white blouse that emphasised her breasts and a thin loose skirt that hung just above her knees. Her cheeks had more colour and was he just imagining it, or did her lips look fuller and a deeper colour of red? And she smiled more. She smiled at Horace – not Flapper or John Knight – Horace.

Flapper Garwood noticed too. He made a comment that could be loosely construed to suggest the young girl might just have a little affection for Horace.

'Make no mistake, Jim, she wants that big cock of yours inside her,' he said, grinning.

Over the coming weeks their relationship developed and Rosa's father seemed happy with his daughter's progress in the English language. So much so that he was quite comfortable leaving her on her own in the company of the English prisoners.

It was on her fourth visit that Horace asked her what sort of work went on in the workshops. She explained about the lathes and the grinding machines and how frustrated her father was at not having the men to utilise them.

'My father and Ackenburg the foreman are the only ones ever in there. The truth is, all the skilled men are either dead or fighting in the war.' Rosa threw an expression that Horace remembered seeing in Ibstock and Torquay and at the dances in Leicester. It was an expression of interest. 'My father says there's a real shortage of good men in these parts.'

It was at that moment that Horace decided to set the foundations for their first date. Was he just imagining it, or was she giving off the right signals? He hadn't seen the signs for so long, but they seemed to be happening right there in front of his eyes. The constant smiles, the flick of her hair, grooming, a gentle brush of the hand and just generally standing too bloody close to him. Then he delivered it. The greatest chat up one-liner in history.

'I don't suppose you could show me the machines, could you?'

Rosa paused. She looked over to the workshops then back to Horace. An uncomfortable silence ensued and Horace wanted to say so much. She shook her head and looked at the ground.

Horace wanted to tell her how beautiful she was and how he wanted to take her in his arms. He wanted to tell her how he lusted after her, how every waking moment was spent wondering what she looked like under those clothes and how much he wanted to make love to her. But he kept silent and remembered that she was a German, strictly off limits.

He didn't want to make love to her... he wanted to screw her, wanted another small Allied victory. He wanted to put a German *Fräulein* on her back and use her for his own pleasure. Nothing more, nothing less.

Then something caught his attention: the door to the

workshop opened. Rauchbach and Ackenburg walked out. They paused for a moment, studied some paperwork and then walked towards Rosa and Horace. Horace walked away, passed them in the opposite direction and strolled nervously over to the workshops. The door was unlocked and he turned the handle and walked inside. A huge dusty wooden workbench took up half the floor. Bolted to it every few feet was a lathe or a vice, a machine to sharpen the drill bits. Over on the far side of the room, also covered in dust, were two large grinding wheels.

Horace turned round and peered out of the window. The guards were gone, probably on a coffee break. Groups of prisoners went about their tasks unwatched. Rosa stood talking with her father. Ackenburg sat on a pile of broken marble, watching work in progress. How stupid did Horace feel as he lowered himself onto the bench – who was he kidding? The looks and signals were fantasy, figments of his imagination. How could a German girl even entertain the thought of a relationship with an enemy prisoner? The civilian girls would hardly speak of the one relationship that had developed within the camp.

Horace continued to stare out of the window. He eased himself up off the workbench and wondered how long it would be before he'd be missed. The German guards disappeared three or four times every day to brew up a coffee; they didn't seem to care. He was lost in his thoughts when the door opened. He expected a German guard or Ackenburg; he expected a scolding or worse.

It was Rosa. She stood in the doorway, a fierce glow in her cheeks and as she breathed deeply, nervously, her beautiful breasts seeming to surge up and down. That familiar feeling grew inside him. His eyes took in the wonderful splendour of her young form. She took a step forward, spoke. 'I should not be here, it is too dangerous. I will...'

Horace shook his head, moved towards her. Their faces were only inches apart and he could smell her musky female aroma. There was no need for any more words. Their eyes locked and they moved ever closer. And with the greatest natural reaction between man and woman, their lips met. Gently at first. A slow, delicate nervous movement, then more anxious, greedy, desperate. They touched each other's face, embraced tightly, broke apart and just stared into each other's eyes. They repeated the sequence again and again. Horace reached for her breast, she moaned in approval. He had forgotten the soft touch as he felt for her stiffening nipple and squeezed. He'd forgotten how the blood flowed and pumped around his body with such a simple touch of the female form.

It was impossible to control the urge. He wanted to stop, wanted to tell her how crazy this was and run from the workshop as fast as his legs would carry him. He didn't. He couldn't.

A different feeling welled over him, a feeling he'd never experienced before. His hands moved around to her backside as their kissing intensified and he pulled her into his hardness and pushed rhythmically against her. She gasped, broke the kiss and tried to break free. Horace pulled her in even harder; his battle-hardened rough leathery hands clenched around her tender buttocks and as he kissed her with a gentle yet firm, determined aggressiveness, she responded. Slowly at first, barely a movement, but then her legs parted slightly, she relaxed and she threw her head backwards as she reciprocated and copied his movement. She was clumsy, they were clumsy, but slowly and surely their movement was one. Her hair fell over her face as she began to pant and her mouth fell open as she moaned gently. He cupped his hands in the small of her back as he took her full body weight and she hung there for an eternity as she pushed and ground her pelvic bone into the unmistakable feel of his erection.

He was breathing harder now, almost grunting like an animal in the jungle. He'd passed the point of no return as he released his double-handed grip and his right hand moved from the small of her back to her buttock and down to the back of her thigh. Her head tilted forward and their eyes met once again. She leaned forward, kissed him again, and he let it linger for a second. She gazed at him with a puzzled, almost frightened expression. Horace stepped back and reached for the buttons on his flies. She looked across to the window but remained in exactly the same position. There was no resistance, no attempt to run.

Horace dropped his trousers to the floor and exposed his erection. He paused, their eyes locked on each other again, he wanted to stop, call a halt to this madness. It was the longest few seconds of his life. He was about to make love to the enemy, about to screw the opposition. Getting caught would mean a charge of rape and certain death, perhaps the same fate for Rosa unless she could convince the authorities otherwise.

Horace took a step forward and took Rosa by the shoulders. He flung her round roughly and pushed her face forward onto the grime-covered bench. He reached for the hem of her skirt and pulled it upwards over her hips. Her modesty was covered by the thinnest of cotton, snow-white panties. Horace reached under her and pulled the material to one side as he eased two fingers into her moist vagina.

Rosa looked over her shoulder. 'We'll be caught.'

Horace wanted to stop. It was madness. The war was madness, Polish prison camps were madness, throwing shit from trains and being starved to death was madness, claiming a tiny victory against the enemy was madness and yet he couldn't help himself. Horace stepped forward, took a firm grip of the material of the panties and tore them from her as he cast them onto the dirty floor. He took a step forward and edged her legs apart with his knees. Her breathing became laboured; the muscles in her buttocks seemed to tighten as Horace placed a hand on each hip. His penis hovered and probed at the entrance of her vagina and in one swift, well-executed movement he thrust deep inside her. Rosa let out a squeal. They would be heard; someone would surely hear them.

Horace was past caring. A bullet in the back of the head would be worth it as long as he could get through the next few minutes. Horace pumped and thrust for all he was worth. The German girl was the enemy and he, Joseph Horace Greasley, was having full blown sex with one of the enemy's girls while they kept him captive... there was no greater feeling in the world.

Rosa squirmed and yelped beneath him as her own hand muffled her cries while Horace pushed her hips roughly into the hard wooden work surface, thrusting as hard and as deep into her as was physically possible. Within a few short minutes he had climaxed and collapsed forward, breathing heavily as his face lay inches from hers. He could feel the silken texture of her hair on his face, smell her sweet breath expending in spasms as she recovered. And he wanted somehow to lie with her forever.

But he couldn't. She was the enemy.

He reached to the floor and pulled up his trousers, gazing at the beautiful shape of her young backside, the form of her hips and her firm thighs still tantalisingly parted, revealing the downy cleft of pubic hair.

Rosa made no attempt to move. She whimpered quietly, almost purred like a cat. He wanted to hold her; he wanted to tell her how special the moment had been. He wanted to kiss and caress her and walk in the summer sunshine discussing the lovemaking like he had with Eva oh, so long ago. He wanted to plan their next tryst, their next forbidden moment of death-defying passion.

Without a word Horace turned and left the workshop. He strolled almost casually into the still, warm afternoon air as a tear ran the length of his face and fell onto the parched dusty ground.

It wasn't a dream. It had happened. The first rays of the early morning sun strained through the barred windows and picked their way through the tiny particles of dust that always seemed to hang in the air. Horace lay awake, the only one of the 30 prisoners.

It had happened. He'd screwed one of the enemy's girls right there in a prisoner of war camp, right there under the noses of the German guards, of the camp commandant and even more incredibly, under the nose of her father who couldn't have been more than 25 yards away.

It wasn't a dream. He lay there with a peculiar satisfied smile on his face. Half-starved, incarcerated, a slave and a puppet to the enemy who could command of him anything they wanted and take his life anytime they wanted, yet he was still smiling. Oh, how he wished he could tell them everything he'd achieved. How he wished he could tell these fucking bastards about how much shit he'd thrown in their comrades' faces, how he wished he could tell them about the many victories he'd achieved during his time with them.

But most of all he wished he could tell them how he'd fucked one of their own, right there under their noses. She chose me, he wanted to tell them. Even as a downtrodden, filth-ridden, half-starved, enslaved creature with a status lower than a sewer rat... she'd chosen him above them. His hair was unkempt, the flesh hung from his bones, his second-hand, ill-fitting dead man's uniform flattered him little. As he remembered the SS soldiers' lectures at the first camp and their claims that the German man would always be his superior, he laughed out loud at the fact he'd just blown that theory out of the water.

'What the fuck have you got to laugh about, Jim, you mad bastard?'

It was Flapper.

Horace leaned over the top bunk. Flapper's eyes had just opened.

'Don't you see how they'll never beat us, Flapper? They can take our freedom but they'll never beat us. We're better than them, bigger than them '

He wanted to tell his friends and comrades, his fellow prisoners all about his conquest. He wanted to tell them, boost their morale; he wanted every single one of them to laugh behind the Germans' backs. But he couldn't.

Flapper groaned then let out a deep sigh. 'Like I say, Jim, you're one mad bastard.'

Horace leapt from his bunk. He had to tell them to be strong, never to give up hope. He didn't know where the inspiration came from or who or what had given him the power of oration, but something strange happened as he delivered his lecture to his friend. A few others around them had begun to wake; he turned to face them.

'We'll win this war, lads, I'm telling you, we just need to believe it deep in our hearts and if we want it badly enough, if we want that Austrian eunuch to get his comeuppance then that's what will happen. We must hold our heads up high. When they turn that key at night, when they dish out the orders and the beatings, we must believe in ourselves, believe we are better than them.'

To a man they had congregated in front of Horace. Several lay on the floor in a sleepy trance listening to the emotional rant of a miner's son from a small village in Leicestershire. They could have been listening to one of Churchill's finest speeches, such was his impassioned delivery.

'Have you noticed lately how quiet the Germans are? Remember how they taunted us almost weekly about the bombing of London and how the Luftwaffe controlled the skies over Europe? Remember them singing and dancing as they announced that Coventry had been razed to the ground, and how they'd bombed Liverpool and Bristol? Remember, lads, remember?'

A few heads nodded, a few murmurs of agreement. The moments when the German soldiers and camp commandant delivered their version of the way the war was going were the low points for the prisoners. They had no way of knowing whether the Germans were telling the truth. Sure, they would exaggerate, everyone knew that, but just how far would they go? Had a few bombs fallen on the outskirts of Coventry or, as the Germans were suggesting, had it been decimated and flattened? No one knew. The civilian workers in the camp had offered titbits of information but even they were listening to their radio sets in an occupied land. Just how much were the news reports influenced by the Germans?

'Well, they aren't fucking singing and dancing now, are they? In fact when was the last time you saw a smile on the bastards' faces? That's because we are winning, lads. The tide is turning.'

In reality nobody was winning the war. Every country involved was on the losing side. The young men of Britain and France and Russia and Germany were being massacred. The broken bodies of civilian men women and children right across Europe and beyond littered the city streets.

But far worse things were happening in the concentration

camps in Germany and Poland and Czechoslovakia as Hitler began to implement his master plan for world domination. Hitler and his generals had begun the mass extermination of whole nations, ethnic and religious groups, gypsies, homosexuals and the mentally unstable. Although at the time the POWs didn't know it, the Second World War would become the deadliest and most destructive war in human history, claiming an estimated 72 million lives. Hitler's regime would wipe nearly five million Jews off the face of the earth, gassing them in the concentration camps of Eastern Europe. The Polish nation would lose over 16 per cent of its entire population and by the end of the war nearly 27 million Russians would have lost their lives.

Unfortunately, by the summer of 1941 the war was showing no sign of slowing down. In 1941 alone, Yugoslavia, Russia, Bulgaria, Finland and Hungary were dragged into the conflict. Towards the end of the year the Japanese would attack Pearl Harbor in Hawaii where a huge American naval fleet lay at anchor, dragging the most powerful nation on earth into the Second World War. Horace didn't know any of this as he continued.

'So you think the war's coming to an end, Jim?' asked a corporal from the King's Own Scottish Borderers.

Horace spoke with a passion, with a sincere belief that it was. He wanted to believe it, simply had to believe it, but nothing could have been further from the truth. Little did he know as he sat on Garwood's bunk while the entire dormitory listened to him, that he would be involved in the conflict for another four long years.

'We must laugh at them, laugh at them behind their backs. Sure they can turn the key each evening and they can make us work ten hours a day, but the irony is we are working on the gravestones of their comrades.'

Horace grinned like a Cheshire cat. 'How fucking great is that?'

The assembled men broke out into raucous laughter.

'Let us work harder, let's smile and laugh and joke as we cut each slab. Let us taunt the Germans as we carve each cross, tell them "This one's for you" with a big smile.'

'Only the ones that don't speak English, Jim,' Ernie Mountain interjected. 'Remember, you took a good beating at the last camp because one of the bastards spoke English.'

Horace paused for a few seconds as he recalled those dark days. But he also remembered how he took strength and an inner pride from the incident. He remembered those first few tentative steps from the medical room and although physically he was as weak as a kitten, mentally he was as strong as two lions. He remembered looking at the men in the back of the lorry as they left that hell hole. A mass of human misery – dejected, almost defeated, skin pulled tightly round their cheekbones, eyes hollow and sunken. Some wore hats to protect them from the cold, some had none, just shaven heads with sporadic tufts of straw like hair. Living, breathing corpses.

Horace's impromptu speech came to an abrupt end.

'*Steigen Sie aus*!' – 'Get out!' – the German guards screamed as they burst into the dormitory. Horace couldn't help feeling their tone appeared more aggressive than normal. His suspicions were confirmed as they took their place on parade and two German SS officers stood talking with the camp commandant over on the far side of the compound. At the sight of their uniforms Horace's blood turned to ice. The memories came flooding back: the cruelty of the SS men on the long march to Luxembourg and the pleasure and joy they seemed to radiate during the beatings and killings in the first camp.

They walked over towards the POWs on parade. Even the camp commandant looked ill at ease in their company. They looked evil, stone-faced and thin-lipped. God knows what evil acts these two men had carried out. Horace recalled the rumours of the death camps, the massacres and mass executions of the Poles and Slavs and wondered, just wondered, if the stories could be true. He wondered about the selection and recruitment procedures for the SS. Did they deliberately choose the evil-looking ones? Was there a series of initiation ceremonies they all had to go through? Did they need to demonstrate just how bad they were before they were accepted into the ranks?

One of the SS officers stepped forward. He spoke perfect English, almost fluent. He announced that the SS would be inspecting the camp once a month. He'd heard reports that the current regime was too soft. The prisoners must remember that they were prisoners, slave workers, and they must show respect to the master German race.

He announced that the working day would be longer. Horace didn't mind, more time with Rosa, more German crosses. He smiled.

In an instant the SS officer caught the look and walked over to where Horace stood. 'Is something funny, English pig?' he bellowed, inches from Horace's face. He drew his Luger pistol from his holster. He waved the gun in front of Horace's face. 'Do you think this is funny?'

Horace's experience told him to keep quiet. Anything he said, any gesture he made would be turned around and construed as an insult.

'Answer me! Do you think this is funny?'

Horace remained silent.

'Don't you understand your own language, you English dog?'

117

The SS officer cocked the pistol and held it at arm's length, inches from Horace's face.

Horace's legs took on an involuntary tremble as beads of perspiration appeared on his forehead.

'Sweating like a little English pig,' the officer announced, and in one swift, powerful movement with all the strength he could muster, he clattered Horace across the side of the head with the handle of the gun.

It was a blow that would have felled an elephant. Horace staggered sideways as the pain from the blow registered; blood trickled from a wound above his temple. He bounced into John Knight, the camp outbuildings spun around him and the SS officer who had assaulted him seemed to become two or three. He wanted to collapse, wanted to fall to the ground and sleep, nature's way. He steadied himself, took a second or two and resumed his position in the line-up. He stood to attention, puffed out his chest and bit into his bottom lip in an attempt to quell the pain.

The German officer had already turned to walk away. Perhaps he would have been happy knocking the prisoner into unconsciousness. A show of strength, a warning, the end of the matter? Not now. The prisoner had defied him; insulted him. He had taken the full force of the blow and remained standing. It was time to teach him a lesson. Flapper Garwood looked into the SS officer's eyes and knew what he was thinking. A fist this time propelled into Horace's solar plexus. It was a good shot. Horace winced and fell to his knees, his head resting in the dirt. Already he'd tensed up and was preparing to make a huge effort to get to his feet.

Flapper looked down at the ground, hoping and praying his good friend would stay there. 'Stay down, you stubborn bastard,' he whispered out of the corner of his mouth. The German officer heard him and now pointed the gun at Flapper in confusion. He had hate in his eyes and his finger on the trigger.

'What did you say?' the SS officer screamed at Garwood, his attention now focused on the big man from Essex. He took a step nearer, venom in his eyes. The other guards had run towards them, rifles trained on the prisoners, and the camp commandant stood in between, trying to calm everyone down.

'Please Hartmut, leave them, let us go. We can drink some coffee, have some nice cakes.' The commandant had a hold of the officer's sleeve. 'The men from Switzerland are here again next week – please don't give me any more problems.'

A silence ensued. The SS officer paused. The line of POWs stood terrified, wondering whether they were about to witness another execution, or even two. The decision was resting solely on the shoulders of one man. As the officer thought long and hard, he turned and together with the camp commandant, made for the mess hall. As the door to the building was opened the officer stepped through. If he'd turned and looked back towards the line of prisoners he would have seen a slightly out of breath prisoner, bruised and slightly bloody, standing unaided on his own two feet with a broad grin etched across his face.

CHAPTER
NINE

Sixteen express trains thundered through Horace's head when he awoke in his bunk the following morning. His whole body ached as if he'd been kicked and stamped on by an entire regiment of German soldiers. 'Jesus, Flapper,' he called to his mate below, 'I don't half hurt.'

'Serves you right. You're a stubborn cunt. That's why you hurt, because you wouldn't go down when the Nazi bastard hit you with his Luger, because you wanted to prove you were better than he was.'

'I am better than he is.'

'It's gonna get you killed though, mate. You have to learn to play the game. Everyone here knows you're better than them; you don't have to keep proving it.'

Horace could remember very little about the incident. The blow from the Luger had been a good one. He remembered standing to attention and grinning, and he remembered the taste of the blood as it crept into the side of his mouth, but the rest was a blur. Flapper explained the full story as Horace sat and listened with pride and a feeling that he'd been a little bit stupid, all for the sake of another small victory.

Gradually over the next few hours his memory returned.

He remembered the camp and the guards and the quarry and the work and the workshops, and then he remembered Rosa and that moment.

Rosa reappeared exactly two weeks after her last visit. Horace remembered the moment with clarity. She was wearing a steel-grey pair of riding britches and a pair of black leather boots. He would later find out that she was an accomplished horsewoman and spent every spare moment she had tending and riding the horses on a nearby farm. Unusually, her hair was dishevelled, a little unkempt and her clothing was soiled, her hands a little dirty. She seemed a little embarrassed as she spoke. 'Please forgive my appearance, gentlemen. I have been tending to the horses. Today they needed cleaning.'

Forgive my appearance? Horace thought. My foot! She looked positively stunning. It was a hot day and the exertion of her work in the stables had brought a natural glow to her face. Her skin shone, glistening with a fine sheen of perspiration. Her slightly damp clothing clung to her beautiful form and her eyes were bright, her pupils fully dilated as she gazed at her incarcerated English lover – the sexual tension could have been cut with a knife. Horace's heart began to beat a little faster and his breathing intensified. He became aware that he too was beginning to perspire and in an instant those familiar feelings welled up inside him as the blood began to pump round his body. She certainly hadn't ignored him. Horace thought this might have been her reaction after she'd left the workshop and realised the danger they had placed themselves in.

But surely it couldn't happen again, could it? It was a one-off, a chance in a million that they'd taken and through sheer luck managed to get through without being caught. His thoughts drifted back to the workshop, the moment his fingers had first entered her tender, moist vagina and how she had squirmed and moaned. He recalled the moment he had first thrust into her, how she had gasped with pain and pleasure and how he had pumped and thrust for all he was worth until he had eventually climaxed.

It was a one-off, he reminded himself, something that would never happen again. He had his memories. They couldn't be taken away from him, but there was simply no way he would entertain any thoughts of placing this beautiful young girl in such danger ever again. It would be their secret and they would survive.

Rosa had never felt this way before. This man had awoken emotions in her that she had never before experienced. She couldn't pinpoint what it was exactly. Was it the danger of being caught that had heightened her pleasure so much? Was it the fact that this man had been the first, or was it something deeper? Perhaps even love?

She didn't know. He'd been so aggressive and yet at the same time so tender. He'd hurt her as he'd entered her and yet awoken feelings of sexual desire she could only have dreamed of. As she looked at him right now, standing there in a dirty shirt and trousers that hung loosely on his tortured skeletal frame, bruising around his head and eyes and an embarrassed impish schoolboy look on his face, she trembled as she thought back to that earth-shattering moment when he'd ejaculated inside her and something incredible had happened to her right there and then as she lay face down on a dirty workbench.

She had wanted to scream and shout. Every muscle, every sinew of her body, every nerve ending had seemed to explode at the same glorious moment. It was a crazy, stupid moment, one that if discovered would have ended up with them both facing the firing squad. She recalled the story her father had told her about the poor girl pregnant with the Frenchman's child. She trembled with fear as she realised the sheer magnitude of the danger they had placed themselves in. No matter how good the feeling, how exciting the moment, it had been senseless.

Rosa looked over at her father in conversation with the commandant. What would have become of him? Would he too have been castigated for failing to control his daughter? Perhaps he too would have faced the German rifles with a blindfold. She had been selfish, headstrong. It would not, could not happen again.

Horace was working on the far side of the camp, the door to the workshops clearly visible. He tried not to look, tried not to remember that wonderful moment of passion. It was difficult. He pictured inside the workshop, the machines, the dirty bench. It was still so fresh in his mind, so vivid. He wished he'd been working somewhere else. Why did she have to be there, walking around as if she had not a care in the world, smiling, laughing with her father and the guards? And those riding trousers and the beautiful shape of her thighs. Each time he lifted the sledgehammer his eyes scoured the camp, pinpointing the exact location of Rosa. She was like a magnet, almost hypnotic. Rosa toured the camp with her father, never far from his side as he checked on the men drilling into the marble, and the civilian workers handling the explosives charges that would break the huge slabs apart.

Several times they went into the camp offices and twice the camp commandant came out and joined them on an impromptu inspection. On one occasion the commandant and Rosa's father came over to where Horace and Garwood were working. Rosa had lingered near the door to the offices. This was it, thought Horace, the cold shoulder, the end of a sweet but oh, so short relationship.

Lunchtime came round. It was as if the German guards had analysed the mood of the prisoners all morning, assessing the dangers of any potential escapees. Once again, because of the geographical location of the camp, they decided they were minimal and the four guards patrolling the area became one. They were hungry and bored, and the pattern was familiar. The lone guard would sit on a log and five minutes later one of his colleagues would bring him coffee and a snack. For one hour he would sit alone, and sheer boredom and the heat of the sun would send him to sleep within 20 minutes.

John Knight noticed him first. 'He's kipping, Jim. Whose turn is it today?'

The POWs drill had been well practised. As the guard drifted into his peaceful slumber the prisoners could take a break too. There was no official lunch break, no food, but a sleeping guard meant the prisoners could down tools and take a rest. Some would chance forty winks and with one prisoner effectively on watch against the guard waking up or anyone coming out of the offices unexpectedly, it meant they could relax for a while.

'I'm not tired, John. I'll take watch,' replied Horace.

Knight was a little puzzled. It had been Horace's turn only three days back.

'But you took your...'

'I'll do it, John. Hush your mouth; I'm not in the mood.'

Knight shrugged his shoulders.

'Suit yourself, Jim. But I'm telling you, you need to take it easy.'

'Maybe, but not today. Give the signal.'

Knight shrugged his shoulders. Like a turf accountant's tick tack man, he gave a series of hand movements that indicated Horace was the man on watch. The men settled down. A few of them chatted among themselves; most sought a spot in the shade and closed their eyes. Horace's eyes scanned the camp. Rosa was nowhere to be seen. Likely having lunch with her father and the commandant, he thought as he took the opportunity to stretch his legs. He walked over to the guard whose mouth lolled open, a trickle of saliva rolling down his chin. Two arms cuddled his Karabiner 98k rifle like a sleeping baby.

Thoughts of escape were never far from Horace's mind. He'd been instrumental in negotiations to form an escape committee. Only last week they'd had their first official meeting. To a man they all agreed that the very idea of escape was preposterous. The Germans had chosen the location of the camps well. Security wasn't tight because it didn't need to be. No perimeter fence, a handful of guards, and hundreds of miles of hostile, German-occupied land. Impossible.

Was suicide a more viable option? Surely it couldn't be any worse than this existence? They'd heard the stories about the Japanese kamikaze pilots, hell bent on taking as many of the enemy with them as they could in a mission of death for the glory of the emperor. He'd laughed at how small minded and stupid they were, and yet here he was thinking exactly the same way. It would be suicide, but how many Germans could he take out before they overpowered him?

'Don't do it,' a voice behind him whispered, 'you'll be killed.' Rosa tugged him by the shirt sleeve, conscious of the sleeping guard.

'Do what?' he asked. Rosa looked into his eyes. She knew exactly what he was thinking. He could smell her now, a sweet feminine perspiration mixed with a delicate perfume.

'You have a life, Jim – a life after the war.'

Horace shrugged his shoulders. 'And when will that be, Rosa? How many more months or years do I have to spend in here?'

'The war is turning Jim. The Germans are fighting on too many fronts.'

'"The Germans", Rosa? Why do you say "the Germans"? They are your men, but you speak as if you are not one of them. We were told your father is German.'

Rosa looked over Horace's shoulder; the guard was still snoring.

'Come.' She walked away out of earshot of the guard. Horace followed. She looked angry as she turned to speak.

'I am not German. Do not ever call me a German again.'

Horace stuttered 'But you speak German. You…'

'The Germans marched into Silesia many years ago. They raped and murdered my ancestors; the pure blood of my family stains the soil of Silesia. Silesia will never be a part of Germany no matter what the politicians and the generals say.'

Horace stayed silent as Rosa continued, tears in her eyes.

'Silesia has been part of Poland since time immemorial, but we have always felt a deep independence, a country within a country so to speak, not unlike Scotland in your country. Silesia has its own language, its own culture. My parents taught me the traditions and history of our land as a small child.'

Her eyes glazed over; she stared right through him.

'But alas, it seems man must always conquer, must always kill and must always want more land, more power, more territory. It seems our small country has always been involved in some sort of conflict. In recent times the country has changed hands many times. Poland then Germany, a brief spell of independence and then we belonged to Germany again.

'1871 was a dark year in Silesian history. In 1871 the Germans forbade us to speak our own language, play our traditional instruments or even wear our own clothes. They made everything associated with past Silesia a crime, as if they wanted to wipe everything Silesian off the face of the earth. They brought in thousands of German nationals to dilute the population. They brought them in to teach in the schools; they took the best jobs in the town halls and any prominent position in Silesia was taken by a German official given money to relocate. We were in effect second class citizens in our own country.'

'You are Polish?'

Rosa shook her head.

'I am Silesian, neither Polish nor German. The Silesians rebelled against the German occupiers many time. Each time we were crushed with a brutal force. It is the German way. Whatever you feel you are suffering at the hands of the Germans, my people have experienced it all before. And now they do it all over again. They massacre anyone and any country that stands in their way. The stories filtering through from Russia and Poland – and indeed from our friends and family in Germany opposed to the Nazi regime – you do not want to hear.'

She turned and stood before him. Her face was flushed red, a tear trickled from her eye and Horace followed its slow trail down her delicate soft skin.

'I'm not sure if I believe them all... they are so bad. Tales of women and children and...'

She broke off. Her hand covered her mouth. She took a minute to compose herself. She continued, the tears flowing freely now, dropping onto the dusty ground where Horace watched them form a small damp hollow in the parched earth.

'However much you hate your captors, Jim, I hate them just as much.'

Horace stood in stunned silence. A thousand thoughts ran through his head.

'I would simply ask of you never to think of me as a German.'

He thought of the sex in the workshop and how at one point he had hated the female he was thrusting into.

'I am a Silesian and I am Jewish.'

'You are what?'

'My family is Jewish.'

'But your father... the camp, he is the owner and...'

'The name Rauchbach is not German, Jim. It's from Israel.'

Horace was shaking his head, thinking that it wasn't possible. Rosa's father was working with the Germans; he seemed to be respected, almost looked up to at times.

Rosa continued with her stunning revelation.

'It was my great grandfather Isaac who first brought the family to Silesia. Even back then he sensed how dangerous it was to be Jewish. He was a wonderful man by all accounts and never forced any religious practices on his children; he allowed them to make up their own minds. My father's father passed on the same ideals to his sons and daughters. Father made up his own mind and when Hitler came to power he cleared the house of anything that told of our past. Even the photographs of his parents on a visit back home to the Holy Land were burned. Books, small trinkets, Hebrew teachings and clothes – everything went into a big bonfire in the back garden. It was just as well; the Nazis made a visit to the house when they took over the quarry. Father knew exactly what it was they were looking for but he was one step ahead of them.'

Horace thought of how the beautiful girl standing in front of him was no longer the enemy. She'd taken on a new look, her features seemed more delicate, her face kinder.

'And I'm on your side whatever happens.'

She was no longer the enemy. She could be trusted; he could talk to her.

She took his hands. 'Listen to me, Jim, please.' Her bottom lip trembled. 'I hate the bastards, Jim... hate them.'

He thought about escape and how this girl might be willing to help him.

Rosa looked him in the eyes then looked down at their hands. In an instant she broke the grip, looked around the camp, praying that no one had noticed, praying that the guard was still sleeping. All was quiet. They breathed a mutual sigh of relief and quickly put space between their two bodies.

'This is dangerous,' she said. 'We mustn't be seen together.'

She turned and glanced over her shoulder as she walked away. Was there any emotion in her face, a sign of a smile, maybe a twitch of a facial muscle as she spoke those few short words?

'The workshops... quickly.'

Horace walked past the snoring guard. He listened. The camp was silent. A few POWs dozed too, those that sat around talking seemed oblivious to the rendezvous that had taken place in the middle of the camp. Surely somebody must have seen them talking, that brief moment of contact? His eyes scoured the camp again. Garwood sat near the entrance of the forest – normally out of bounds – glad of the shade, his cap covering his eyes. He slept.

As Horace entered the workshop Rosa stood against the same bench. They fell into each other's arms. She felt different, no longer the tarnished German citizen he once thought she was. They ate each other greedily, their kisses passionate as they pawed each other like two lovers meeting after an eternity. He took her hair, looked at her beautiful face, that puzzled look, before kissing her again with more fervour, more tension, more frenzy. He pushed against her, his erection in full bloom once again, and she felt it immediately.

'Quickly, Jim, quickly... no time.'

This time she broke away, reached for the buttons on the waistband of her trousers, and within seconds they were at her knees. Horace stood back in bewilderment as her small panties followed. Without hesitation, without instruction she turned around, bent over the workbench and parted her legs as best as she could. It was an awkward stance with a pair of knee length leather riding boots and trousers gathered tightly at her knees but it gave Horace a chance. He stepped forward, reached for her with his hand as the other hand took hold of his stiff penis. Within a few seconds he was inside her. As before her hand covered her mouth in an attempt to contain her noisy pleasure. He held the position, wanting the moment to last. He groaned as he leaned back, looked up to the ceiling and began a slow rhythmical movement.

The guard was puzzled. He was displeased. The prisoners had taken advantage of his moment's weakness. Who could blame him? It was so very hot and such boring work looking over the 20 or so prisoners, none of whom had the slightest intention of escaping. He tried to tell the commanding officer time and time again, but he had insisted they be watched at all times. Two were clearly sleeping, others were leaning on picks and shovels. Idle bastards. He'd make them pay. And where was the one that spoke some German? Jim. Where was that bastard? Did he dream or had he seen him going into the workshops as he dozed in the afternoon sun? He hadn't dreamed it. He eased himself to his feet using his rifle as leverage. He cursed his arthritic knee as it stiffened and a pain shot down the length of his shin bone. And the girl, where's the girl? 'Bastards,' he whispered. 'Someone is going to pay.'

Rosa exploded into orgasm. The sweat had soaked through her blouse and it clung to her back. It was time for Horace to join her and as he quickened his movements Rosa tensed up.

'Please, quickly,' she gasped as her head jerked back and forward. 'I hear the guard talking.'

Panic welled up inside Horace as he heard the conversation too – half German, half broken English. Yet his pleasure seemed to intensify at the danger they were now in.

Within seconds they'd both climaxed, regained their composure, buttoned up their trousers and sneaked out one at a time into the bright sunshine – satisfied, but both wanting so much more. No foreplay, no experimentation, no teasing, no clumsy awkward moments, no laughter, no words of love and expression as he'd remembered with Eva. They'd often lain for hours in the bedroom of her small cottage in Ibstock while her mother and father had been at work. They'd frolicked in the cornfields and the meadows of Leicestershire, making love for hours on end, and he'd touched and stroked and caressed her whole body, teasing and arousing her again and again. Eva had done likewise as she insisted on fitting the French letter each time they made love. Horace lay completely naked with his hands by his side as Eva complimented him on his recovery time and the impressive quality of his manhood. And they'd left the fields laughing and joking, talking about their daring exploits. He recalled how Eva had positively glowed after one particularly energetic session. They'd often wondered if they'd been seen, what might happen if a farmer or even a family friend had discovered them.

It was so different now as he walked the long walk to where Flapper Garwood lay sleeping. No laughing and joking, no swaying cornfields, no touching hands nor a loving embrace – just thoughts of a firing squad and an even greater hatred for the German race. Deliberately avoiding eye contact, Horace focused on his sleeping pal as he walked straight past the guard.

Suddenly the German shouted behind him.

'*Was machen Sie, Scheißkerl*?' 'You bastard! What are you doing?'

Horace froze, turned around as the German marched towards him, rifle pointing at his chest. The guard cocked the rifle and broke into a run, spitting his anger as he got nearer. Horace looked around. Thank God Rosa was nowhere to be seen. She'd disappeared – the guard hadn't seen her... he hoped.

'*Sie meinen, ich bin so bloed*?' 'You think I'm an idiot?'

Instinctively Horace raised his arms in the air.

But the German guard ran straight past him and stood over the snoring Flapper Garwood. Poor Flapper. He was now the focus of attention, and the guard vented his fury with a swift kick to the ribs of the sleeping POW.

'You pig dog! Get up!'

A rifle butt hit the prisoner in the chest as the air was forced from his lungs. He gasped and scrambled to his feet in a sleep-induced stupor. Flapper picked up his work tool, ran over to the huge block of marble and began chipping away furiously. The guard followed, gave Flapper another kick in the pants and a cuff along the back of the neck.

He then turned to face Horace. There was hatred in his eyes, menace in his voice.

'And you my English pig slave, where have you been?'

Horace was in a quandary. Had the guard seen him come out of the workshop? Had he seen Rosa? Had he seen them going into the workshop? The adrenaline of fear swam through him. It was fear for Rosa, fear for her safety. At that moment, as he stood in front of a German guard intent on meting out yet more punishment, he realised he needed to protect Rosa.

He realised too that he had developed feelings for her.

'Speak, you bastard!'

Horace spoke in English. The guard's vocabulary was reasonably good, but his sentence construction and verbs were poor.

'You're a piece of shit, you are.'

Garwood's knees turned to lead. He couldn't believe what his friend had just said. The German took a step forward, raised his rifle and pointed it between Horace's eyes. He looked confused, almost shocked. Had he understood correctly?

'What did you say?' he snarled.

'I needed to do a shit, sir.'

Horace stood to attention. The guard lowered his rifle.

'Speak German, prisoner. I know you speak it well.' He grinned – an evil smile. 'It will be the language of the world in a few short years, you might as well get used to it.'

Horace repeated his statement in German, told the guard he would normally have asked for permission to use the toilets through the workshops but didn't want to disturb the guard's well-earned rest. The guard lowered his rifle, seemingly satisfied. As he walked away he signalled for the prisoner to resume his duties and Horace released a huge sigh of relief deep from within his lungs.

It was late August 1941 and the summer weather had been quite pleasant on the whole, with lots of sunshine and warm, sultry days. The German offensive into Russia was stalling: although they'd captured Smolensk and over 300,000 Russians, the first signs were beginning to appear that a siege of Leningrad was materialising. On 30 August the rain began in earnest. It came down in torrents hour after hour and the men in the quarry were soaked to the bone. Horace shivered and struggled with his pickaxe. On more than one occasion it slipped from the marble, coming to rest on the ground a few inches from his foot. He looked across towards the German guards standing under a makeshift tarpaulin shelter, smoking cigarettes and smiling. In his best German and with his most doleful eyes he pleaded with them.

'It's too dangerous, sir. The marble is too slippery.'

'Continue,' one of them said with a gesture of his hand. Rosa's father looked on.

For another two hours the men half-heartedly chipped and picked away at the slippery white rock. Two at a time, when the marble had been chipped and shaped to an adequate size, they moved each slab the 50 yards or so to a flatbed lorry. John Knight and Danny Staines shuffled across slowly, their fingers tenuously gripping the wet marble as best they could. Danny Staines was tired. He was visibly shivering and of course he was hungry. He was thinking of his ration of cabbage soup later that day, he was thinking about the fistful of bread he had saved and how he'd cleverly hidden it in a dry spot beneath his bunk. He wasn't concentrating and as John Knight signalled by way of a nodding head, the two men heaved upwards with the huge effort needed to lift the marble onto the wooden floor of the lorry.

The result was catastrophic. Staines' timing was just a split second slower than John Knight's and the slab tipped unevenly towards him. On a normal day the men's grip on the marble would be firm, their concentration would be better and the two men would immediately right the marble with a quick twist of the wrist or a pull of the shoulder. Not today. Both men realised the danger immediately and they reacted accordingly, tightening their grip on the rock. It was futile. The wet surface of the marble was impossible to hold and the 40lb load tipped violently and dropped three feet onto the bridge of Danny Staines' foot.

The crack of the bone and the subsequent squeal could be heard by every man in the quarry. Rosa's father came running from the workshop with the camp commandant in close pursuit. Rosa's father was angry and shouted at the commandant.

'I told you this would happen!' he screamed at the German guards.

'Too dangerous,' Horace picked up in a heated German conversation. Then, 'impossible conditions'. Within 20 minutes all of the men were confined to their respective huts.

Danny Staines' foot was reset into a position that loosely resembled the shape of the foot he'd started the day with, but without any anaesthetic or even a mouthful of whisky to deaden the pain. It was crudely splinted and bandaged up with strips of flannelette. He would be reprieved of his duties for nearly six weeks but would walk with a limp for the rest of his life.

The rain continued for many days. At first the men were glad of the rest, a chance to recuperate and recharge their batteries. Some had worked non-stop, without a day off for over two years. But then boredom set in and the continued noise of the heavy rain on the roof of the wooden hut began to take its toll. A few arguments broke out for little or no reason and then a full-blown fist fight developed between two men over a matchstick during a card game. Sergeant Owen, the official go-between, decided to take some action, and after helping break up the scrap, made his way over to the commandant's office. He returned within 15 minutes with a smile on his face as big as the mouth of the Thames.

'Come on lads, time for some sport.'

'What sort of sport?' Horace asked him.

'You'll find out soon enough.'

As Horace left the hut along with the rest of the men he imagined the rain just might be getting a little lighter. And yes, he looked up, pointed overhead and turned to John Knight.

'Blue sky, John. I do believe it's beginning to clear up.'

The men followed on behind the sergeant as he led them

through the compound and up the hill towards the area where the blasting and splitting of the marble seams took place. Six German guards accompanied them. The sergeant scrambled up the hill and stood looking over the huge natural basin carved out by nature and man-made dynamite in more recent years. It was completely flooded and filled with water, the size of a football pitch.

'We're going swimming, chaps. Time to strip off.'

Horace hadn't been fully immersed in water for nearly three years. He remembered the day with clarity: Christmas Day 1939. He'd slipped into a hot bath whilst absent without leave in his parents' house in Ibstock. After that it had been army regulation showers, which although pleasant enough, just weren't the same as submerging an aching body in hot water. Then there was the hell of Fort Eight at Posen. Not a bath, not a shower, nothing.

As he stood watching his fellow prisoners diving naked into the deep milky water, a kind of magnetism drew him forward and he began to unbutton his shirt. He was wary, always had been. His father had taken him and Harold as youngsters to the public baths in Leicester every Saturday. He'd stressed the importance of being able to swim and Horace remembered with clarity the moment he'd scrambled and struggled across the short distance of the width of the pool to claim the prize of an official swimmer. He remembered being presented with a sheet of paper that announced he'd swum the required 25 yards.

But he had never been totally happy swimming in water. Several weeks later on a warm summer's day trip to Skegness, Daisy and Harold and their father had frolicked in the sea and although Horace had wanted to dive head first into those breaking waves, wanted to swim far out like his dad, something held him back. There was a certain wariness, a certain respect for the powerful breakers crashing onto the shore and a fear of the massive expanse of water as far as the eye could see. Harold hadn't helped when he'd explained that the eye could see eight miles out to sea until the natural curve of the earth forced the ocean to disappear from view. He'd been out as far as his waist that day, but hadn't even attempted anything that resembled a swim.

But today was different. Today he would swim. Today he would immerse himself in the warm waters of this natural pool. That's what he told himself as he removed his trousers and stood naked at the water's edge. It was a swimming pool. Just like the baths in Leicester. He watched the men jumping from the huge logs that now floated in the water. The logs were used to roll the huge slabs of marble to different areas of the quarry and had been neatly stacked up at the far side the last time he remembered. Now they acted as diving platforms as they bobbed up and down, half submerged in the milky water in front of him.

Rosa's father stood close by, muttering to himself as he surveyed the scene. 'It will take bloody days to pump this water out. More production lost.'

It was an unreal moment. Horace standing naked as Herr Rauchbach looked on.

'Come on, Jim, take a swim with your friends.' He looked around and surveyed the scene, shook his head and laughed. 'So many bare arses, Jim, so many English dicks.'

Horace looked straight at him and grinned.

'And you, Jim, more lucky than most, a popular man with the ladies back home, eh?'

If only you knew, mate, Horace thought to himself as he leapt into the water.

The cold water took his breath away as the initial shock kicked in. Within 20 seconds, however, Horace was in a world he'd never experienced before. He'd lost his fear and for the first time in his life he swam for real. Perhaps because he'd stared death in the face, witnessed awful events since the beginning of the war, the fear of it didn't seem to matter anymore. Twenty feet from the shore now, he pushed out, breasting the water, his limbs loose in a fluent motion, his breathing controlled. He laughed as he remembered the desperate stiff-armed, stiff-legged, out-of-breath 12-year-old in Leicester baths, the fearful soul at the water's edge in Skegness.

'C'mon Jim, up here!' It was Flapper balancing on a log, ready to dive off. 'It's just like fucking Clacton on Sea in July.'

Darkie Evans, a mixed race Welsh Guard from Cardiff, sat alongside him. 'Up here, Jim boyo. This end of the log is Llandudno.'

Horace struck out for the huge log, his confidence growing with each stroke. Each man was in their own seaside world, his brain beaming him back to a childhood long since forgotten. Horace in Skeggy, Garwood in Clacton, the Welsh in Llandudno and the Scots in Ayr or Dunoon or Portree.

As Flapper dived out over Horace's head the log began to spin. Evans cursed as he lost his balance and fell into the water and Horace reached out for the log, aware that he had begun to breathe just a little harder. The log was still spinning as Horace reached it, and its immense saturated weight made it impossible to stop. It was slowing down and Horace began to tread water, his face just inches from it.

He saw the two-inch diameter bolt for only a split second. Two or three bolts were drilled into every log to give the ropes attached to it a better grip. The bolt protruded no more than five inches. As the three-ton log turned a full circle in the water the bolt crashed into Horace's skull and his world began to spin out of control.

He was under the log now and his newfound confidence had evaporated in an instant. The stiffness was back in his arms and legs as he struggled for air, aware of the foul-tasting water mixed with his own blood entering his mouth and stinging and biting at the sensitive membrane of his lungs. A nauseous feeling washed over him as he vomited, polluting the water still further. And a struggle. A struggle to reach out for the surface, just a few tantalising feet above him. The log had moved, he could see the sunlight above him and legs and faces peering down into the depths of the water below. Not far to go. Two strokes, three, four at the most and he struck out for the surface, willing his arms and legs to respond to the signals being sent out from his brain.

Something wasn't working. Lack of oxygen, perhaps? The surface of the water and safety and the lifeblood of air were being sucked further and further away. The legs were smaller now... he could no longer make out the characteristics of the faces above him. The shapes blended into each other and then the desperation and the panic subsided and he floated, suspended in a womb-like trance as a smile flickered across his face and a wonderful feeling of inner contentment washed over him.

No more war, no more suffering, just beautiful images of his family. The smiling, always contented face of his beautiful mother and a photograph from long ago of Mum as a 20-year-old, pretty and proud, the most elegant girl in the world. An image of Dad in the fields that day, gun in hand, and rabbits, and Dad's fiercely proud expression as the shot rang out and young Horace beamed a smile that neither Dad nor he would ever forget.

Final images now. Daisy, Sybil and Harold, baby Derick. Christmas, the snow, whisky in tea and a roaring fire. And ultimately a picture of Horace. Someone looking down,

Horace floating... his arms and legs suspended like a puppet with no master. Horace in water, water mixed with blood, and another smile... and then blackness... and peace.

CHAPTER TEN

Rosa lay on her bed crying. She couldn't believe the news her father had delivered only moments before. She'd needed to hide her feelings as he'd explained about the accident and how they'd fought in vain to revive the prisoner known as Jim, on the banks of the flooded quarry. They'd pressed and pounded at his chest for what seemed like an eternity and after a few minutes Henryk Rauchbach had left, realising that the frantic prisoners were pursuing a hopeless cause.

The shock at hearing his name had stopped her heart beating. The first man she'd loved, the only man she'd given herself to freely... dead. She managed to control her emotions for the briefest of moments and made a lame excuse about returning to her room. Now, in the confines of her attic room of her parents' house, she buried her face into her pillow as the tears flowed in torrents.

Horace was back in the sick bay again. He remembered nothing of the incident – nature's way. His first recollection was of spewing a torrent of foul-tasting water from his lungs and the smiling faces of Darkie Evans, Flapper, and Sergeant Owen. The German guards showed no emotion at all. They cared neither one way nor the other whether a prisoner lived or died. It was just one less mouth to feed.

Darkie Evans explained how he'd saved his life. Somehow, Horace thought, the Welshman would never let him forget it. 'I could barely make you out under there, Jim. The water was like bloody milk, boyo!'

Flapper looked on smiling, content to allow the Welshman his moment of glory and say how he deserved it. Flapper had gone under too and thought it was hopeless: the water was clouded from the chalky silt at the bottom and he could barely see a few feet in front of him.

'You must have been 20 feet from the surface. You weren't moving at all, my friend,'

How Evans had spotted him Flapper would never know.

'I went back to the surface for a deep breath, told the laddos and Flapper here I'd seen you.'

Flapper spoke. 'Darkie got to you first; two of us followed him down. He must have the eyes of a fucking owl, Jim, I swear. I couldn't see fuck all, just the legs of our Welsh friend.'

Darkie Evans looked on smiling, his chest swelling by the minute.

'I managed to hook a hand under your armpit and started pulling you up. Fuck me, boyo, you were a heavy old lump!'

'I took a hold of the other arm,' Flapper said. 'And Robbie Roberts helped drag you to the shore. I swear the MO worked on you for ten minutes, Jim. We all thought you'd had it.'

'I don't remember a thing,' Horace said in a voice that resembled a whisper, aware of how tender his throat was.

Henryk Rauchbach delivered the good news to his daughter the following evening as they sat around the table having the family evening meal. Again, Rosa congratulated herself at her ability to conceal her emotions. Her father and mother would not suspect a thing, she thought to herself.

As was the nightly ritual, she cleared the table and prepared to wash the dirty dishes. As she made her way into the small kitchen her parents looked at each other. They thought it most unusual that their daughter hadn't eaten a bite since Herr Rauchbach had delivered the news on the prisoner known as Jim.

Horace followed Rauchbach through a small copse, weighed down with a heavy drill and a canvas bag containing several drill bits. Horace had been stood down from the morning's roll call and asked to report to the office. Rosa's father explained Horace was being assigned to a new part of the camp for a different duty.

'I chose you, Jim, because you are intelligent and you have a way with your hands,' Rauchbach explained as they made their way to the top of the hill that looked over the once-flooded quarry. 'I have watched you cutting the men's hair. So precise and careful. This is what I need for this job.'

He made his way across to the huge marble slabs. 'This marble is too big to move and must be broken down.' He dropped to his knees, took the pack from his back and unzipped it. 'We do this with dynamite.'

He opened the bag, exposing the small sticks of explosive about the same size as a small candle. 'But we must do it carefully and precisely and each stick of dynamite must be positioned exactly right in order to split the marble, not blow it to hell.' He smiled. 'It's a skilled job, Jim. One I think you can handle. But before you go getting any ideas you won't be working the explosives. No. You will be the drilling man. The explosives will be the job of a German. Can't go letting you prisoners loose with bombs now, can we?'

Rauchbach stood up and laughed again. 'This morning you watch and learn, this afternoon you take over.'

For the next four hours Rauchbach drilled a series of strategically placed holes in the huge slabs. He explained to Horace how to spot the seams and the natural fault lines in the stone where the marble would be at its weakest. Horace watched as the explosive charges detonated and how the marble seemed to fall apart effortlessly as if a huge knife had separated a block of butter. On one occasion Rauchbach cursed in German when the marble cracked rather than split. 'I fucked up there, Jim,' he said as he examined the marble. 'Here, see.' He pointed to the rock face. 'The hole was a fraction out of line and this is the result.'

Rauchbach stretched, rubbed at the base of his back and squeezed gently. He kicked the handle of the drill so it was pointing at Horace. 'Your turn now, Jim. I think you've seen enough.'

Horace took to his new job well. He'd been given a break, a chance to escape the back-breaking ten-hour days of labour-intensive, monotonous work. This was a job that needed a little thought, a little skill, a little patience. Horace drilled and Rauchbach filled the holes with the explosive charges. As the first seam split along the line of perfectly placed holes, Rauchbach grinned.

'You are a natural, Jim. It's time for my lunch – you get on with it.' Rauchbach pointed at the slabs lying ten feet from the forest. 'Make a start on those; we'll split them after lunch.'

Horace looked around. No guards, no other prisoners. Rauchbach caught the look.

'Yes, Jim, I trust you. Don't go letting me down and running off.'

And then Rosa's father said something that sent a shiver up his spine.

'Somehow, Jim, I don't think you will. This camp has certain attractions; it's by no means the worst.'

He winked as he started to walk away. 'And you, Jim, are luckier than most.'

Horace had drilled his third line when the unmistakable smell of his lover filled the air. He stretched up, wiped the sweat from his brow, and then sensed it. He turned around and there she stood like a goddess, the breeze tugging at her light dress. She rushed into his arms and they kissed passionately. He became aware of the salty tears flowing down her cheeks and the tremble of her young form.

'What is it, Rosa?' he said as he held her at arm's length and gazed into her moist eyes.

She turned her head, not wanting Horace to see her that way.

He took hold of her chin gently and kissed her on the lips. 'Tell me, Rosa.'

Rosa pulled a handkerchief from her sleeve and wiped the tears away. She'd composed herself a little, tried to smile as the tears subsided. She moved forward, kissed him again and wrapped her arms tightly around his perspiring body. The trembling started again and she whispered in his ear between sobs. 'I thought you were dead, Jim. Father came home, said you had drowned. I thought I'd lost you, thought I would never see you again.'

And then it became clear. At that moment Horace realised that this young girl loved him more than anything else in the world. Right there and then something changed in Horace. Something changed that he couldn't quite put his finger on as they walked hand in hand into the forest. He felt different, he felt at ease, content. He was incarcerated in a prisoner of war camp but he could put up with whatever was necessary to get him through till the end of the war as long as Rosa was here with him.

They made love on the grassy floor of the forest in among

the dead pine needles and wild flowers. They were naked, the first time they'd experienced each other that way. They made love slowly, Horace facing his lover, looking into her hypnotic eyes. They never spoke, each enjoying the moment as their breathing intensified. In the workshop they'd had sex; here they made love.

Horace raised himself up as his arms straightened and he took the full weight of his body. Rosa reached up and cupped her hands around his neck. He marvelled at her small perfectly shaped breasts rising and falling in time with her heavy breathing. A light sheen of moisture covered them as she began to groan gently while he continued his slow rhythmic movement. He lowered his body again and crushed her breasts with his chest as he quickened his movement. All at once they were one. Her pelvic thrusts were in time with his, lovers who instinctively each knew the exact timing necessary to climax together.

Afterwards they lay on their backs on the forest floor, at one with nature. They were satisfied, their hands coupled together as their breathing returned to normal. They wanted to lie there forever, wanted to make love over and over again. Eventually the cool autumn breeze forced them to dress. Fifteen minutes later Horace had started drilling again with a new found energy and Rosa sat with her father as he finished the remains of his lunch.

Willie McLachlan would never have considered himself a poofter back home in Helensburgh, just north of Glasgow and a few miles from Loch Lomond. He hadn't given it a second thought. He'd had his girlfriends like anyone else and he remembered the day as clear as a bell when Jenny Murray had taken him into her father's garden shed to show him her chickens. He laughed at the incident now. He'd been 13 years of age at the time, raised on a rough council estate, and had actually believed that Jenny, two years older, had chickens in her garden shed at the bottom of her father's allotment. Why not? A few of the miners and shipyard workers and dockers kept a few hens to supplement the family's diet.

But something didn't quite ring true as Jenny took his hand and led him through the door. The shed was cluttered up with rubbish save for a dirty rug sprawled out in the middle of the shed.

'Whaur's the chickens?' he asked innocently as Jenny smiled and lifted her dress over her head.

'You're jist aboot tae see one,' she replied and in a couple of swift movements Jenny stood with her knickers in her hand, thrusting a soft downy pubic triangle in the direction of a startled young Willie. No, he hadn't been a poofter when Jenny had taken his hand and made him explore her inner reaches. As she'd stood and moaned while he'd willingly thrust his fingers into her secret place, he'd became aware of his own stirrings and an uncomfortable tight feeling in his trousers. Jenny noticed it too and within seconds his shorts were down by his knees and she massaged him to a hardness he'd never experienced before.

He'd enjoyed his experience with Jenny in the musty shed in Helensburgh all those years ago. He'd enjoyed the moment she'd eased his hardness into her and cried out in pleasure as he climaxed after a few brief seconds, grunting and groaning as his backside took on an involuntary rhythm of its own. He was no poof back then. But now, after a year's incarceration and only an odd glimpse of a covered female breast or backside, his homosexual tendencies had risen to the surface and he'd developed an attraction to a young man from the 2nd/5th Battalion Leicesters.

It started with a wolf whistle. Whenever Horace walked past

the Scot, be it in private, in a group in the quarry, in the shower block or wherever... always a little whistle and occasionally a wink. At first Horace ignored it, not quite realising the significance of it, but then McLachlan started getting a little bolder. The whistles were getting louder, more frequent and he was doing it in front of the other men. Ernie had made a comment – albeit tongue in cheek – that Horace was 'on the turn'. It was a term used in the camps quite often. Men were men but because of the poor conditions and inadequate food, their natural sexual appetite was suppressed. For some it was still there. Some stuck to masturbation to release the pent up sexual frustration, others turned to homosexuality.

In general it was frowned upon. Those that turned to it kept it secret, didn't brag or boast and any sexual activity was carefully planned so that it took place in private. Worse than the disapproval of the POWs were the rumours on the grapevine about just what the Germans thought about homosexuals. Jews, Poles, Slavs, Russians, the mentally unstable, handicapped, gypsies, freemasons, homosexuals – it was rumoured that Hitler and his henchmen were exterminating them all in the camps of Poland and Germany.

Horace didn't believe the grapevine. He wouldn't believe the rumours, didn't want to – it was just too unimaginable for words. He could understand how Hitler craved power, how he perceived Germany to be a dominant world force. Right through history, men and countries had wanted to force their ideology and beliefs on other men and women of a different creed. From Genghis Khan to the Romans, from the Christian Crusades to the Spanish Conquistadors in the New World. But if these rumours filtering through were correct, Adolf Hitler and his Third Reich were in an altogether different league. He'd witnessed their barbarity first hand on the march and at the first camp. But no... surely not? It can't be, Horace thought to himself over and over again. But what if it was true? And what if the Scot's actions were brought to the attention of the guards? It didn't bear thinking about. Horace would need to take him to one side, have a little word in his ear.

Two days later Horace took hold of his sleeve as he sat on the ground outside his hut finishing the last of his soup. 'Can I have a word, Willie, please?'

Willie looked up. The late evening sun cast a shadow over Horace and Willie squinted as he peered up. 'Sure Jim, nae bother. What is it?'

'In private,' Horace replied, uncomfortable with the conversation he was about to have. McLachlan hung around with other Scots. The Scots always hung around with each other: they ate together, slept together and drank together. It was almost an exclusive club in a prisoner of war camp, and it annoyed the hell out of Horace and the other men. At times they were arrogant, even a little hostile, and while they would tell anyone who would listen how proud they were of their country and their culture, in reality they were anti everybody else (especially the English) and seemed to complain continuously. Flapper summed it up one night when he commented, 'They're well balanced, these fucking Jocks. They have a fucking chip on both shoulders.'

Willie McLachlan raised himself to his full six-foot height. He'd been captured in France a little over a year ago. Although he had lost weight, he hadn't suffered the ravages of the death march or the harsh conditions of Fort Eight. Horace felt a little intimidated as McLachlan took a step forward and towered over him.

'And what fucking word would that be, handsome?'

'Over here.' Horace turned and walked a few yards. McLachlan followed.

Horace turned to face him. The Scotsman was smiling.

'Is this our first date, Jim?'

Horace ignored the remark. 'Look, Willie, I just wanted to say I'm not that way inclined and would appreciate it if you would keep your whistles to yourself.'

Willie McLachlan's face took on a complete new look.

'And what fucking way would that be?'

Horace had dug himself a hole. He wished he'd worded it a little differently. The Scot spoke again.

'Just what are you fucking calling me?'

'Look, Willie, you've been whistling at me and that only means one thing. Where I come from we only use it on girls.'

'And what does it mean then, pretty boy?'

McLachlan inched closer, threateningly.

'Well?'

'Look, Willie, I don't want any trouble. I just want you to stop whistling at me. You've heard the rumours about the Germans and what they do with...'

He paused, then decided to use the word and face the consequences.

'Homosexuals.'

The Scot visibly trembled with rage, raised his voice, poked a stiff finger in Horace's chest.

'You calling me a poofter, English boy?'

'No, Willie... no... I'm just saying...'

Another finger in the chest, a little harder than the previous one.

'Just what the fuck are you saying, then?'

The adrenaline surge started deep down in Horace's veins. He was past the point of no return and his body knew it as the chemical coursed through his body. He wanted to back off, wanted to tell the big Scot he'd been mistaken. But he wouldn't. It wasn't in his nature; he'd never backed down from anyone, not in a playground fight, not in the boxing ring he'd enjoyed so much in his early teens. He'd never backed away or refused a fight even when they'd thrown him in against the 15 and 16-year-olds far bigger than him. McLachlan interrupted his thoughts.

'Just what the fuck are you saying?'

Be tactful, he thought to himself. He looked around. A few of the other men had begun to take notice of the raised voices, the altercation that seemed to be brewing right in front of them.

'Well?'

'I'm saying,' he paused, gathered his thoughts, tried not to antagonise the Scotsman any further. 'I'm saying, McLachlan, that if you whistle at me just one more time I'll fucking punch you into the middle of next week.'

The Scot lunged forward and grabbed Horace by the collar, almost lifting him off his feet. He'd been caught unawares: he should have been more alert and remembered his boxing training – keep the bigger man at a distance. It would be a mistake he wouldn't make twice. Garwood and one or two of the Scots rushed into the mêlée to break things up. A fight in view of the Germans would not be tolerated by the guards and generally resulted in a further skirmish with two or three German rifle butts.

'Fucking cunt's calling me a poof!' screamed the Scot as two or three of his countrymen held him back. 'I'll kill the bastard, let me at him!'

Horace regained his composure. The adrenaline felt good now as it flowed smoothly. The trembling had stopped and he spoke with a renewed confidence.

'In the basement of hut number three, tonight – we'll settle this matter once and for all.'

Flapper looked at him incredulously and pointed at the big Scotsman. 'You want to fight that big bugger, Jim?'

'Tonight. Six o'clock.'

McLachlan started laughing, as if he couldn't quite believe what this small, emaciated Englishman was saying. Then an inner rage welled up as he snarled through gritted teeth.

'Six o'clock, ye Sassenach bastard. I'll be there, I'm gonna tear ya fuckin' heed aff ya shoulders.'

Horace walked away with Flapper as the Scots returned to their original position to draw up battle plans. Garwood had done a bit of boxing in the past too, and as the two friends prepared for the fight of the year, Garwood assumed the position of unofficial trainer and corner man, offering tips and suggestions on how to beat the big Jock. The odds were against Horace, giving away at least five stone and nearly six inches in height. McLachlan's hands were like great shovels attached to huge powerful arms that Horace swore would trail the ground when he walked. And word filtered back from the Scottish camp that street fighting was in McLachlan's blood, that he'd run with a gang from a tough area of Glasgow and killed a man in a street fight.

Horace stood, boxing in the traditional stance, left hand leading as Garwood held up his heavily strapped hands covered in swathes of flannelette. Garwood tried hard to dodge and avoid each blow but Horace connected with more than he missed. At 5.30 Garwood drew to a close the training session and made Horace take to his bunk for 30 minutes' rest. Horace felt good. The natural boxing rhythm had returned as if it had only been yesterday and he knew that if he could just keep McLachlan at a distance he'd have a chance of winning. Whatever happened he'd give it all he had.

Five minutes before the scheduled fight a crowd had gathered in the basement of the hut. This was big news. There had been many a fight in the camps since Horace had been captured, sometimes one a week, but they were always broken up by the other prisoners for fear of recriminations from the Germans. This was different. There would be no Germans around to break up proceedings. A small ring had been crudely constructed in the basement and men were betting on the result. It was entertainment, a break from the normal monotonous routine of supper, rest and lights out.

It was ten past six before Flapper Garwood allowed Horace off his bunk. The Londoner's theory was that it would make McLachlan anxious, complacent, thinking his opponent had bottled it. At 14 minutes past six Horace and his corner man burst through the door of number three hut. 'He's here!' a voice shouted down the stairs to where the restless crowd stood and jockeyed for the best view. A muffled cheer drifted up and the hairs stood up on Horace's neck. He turned to Garwood.

'Do you know, Flapper, I think I'm going to enjoy this.'

'Just don't get in too close, Jim. He's a brawler not a fighter. Keep your distance, jab and run. Keep jabbing and keep running until you see the opportunity. Keep doing that and you'll win and for fuck's sake, be patient.'

Garwood's game plan mirrored the one Horace had devised almost as soon as the gauntlet had been thrown down. The last thing he wanted was to get in a wrestle or a brawl. Controlled, measured boxing, just like the art he'd perfected in the boxing club in Ibstock.

McLachlan stood in the corner of the makeshift ring stripped to the waist, a huge smile on his face.

'So you've eventually turned up, chicken shit? We thought you'd cocked, shit yer wee English pants.'

Horace said nothing. He climbed through the ropes and skipped a little shadow boxing as Garwood placed a bucket and a tin full of water in the opposite corner. Corporal David Valentine from the Northumberland Fusiliers had assumed the position of referee as he brought the two fighters together. 'I want a good clean fight, lads.' McLachlan stepped forward, trying to intimidate. 'No hitting below the belt and break when I say "break".'

'I'll break his fucking neck,' said the Scotsman with a grin.

Horace said nothing.

The referee ordered the two men to their respective corners. A gaggle of Scots surrounded McLachlan, slapped him round the shoulders and screamed encouragement. Flapper offered Horace a drink of water and reminded him to keep his distance. Valentine beckoned the two men forward and when they were a couple of yards apart stepped out of the way, shouting 'Fight on!'

Another cheer went up as Horace went into his familiar boxing stance, his eyes fixed on McLachlan. This time he was ready.

McLachlan rushed forward, heavy-footed, his arms stretched out in front like a wrestler. Horace danced on the balls of his feet, ready to spring in the right direction at the last second. As McLachlan came within range Horace powered a left jab into the bridge of his nose. It connected perfectly and the Scot's nose popped like a balloon. In the same fluid movement Horace turned and fled before McLachlan knew what had hit him. He stood in Horace's corner now as the blood started flowing freely down his face. Horace stood inches from the Scottish corner men.

'Ye lucky cunt,' snarled the red-haired man behind him. Horace ignored him and stalked towards McLachlan, his confidence growing by the second. The Scot was more canny this time, aware of how foolish his last move had been. He raised his fists towards his face to protect himself. He now realised he was in a real fight. Horace moved forward, within reach of his opponent. McLachlan couldn't resist it; he lunged forward with a telegraphed swinging right hand. Horace bent backwards and the Scot's fist flailed at fresh air. Horace counteracted with a quick combination, a left cross to the temple stunning his opponent as his right fist powered into McLachlan's solar plexus.

The crowd cheered. McLachlan fell to his knees. Horace walked over and bent down to speak.

'Had enough, Willie? Want to call it a day?'

McLachlan spoke. 'Aye... right enough, geez a hand up.'

Horace felt sorry for him. The fight was over, he'd shown the tough man up for what he really was. Horace extended his hand. As the Scot raised himself to his full height, he smiled and shook Horace's hand. As Horace lowered his guard, McLachlan powered his forehead into Horace's face.

As Horace lay on the floor – he must have been out for a second or two – the Scots whooped and cheered as David Valentine delivered a stern lecture to the smiling, apologetic Scot.

Garwood spoke just once, another pearl of wisdom. 'Rules out the window, Jim. Get the dirty cunt.'

Horace was aware of the blood covering his face and of a different surge of adrenaline coursing through his veins. It was anger this time as he raised himself to his feet. The English boys roared him on as the Scots booed and hissed, called him an idiot. One shouted at McLachlan to 'murder him.'

But McLachlan didn't hear him. He had seen the look on Horace's face and was more than a little worried as the bloodied battler came towards him. Horace's hands took up the guard again and he was grinning through the blood.

'Right, you dirty Scottish bastard, time to fight your way.'

Horace wasn't controlled. He didn't jab and run. Instead he

launched into McLachlan with a venom and a fury that the Scot just couldn't cope with. McLachlan's hands covered his head as he stood slightly stooped. Horace rained punches down on him and hammered two perfectly executed upper cuts into his chin, picking his spot perfectly between the elbows. The Scot was on the ropes and his corner men silenced as Valentine signalled the end of the first round.

McLachlan sat on the stool as his fellow countrymen plied him with water and attempted to stem the flow of blood from his right eye, his nose and a huge, protruding fat lip. The big man was a mess, breathing heavily.

As Valentine announced round two Horace sprang to his feet. The Scot was almost pushed into the centre of the ring and Horace continued where he left off. McLachlan's hands were no longer able to protect his head and Horace moved in for the kill. Two left jabs, each one delivered with accuracy and power. McLachlan's head jerked back. His legs were gone and his crossed eyes focused on no one in particular. Horace moved forward and tightened his right fist. The Scot stepped back and made a last attempt to protect himself. Horace almost felt sorry for him as his perfectly executed right cross smashed into his cheekbone and McLachlan hit the deck.

Garwood gave a slow, dignified clap as he returned to the corner. The English boys cheered as the Scots licked their wounds.

'One more thing, Flapper,' Horace said as he took a drink of water and turned. 'I'm not quite finished.'

He walked casually over to the assembled Scots, where McLachlan was showing slight signs of regaining consciousness. Horace spoke. 'You called me a cunt, didn't you?' McLachlan looked up just as Horace threw his favourite right cross. Another perfect strike, another Scot on the floor of number three hut.

Horace looked at the rest of them. 'Anybody else want a go?'

A deafening silence ensued.

The following morning McLachlan was led out onto parade by two of his mates. His legs were fine, his balance perfect – it was just that his two eyes were closed and he could not see an inch in front of him. The German guards questioned him immediately. McLachlan played the game and explained he had slipped in the shower and fallen. The Germans doubted his reply but reluctantly accepted his explanation. Strangely, Horace felt sorry for him. It would be another 24 hours before he regained his sight.

Life in the camp returned to normal, and the animosity between the Scots and the English did not fester. There was a kind of accepted respect for Horace, though not many words or conversations were exchanged. And as expected, McLachlan's whistles were no more.

CHAPTER
ELEVEN

It was December 1941. The Japanese were about to make a mistake they would regret for many years to come. They were about to bring America into the Second World War. As they eyed up the majority of the American fleet stationed at Pearl Harbor, they figured a quick, aggressive strike would break the back and resolve of the US Navy.

About three times a week Horace was appointed to drilling duties on top of the hill overlooking the camp. His skill with the drill improved almost every time. Once, sometimes twice a week, Rauchbach would leave him to his own devices and every so often Rosa would appear. It was here in the forest above the camp that Horace continued his love making with the owner's daughter – Rose, as he'd now begun to call her – right through the winter of 1941/42. He had explained that he didn't want to make love to a German girl and asked if she had any objections to being rechristened. He wanted her to become his English Rose, and she seemed to positively revel in it. It was their secret, their path to a new life.

The winter was not as severe as the year before in that hellhole of a first camp. Horace thought back and wondered how they'd survived. The two of them made love in warm rain and cold rain and several times on a carpet of snow as the winter weather turned, the bitter piercing cold penetrating their bodies and taking their senses to a heightened level of arousal. They laughed as they collected their damp clothing and shivered as they dressed each other and marvelled at their daring exploits just a few hundred yards from the German guards.

Life in the quarry camp was bearable for Horace, especially with his English Rose, but he could not control the guilt and often thought of escape as winter turned to spring. He discussed it with Rose. Always she tried to talk him out of it. She explained the geography and the lack of success of previous escapees and of course it all made perfect sense, but it was something he couldn't shake from the back of his mind. He asked Rose if she could bring him a map and reluctantly, between tears, she agreed. Horace felt he had spent enough time in the quarry camp, enough time with his captors. The map never arrived. After a few weeks he stopped asking. Without a map escape was impossible. Rose knew this.

The following week Rose approached him on top of the hill as he finished the last of a line of strategically measured holes in a particularly large slab of marble. He noticed her eyes immediately – they were glazed over with tears. Her bottom lip trembled and she quivered all over. The map, he thought to himself, she has the map. And he thought of the danger he had forced her into. He was wrong. There was no map.

Rose was crying now as she delivered the news that her father had told her the night before. Horace and his companions were to be on the move again. They were being transferred to another camp. Rauchbach delivered the news personally while on parade the following morning. He looked sad but resigned to the fact that the German hierarchy had decided to rid him of a band of men he had personally trained to a highly productive, well-oiled machine. He wished the men well, and said that conditions in the next camp were better than he could provide. There were more showers, more facilities and even hot running water, and he hinted that the rations would increase too. It was a more modern camp with a concert hall and games facilities, he went on to say. On the whole Horace's fellow prisoners seemed pleased – a little wary, but pleased.

There was no reason to doubt this German standing in front of them. He had been honest and fair in everything he had said. He had increased their food, improved conditions and seemed to have the welfare of the prisoners genuinely at heart. Some would argue in the huts at night that he was only interested in production and the prisoners were merely a tool with which to meet his objectives, but nevertheless Rauchbach delivered his final address well as the German guards looked on uncomfortably. In a final goodwill gesture Rauchbach explained that the prisoners would be spared their work detail that day. He had organised a last supper with extra bread and coffee and biscuits by way of a thank you to the prisoners. They could relax and recharge their batteries and prepare for the long journey ahead the following morning.

The men hung around their huts for the rest of the day. They chatted about the new camp and what their new surroundings would bring them. Most seemed happy, almost excited at the prospect of new surroundings and the improved conditions that Rauchbach had promised. Horace lay alone with his thoughts on his bunk. He did not care about improved conditions, was not interested in increased rations or concert halls or games rooms. It was at this point he realised how much he would miss Rose. Horace understood that for the first time in his life he had fallen in love. It was a forbidden love; one he should never have embarked on. It was a love that the Germans had brought to a premature close.

The following morning Horace sat in an all too familiar position in the back of the German troop-carrying lorry as it left the camp. Flapper sat opposite. It was déjà vu. Horace peered out of the back of the lorry, watching carefully mile after mile. He tried to take note of the landmarks, the twists and turns in the road and the T-junctions and the signs. It was all so futile.

Horace realised the impossibility of the situation: he didn't even know the name of the village in which Rose lived. Why hadn't he asked her on that last meeting? An hour into the journey it dawned on him that even if he did manage to escape from the next camp, it would be simply impossible to find his way back to Rose.

He had never felt this way before about any girl. His heart ached. He felt nauseous, his mouth was dry and he wanted to burst into tears and sob like a nine-year-old schoolboy, such were his feelings for this girl. His good friend Flapper tried once or twice to strike up a conversation but almost telepathically understood. Horace buried his head in his hands and fought back the tears.

CHAPTER TWELVE

After a three-hour journey, the men were welcomed at the new camp with lunch. It was the same old cabbage soup, but with flecks of meat and whole vegetables. A big bucket of bread sat in the middle of the new compound and the men were allowed to take as much as they wanted without restriction. A sign of things to come, perhaps?

The men seemed happy as they chatted in the early afternoon sunshine. Flapper tried once again to strike up a conversation with Horace, his speech impaired by the overloaded portions of bread hanging from his mouth.

'Come on, Jim. Aren't you eating?'

'I'm not hungry,' Horace replied. 'A touch of travel sickness,' he explained limply.

Flapper spoke again as flecks of bread exploded from his mouth.

'I don't understand you. The cunts have starved us for two years, then they lay on a fucking feast and you're not fucking hungry. I swear, Jim,' the big man said, 'there is something seriously wrong with you.'

I wish I could tell you, mate, Horace thought to himself. I wish I could tell you.

Rauchbach had been right about the new camp, at Freiwaldau in Czechoslovakia. It was altogether different, with more food, better sanitation and washing facilities, and a new shower block with ten shower roses in a row. And for the first time... warm water.

There were no sentries in watchtowers and not much barbed wire – another indication that the Germans knew escape was pointless. The main camp compound was roughly the size of two large football pitches with outbuildings containing guard rooms, staff rooms, a main office, a shower room and a small concert hall. The walls of these buildings formed the walls of the camp and on the edge between the huts and the forest, a huge vegetable plot. In another huge L-shaped position were the barrack rooms where the prisoners slept and ate and a huge toilet block where 40 men could sit and shit at any given time. Still no privacy, but nevertheless a little cleaner than the last camp.

The buildings formed a huge square and at the top end of the camp was the main entrance, watched over 24 hours a day by at least half a dozen guards. The gaps between the buildings were protected and secured with impregnable barbed wire.

Horace met another prisoner, Billy Strain from Falkirk in Scotland, who would become a great friend. Like most prisoners from Scotland he would become affectionately renamed Jock. His cooking skills had been discovered by the Germans and he worked the prisoner kitchen, sharing the staff quarters with Horace and a number of other key workers.

Later that week, for the first time in over two and a half years, Horace would receive a letter from home. It was written by his mother. The letter was as expected: it had been vetted by the English bureaucrats in the UK and the German authorities in the camp. Everyone was well, his mother wrote, though no mention of any names. Horace wondered about Harold. Where was he? Was he alive? Mother hoped the war would soon be over, but again no mention of any news on how it was going or who was winning the fight. The letter was more or less chapter and verse the same as the dozens of other letters that had been sent to the other prisoners, as if the writer had been told what to write by the official at the war office. Still, the delivery of the letter pleased Horace, and he breathed a mighty sigh of relief that his family knew he was still alive.

But nothing could shake off the depression he was feeling at the loss of Rose. She was in his waking thoughts and was the last thing he thought of each evening. He tormented himself over her safety and although she had expressed her undying love that final time they lay together naked in the forest at the quarry camp, he wondered how long it would be before she found another lover to replace him. She was a young attractive girl in the prime of her life. He had introduced her to the pleasures of the flesh and she had responded eagerly with an unbridled passion. She had been a willing lover, eager to please and keen to experiment and after that oh, so special first orgasm she had wanted more and more. Of course she would find a new lover. Horace just prayed he would not be German.

It was late September 1942, and the first chills of the oncoming winter had begun to be felt on the early morning parades. On the Russian front the German troops had reached the suburbs of Stalingrad. Horace tried desperately to shake off his depression, but it was not easy. Gradually he thought of Rose less and less, but still she was with him every day.

One morning, for the first time, the men were issued with Red Cross parcels. They contained chocolate and cigarettes, matches, candles, tins of bully beef and powdered Nestlé milk. The camp was comfortable, and again Horace's guilt rose to the surface. He was well fed, slept well on an individual bunk with a mattress of sorts, and the working day was a manageable eight hours. Again Horace was the camp barber. He worked hard on the conversations with the prisoners whose hair he was cutting. In camp three there was no need to shave the heads to the bare scalp: body lice were an exception rather than the rule. The familiar skill of cutting hair, as opposed to simply shaving it all off, returned quickly. Maintaining the conversations was hard work. They had been in Leicester and in Torquay and in the previous two camps, but a good conversation was a distraction and squeezed out all thoughts of the lover he had left behind.

Most of the men he talked with were working on the log piles in the camp grounds. The logs were cut into manageable piles that were loaded onto flatbed lorries and taken to a factory on the perimeter of the camp. It was here that the wood would be cut into fine shavings and used as 'wood wool' for bedding and upholstery for the German war effort. Other men worked in the huge pine forests that surrounded the camps, felling the trees, stripping them of their branches before bringing them back to the camp. It was one of these men returning from his duty one day who would give Horace the fright of his life.

Dave Crump sat down in the barber's chair with a huge grin on his face.

'What are you so happy about, Dave?' Horace asked.

The man could contain his good news no longer.

'I saw Rose today,' he grinned. 'At least that's what she said her name was.'

Horace's scissors took on an involuntary life of their own as he lopped a big chunk from the prisoner's head.

'Whoa, Jim, you'll have my bloody eye out. Just put the bloody scissors down for a minute, please.'

Horace did as he was told but was unsure if his so-called friend was playing a sick joke. No, he couldn't be. If he'd said Rosa, perhaps – but no, he'd said Rose, he'd definitely said Rose.

'What do you mean, you saw Rose? We were on that bloody truck for three hours. You've been working less than a mile away from the camp. How... what...?'

'If you shut your face, Jim, I'll tell you.' The man paused, took a deep breath. 'Rose told me she's been looking for you for months. She came up to this camp sometime last week. It takes about an hour by train from the village she lives in. She said she recognised some of the men on the outside party. She plucked up courage to speak to me, asked if there was a barber in my camp called Jim.'

Horace couldn't believe the man sitting in front of him. It did not seem possible. Dave reached into his pocket. He pulled out a letter.

'It's for you, Jim. She's written it for you.'

He handed the letter to Horace who sank onto the floor as his legs buckled and gave way. Dave excused himself and said he would return later to have his hair finished. He didn't fancy a date with the scissors in Horace's current state.

Horace's hands were shaking uncontrollably as he broke the seal of the envelope. The letter was not signed, nor was it addressed to him personally. Rose had been clever, all too aware that the letter might fall into German hands. Horace brought the paper to his nose and breathed in hard. He detected the faintest aroma, the musky, slightly perfumed smell of Rosa Rauchbach. Her written English was faultless.

Dearest
My Father would not tell me where it was you had been
sent, only that the conditions were much better and the

food would be good. I hope you are keeping well. I miss you. I miss our times together and wonder if there is any way I can see you.

You are not on one of the outside working parties. I have checked them all. I have been searching the camps for many months now, almost given up hope of seeing you ever again. I have taken the train to many places and walked through the forests to Lamsdorf, Sagan, Teschen, Silberberg and Sternberg. I have seen many sad men but no one that I recognised until I walked to Freiwaldau just over a week ago. It was six kilometres to the forest where the men work and gradually I began to recognise some men from the quarry. I looked and looked but could not see you. I returned back home each evening and as soon as the train starts moving I cry. Goodness knows what the other passengers must think. Eventually I found the courage and spoke with your friend and he tells me you are confined to camp cutting the men's hair. I had so hoped you would be working in the forest and we could have seen each other.

Perhaps it is not a good idea to try and meet up, it is too dangerous. But I want you to know that I think of you always and as soon as this damn war is over we can be together again. I will be waiting forever. I shall return one last time next week just to see if you received this letter. If you can, please write back and tell me that you are well.

I love you.
xxxx

The letter fell to the floor and Horace wiped at the tear that fell onto his cheek. He couldn't comprehend what he'd just read. She was right: it was too dangerous. How could he possibly see her? No way would the Germans give him permission to abandon his barbershop in favour of forest work. His lover, his English Rose... so near and yet so far.

Horace lay on his bunk in the small staff room containing the 12 beds of the camp chef and his assistant, a cobbler, two sergeants, a smattering of other work prisoners including Flapper Garwood, who had been appointed head gardener. Horace was studying the window two feet from the bottom of his bed. Then he began dismantling the architrave that surrounded the glass pane, housing six half-inch iron bars that ran from top to bottom of the window.

'What are you doing?' Flapper asked as he looked up from the letter he'd received earlier that week.

'A little bit of joinery,' replied Horace. 'Get back to your letter, you've only read it 27 times.'

It was true. Flapper had read the print off the letter since it had arrived. It was from his wife Cissie and told of the progress of young Shirley, Flapper's little girl, three years old when he left for the war. She missed her Daddy, looked forward to her next birthday and prayed every night that Daddy would be home to celebrate it with her. Every POW devoured every word from home over and over again. It was a link with their family, their loved ones, wives and girlfriends, brothers and sisters. Words... and yet words that tore his heart from his chest. He placed the letter carefully under his mattress and walked over to where Horace was studying the bars.

'Speak to me, country boy. What's going through that turnip-filled head of yours?'

Horace pointed to the bottom of the bars. They ran to the length of the floor but were split in two and each one held together with a cotter pin.

'See here, Flapper?' he pointed at one of the pins. 'I reckon if we could get these pins out, the bars would separate and we could get out through the window.'

'And then what?' Flapper asked as he shrugged his shoulders. 'Then where do we go? Straight into the arms of the Bosch, that's where.' Flapper relayed the all too familiar statistics. 'Hun after fucking Hun as far as the eye can see. No one has ever escaped from this camp and made it back home. The longest escape was three days and even then they shot the poor bastard there and then in the forest because he'd dared to wear civvy clothes.'

'I know, Flapper, I know. I've heard it all before.'

'Three days, Jim. We reckon it would take at least six weeks of activity to get out of German-occupied land, then you've got to cross the Bering Sea or travel up as far as Norway and pray that your ship isn't sunk on the way over to England.'

Horace whistled as he began to loosen the cotter pins. He leaned forward, spat directly at the pin securing the third bar and the moisture lubricated the pin just enough to remove it from its housing. He worked on another bar and figured that a man of his build could squeeze through quite easily. He turned around and faced his good friend with his arms outstretched.

'Hey presto, Sir Flapper! That's magic.'

Flapper shook his head.

'You're not listening to a fucking word I'm saying, are you, country boy?'

Horace grinned. 'Not really, Flapper. When did I ever listen to anyone? I'm my own man. The last time I took notice of anything anybody said, my own sergeant major surrendered me to the fucking Germans.'

Flapper sighed. 'Same old tune, Jim.' He had heard the story a hundred times. He had been there on the death march when his good friend had caught up with Sergeant Major

Aberfield and laid him out like a kit inspection. 'Listen to me, Jim. You can't...'

'I am listening to you, Flapper. I hear what you are saying, but who said anything about making it back to England? I know it's stupid and now that the Americans are in the war it shouldn't be too long before it's over. I'm sitting here tight like the rest of you, I ain't going anywhere. But who's to say we can't have a few nights of excitement while we sit here waiting?'

Flapper Garwood let out a sigh and looked at Horace incredulously. He did not want to believe what he was hearing. Horace had loosened off the bars in the window and created a perfectly acceptable gap through which he could escape. The window was 50 yards from the forest and although the German guards routinely patrolled the perimeter of the camp, Flapper admitted escape was not difficult. The difficulty lay in what was beyond and as the two men faced each other, one with a stupid grin on his face, the other with a look of dismay, Garwood knew, just knew, that his friend could not have been more serious in what he was implying.

Horace replaced the bars and cotter pins and pushed the architrave back into place. He turned round and walked towards Flapper. As he drew alongside him he slapped him playfully on the cheek twice.

'Boys will be boys,' he grinned.

'You're a fucking nut, Jim,' replied Flapper, 'A prize fucking nut.'

The following evening Horace lay on his bunk. There was no official lights-out time in the prisoner staff hut, but the men were generally quite exhausted after their long working day with little or no break so the lights were generally turned off between 10.30 and 11pm. The POW staff quarters were slap

Above: Before war broke out, Horace enjoyed ploughing the fields with his father, Joseph Greasley Senior (pictured).

Below: During World War Two, Horace was called up to join 2nd/5th Battalion Leicesters by the government, but it wasn't long before his unit surrendered and became prisoners of war. Horace pictured (*top right*) with other prisoners, including Billy 'Jock' Strain (*below left*).

Above and below: Horace's camp was situated close to a huge marble quarry. It was in this quarry that Horace was to endure backbreaking work. Rose's father owned the quarry.

Above: Prisoners of war.

Below: Horace and Jock (shirtless). They'd stuck together through thick and thin and the hell of a war that nobody wanted.

Horace (*right*) wearing the Polish uniform in 1940.

bang in the middle of a long wooden hut. On one side were the German guards' sleeping quarters and on the other side the larger barrack room of another hundred prisoners.

Horace loitered in a shadow several feet from the barred window he had so easily dismantled the previous day. About 25 yards from the perimeter of the hut were two huge arc lights which lit up that side of the camp. A four-guard patrol walked the perimeter of the camp on a regular basis. They walked in a clockwise direction past the window, passing the large barrack room to Horace's right. After about 50 yards they took a right turn, walking around the far end of the barracks, walking another 100 yards past two more barrack rooms before turning right again, completing a big square by returning to the camp gates just to the left of Horace's window. Horace timed the walk as averaging nine to 11 minutes, depending on how quickly the guards walked and whether they stopped to light any cigarettes.

Horace could just make out the camp gates to the left of the window. The guards always lingered for a minute or two at the gates and every so often one of them would disappear inside the guard room to relieve himself or perhaps take a quick coffee.

Horace did not have a watch. He counted the seconds and consequently the minutes with a tap of his finger on the window ledge, simulating the second hand of the clock. That first evening Horace watched the patrolling guards until three o'clock in the morning. Not once did they deviate from the route, and the timing of the patrol always fell between nine and 11 minutes. At 11pm the four guards became two as they scaled down their evening watch. Horace could not quite understand this. If anyone wanted to escape it would surely be during the hours when the night was at its quietest, the very hours the Germans relaxed the patrol. Horace looked out over the vegetable garden that stood between him and the cover of the forest 50 yards away. It was a wide open expanse. The garden was planted and tended by the prisoners but the German guards took pick of the crop, leaving what they didn't want for the soups and stews made for the incarcerated.

There was no cover and Horace wished that the men had been allowed to plant something a little taller in order to obscure his form. A small cornfield would have been ideal but no, they had planted carrots and onions and of course cabbages – the mainstay of their diet. Horace cursed: nothing grew more than four or five inches in height.

Horace stayed up again the following night observing and studying the guards until sheer exhaustion forced him to collapse onto his bunk at around 4am. He watched them the next night too and the night after that, and not once did they deviate from their routine. He had to hand it to the Germans, no matter how much he hated them. They were organised and well planned, and once a plan had been cast in stone it was adhered to.

When the Germans scaled the patrol down at 11pm, Horace observed that as the four guards became two, the first patrol setting out afterwards always seemed to be a few minutes late. He figured the four guards would quite naturally be saying their goodbyes for the evening. The two remaining men on patrol also may have been a little reluctant in starting their long shift. While each circuit of the camp had a real pattern in timing, the patrol prior to 11 o'clock always lasted three or four minutes longer.

Horace decided on the optimum hour of escape. He would wait until the four-man patrol passed his window at around ten minutes to 11pm. He would give them five minutes, then check the corner of the barrack building to make sure they had not stopped for a cigarette break. He figured their five-minute walk would take them to the furthest point of the camp, a good hundred yards from the tampered window. It would take no more than two minutes to dismantle the architrave, remove the cotter pins and drop down the bars. Horace would be through the window and make good his escape across the vegetable garden and into the forest beyond. Two of the men would replace the steel bars with false bars they had made in the workshops one week before, allowing Horace to break back in. There was a two- to three-minute margin for error before the German guards passed the window again. While the plan was by no means foolproof, Horace was willing to give it a go, even though a sighting from a stray guard meant certain death from a bullet or two in the back.

CHAPTER THIRTEEN

Early the next morning Horace caught up with Dave Crump as he made his way over to the barber's shop. 'Dave!' he shouted as the young man from Worcester turned round. 'Are you out on the working party today?'

Dave nodded. 'Yeah, as always, Jim. Why do you ask?'

Horace handed him a piece of paper sealed at the edges.

'I'm figuring Rose might be around one of these days and I was hoping you might give her this letter.'

Dave smiled. 'Sure, Jim. If she's there I'll see she gets it. What is it with you and her anyway? You haven't been shagging her, have you?'

Horace did not answer. There was no need. The twinkle in his eyes told Dave Crump everything he wanted to know.

Rosa shook from head to toe as she eased the envelope from her breast pocket sitting on the train taking her back to her home village. She read the letter yet again, not quite believing the words her lover had written. The note was short and to the point. Her heart skipped a beat as she read the first line.

My English Rose
I will be escaping from the camp at around 11 o'clock
next Wednesday. I will be making my way northwards
into the forest. Is it likely you can meet me there? No
need for another note, they are rather dangerous. Just
tell our friend yes or no.
Xx

Garwood, although totally against his friend's plan, was as ever a willing participant in its execution. Horace had studied the pattern of the guards' patrol for over a week, keeping detailed notes of their movements. The letter had been delivered and Dave Crump had returned with a 'yes'. Dave was in the dark. He knew nothing about the escape. He had simply delivered the one word answer from Rose. Horace lay nervously on his bed. He was aware of a slight trembling in his legs. Fear, perhaps adrenaline – he did not know what was bringing on the involuntary movement, but he hoped that it wouldn't be there as he made the 50-metre sprint across no man's land into the forest about an hour from now.

A voice came from behind him. It was Flapper.

'Are you still going for that shag, country boy?'

'I'm afraid so, Flapper. I'm past the point of no return.'

'What do you mean by that, Jim?'

'I mean, pal, my cock is harder than a blacksmith's anvil and a cat would have difficulty getting its claws into it, it's so damned hard.'

The two men laughed to disguise their nervousness. Horace had told his immediate sleeping partners in the POW staff quarters about his grand plan to escape and return to the camp, so of course he had no option but to tell them the reason he was doing so.

They had been astounded as he told them about his sexual

escapades in the quarry camp. Dave Crump had backed up Horace's story as he explained how the young attractive German girl had asked for him by name. Horace was a little concerned. Some of these men had been locked up for nearly three years. The nearest they had been to a woman had been a glimpse of Rose in camp two or a village civilian worker passing through the camp occasionally. Of course, most of the men resorted to masturbation but the memories and the imagination needed to perform such an act had long since dulled. The poor diet did not help either.

As 11pm approached ever nearer Horace wondered if he was expendable, if any of his fellow roommates were willing to turn him in or even throw a spanner in the works of his grand plan so he would be shot as he ran to the forest. It would be easy to do. A pan dropped on the concrete floor would bring the guards running, as would removing one of the iron bars from the window. It was all so easy. He would be caught like a rabbit in the headlights. He felt so vulnerable. If he was taken out of the equation, would that allow one of his fellow prisoners to step into his shoes and possibly the arms of Rose? Dave Crump, perhaps? What if he had read the note, given it to Rose resealed, and perhaps whispered into the ear of the nearest German guard? Bang! One shot and Horace Greasley would be no more and Dave Crump would comfort the grieving German girl and worm his way into her affections. Horace bit his lip. He cursed himself for thinking such a thing. Dave had stuck his neck out by simply passing the notes on. He cursed himself for doubting Garwood, too, and the other boys in the room.

'Are you ready?'

Garwood checked his watch. It was the only watch among the roommates of the staff quarters. Flapper had managed to hide it in each of the three camps and hung onto it for dear life. Horace would have liked it to help him with his return timing but he simply would not ask to borrow what was the big man's pride and joy. He hoped Rose would be in possession of her own timepiece; if not, the moon and the stars would help. Horace stood by the window and looked up into the sky. It was a clear night; the moon as well as the arc lights illuminated the entire area and the forest beyond.

Two of the other men had risen from their bunks and stood in the darkness next to the table they had placed under the barred window.

'Any second now,' Garwood whispered.

Horace brushed a small insect from the left breast pocket on his jacket. Incredibly, he could feel his heart beating through the thick material. It was towards the end of September and a noticeable chill lingered in the air as it penetrated the wooden walls of the hut. But Horace felt as if he was in the heat of a furnace. His hands were hot and clammy and perspiration ran down the back of his neck. Flapper noticed the sheen on his friend's brow.

'It's not too late, Jim. You can call it off, you know.'

Horace shook his head. He wanted to call it off, put a stop to all this nonsense. The war might be over in a few months' time. It was not long to wait. Surely he did not need to risk his life for a few moments of passion? He felt a lump in his throat. The hairs stood up on the back of his neck and his damned legs were still shaking. He was not doing this for a few minutes' passion; he was doing this because he wanted to spend time with the woman he loved. He wanted to touch her, smell her, see her smiling face again and yes, he wanted to caress her naked body and feel himself between her naked thighs. The war might well be over in a few months... it might not. But this was a love that would not wait. It would not wait ten weeks, ten hours or even ten minutes. His English Rose was waiting somewhere in that darkened forest, a tantalising 50 yards away and if a whole regiment of Waffen SS stood between the barred window and the edge of the forest, he would still be prepared to give it a go.

Garwood gripped his arm. The four men instinctively ducked down as the smell of a strong German cigarette permeated the air. A few seconds later the patrol of four German guards slipped quietly past the window. The prisoners waited, eyes fixed on Garwood. He signalled as each minute passed. On two minutes Horace unlocked the shuttered glass panes and eased them slowly onto the back of the wooden walls securing them with a tiny bolt on each side. Ever so gently he pressed his face up to the barred window and craned his neck to get a glimpse of the far end of the barrack wall where occasionally the patrol would stand on the corner and light a cigarette.

Nothing.

There was no glow from any matches nor a cigarette. No smoke polluted the air. The guards had disappeared. They would be making their way down to the far end of the camp and in another few minutes would be the furthest possible distance from Horace's escape route.

The men stood together without uttering a single word. Garwood studied the face of his precious watch. Three minutes passed and he gave the nod. Horace and another prisoner began loosening the architrave, exposing the cotter pins that held the bars in place. Horace's hands were slippery and the task seemed to take a little bit longer than normal. The minute or so he took to remove the pins and lower the bars seemed to last an hour. Nevertheless, the bars slipped out effortlessly and they were placed directly on the floor underneath the window. They only had to remove two bars. Horace was not a big man – the Germans and their rations had seen to that – and as he lay on the table next to the window, the men either side of him prepared themselves.

Garwood took his arm and whispered quietly, 'Watch my fucking veggies, country boy, or I'll batter you when you get back in.'

Horace grinned. 'I will, pal… I will.'

The men either side of him signalled and pushed together. 'Heave…' they whispered in unison.

Horace slid quickly over the threshold of the window. The momentum of the push propelled him forward and as he made a dive, he tucked his head and his arms into his body and the quiet, well-executed forward roll brought him back onto his feet again. He crouched down, breathing heavily, and his eyes swept the wide expanse to the front and on each side of him. All was silent, but Jesus, he cursed, it was lit up like bloody Oxford Street at Christmas time. Not for the first time he wondered what the hell he was doing, but then as always that image drifted into his head. That image of innocence, of trust, and those beautiful sad eyes. Those same sad eyes that cried out for the love of an English prisoner.

In just over six seconds he had covered the distance through the middle of the vegetable patch and stood panting just a few yards inside the break of the forest.

He'd made it. Incredibly, he'd escaped from a German prisoner of war camp. If Horace was truthful with himself, it had been quite easy. He stood in the shadow of the dark forest, looking back at the huge arc lights illuminating the barrack rooms and huts, the front gates and the other outbuildings. He slipped back behind a tree and noticed the shadows of the two German guards lengthening as they approached the camp gates. He crouched down, thinking it wise to wait a minute or two until they had started the next patrol of the perimeter.

He smelled Rose a split second before he felt her knock him to the ground. She pounced on him like a lioness taking her prey. As they embraced they spilled out into the opening of the forest. Their cover had been broken but neither cared as they kissed passionately

'I love you, Jim. I've missed you,' she whispered into his ear. The tears rolled down her cheeks as their lips locked together again. Rose clenched her hands together, her nails biting into the back of his neck.

'What was that?' The younger of the German guards asked as he peered into the darkness of the forest.

'What was what?' his partner on patrol asked.

'I thought I heard a voice, thought I saw something over there.' He pointed directly to where Horace and Rose lay.

The sound of a German voice brought Horace to his senses and he lay face down with his hand over his lover's mouth. She too, could see the German soldiers peering over towards them, and her moment of lust and animal instinct was replaced by one of sheer terror. She trembled with fear, sure that her movement would give their position away. Slowly she lowered her head into the forest floor and began to weep. Horace stroked her hair gently. How could they have been so stupid, so complacent? The Germans had seen them, of that he was convinced.

'We must go and check, Helmut.' The young guard was keen for a little adventure, a little sport. He was bored with this duty – the same patrol, the same shift, night after night. He knew he was fortunate to be posted to this camp only four miles from his home village, and he knew he would be safe to see out the remainder of the war here, but he longed for something to happen. At times he almost craved a front line posting. He wanted to fight for the Fatherland, to further the cause of the Third Reich and the Fuehrer's ideals and philosophy. Not

Russia though... no, he would rather stay here than be posted to the frozen Russian front. He'd heard the stories, the rumours. Perhaps he was better off where he was, where the only risk of injury was from a hot pipe or a stray bit of barbed wire.

'We must investigate,' he repeated to the older man. 'One of the prisoners may have escaped.'

The older man was a little bit more reluctant; he'd seen it all before. A fox calling or an owl hooting could give the impression of a human voice on the evening breeze. He let out a sigh. Nevertheless they would need to check it out. The thing was, he couldn't see a damn thing for those huge arc lights shining in his face.

'Why walk all the way over there, Fritz? Come, let us walk round the huts once more. We'll check the doors and windows. If they are secure there is no use getting our boots dirty in the mud.'

'But Helmut, we must...'

'Shush, youngster, do as I say. If we find anything untoward then we'll go looking in the forest.'

Without waiting for an answer the older and wiser German guard struck a match, lit up a cigarette and walked towards the prisoners' barracks. Fritz Handell-Bosch kicked at the heels of his boots, sighed and reluctantly followed in the wake of the senior man.

Horace couldn't believe his luck as he watched the two Germans disappear from view. He pulled Rose to her feet and they ran quietly into the dark forest. When Rose was sure she was out of sight of the camp she pulled out a torch and switched it on. They held hands; Rose led the way.

'You look as if you know where you are going.'

She looked back, nodded and continued her progress through the forest. After about half a mile the forest opened out into a small clearing. Horace looked at the small building Rose was pointing to.

'It's a small church, Jim. There are many in the forests of Silesia.'

'A church? A bloody church? I'm sorry, Rose, but I don't feel much like praying tonight. In fact I think it's about time I told you all about my religious views.'

Rose held a finger to his lips, 'Be quiet, stupid, I've no intention of praying either. It's warm and dry and we won't be disturbed.'

Her smile said it all as she pulled him towards the tiny entrance. She pulled at the door handle and they walked inside. It was an exact mini replica of a large church with an altar and three small pews and even a stained glass window with a picture of Jesus on the cross looking out into the forest. One or two panes of glass were cracked but otherwise the small church was well looked after.

'The villages surrounding the forest take turns to look after it,' she said, by way of an explanation. 'It's seen as a sort of sanctuary where people can be alone, and of course it acts as a shelter in the winter for the woodcutters and the farmers.'

Horace took her in his arms. 'Where people can be alone... I like the sound of that.'

They kissed again, a long lingering kiss. No Germans to disturb them this time. Rose felt his hardness and thrust her hips forward, moaning with pleasure as her pelvic bone came into contact with his ever stiffening penis. Horace had waited too long. Rose had waited too long. Despite the cold air hanging in the ancient place of worship they pulled each other's clothes off, throwing them to the floor in an untidy heap. Rose took a step back, shivered a little and Horace took in the wonderful view as she lay back on the thin narrow ledge of the small pew. As he moved forward she hooked her leg over the pew in front, exposing her moist vaginal opening. Horace needed no further instruction as he lowered himself gently on top. She took his hardness in her hands and delicately guided him inside her as she gasped out loud.

Horace made love to her slowly. This time there was no hurry and he brought her expertly to the point of orgasm. As her back arched and she stiffened up, raking her nails into his back, he quickened his movement accordingly. For once she could cry out loudly with no fear of anyone hearing, and the noise of her passionate wail triggered the involuntary action deep inside that led Horace to his own earth-shattering release.

It was three o'clock in the morning before Horace made it back to the camp. He watched the guards for over 20 minutes. Their routine hadn't changed. He waited a full four agonising minutes once they'd disappeared round the side of the hut then made a quick bolt for the window. He loosened off the temporary wooden bars and leapt through. The old bars were back in place with the architrave set firm and he was tucked up in bed with a full minute to spare before the two guards passed his window again. No one in the staff room had even heard him return. He lay with a satisfied grin on his face and thought if this was the worst the Germans could throw at him then he would sit it out for the rest of the war.

Rose had cheered him up even further as she'd told him about the latest Allied victories. Reports were being heard around the world by people listening to the BBC World Service, but in the camp in Freiwaldau in Silesia, the Allied prisoners of war heard nothing. Stalingrad was now completely surrounded by German troops. However, Germany was being bombed heavily by Allied warplanes. By mutual agreement the Americans bombed in the hours of daylight, and the RAF by night.

Incredibly, Horace broke out of the camp another seven

times that month, his confidence growing with each foray, his lovemaking continuing in the small church in the heart of the forest. Each night they met Rose delivered the latest developments in the war. Although the German propaganda machine tried to stifle the story of the successes of the Allied bombing raids, word filtered through the grapevine of the German civilian population, reaching right into the villages of Silesia.

By mid-October 1942 the Russian system of ferrying troops across the Volga directly into Stalingrad seemed to be working. The German regiments were floundering in the city as the harsh winter began to bite. Huge battles were taking place all over the world. Montgomery was active at El Alamein and Rommel returned from his sick bed in Germany to lead his corps in Africa. On 26 October the naval battle of Santa Cruz between American and Japanese forces began. At the end of the month in London, leading clergymen would lead a protest to register public outrage over Nazi Germany's persecution of the Jews.

If the Allies were lulled into a sense of false security, believing the end of the war may just be in sight, Winston Churchill counteracted any complacency with a speech in parliament. 'This is not the end,' he stated in his powerful tones. 'It is not even the beginning of the end. But it is, perhaps, the end of the beginning.'

On 18 November the RAF inflicted heavy damages on Berlin. In what many believed was a turning point in the Second World War the battle of Stalingrad had turned. General Friedrich Paulus sent Adolf Hitler a telegram saying the German Sixth Army was surrounded. Hitler ordered Paulus not to surrender or retreat under any circumstances. *Der Kessel* – the cauldron – was the description Paulus used to describe the fighting raging in the city.

CHAPTER
FOURTEEN

The peace of the camp was a far cry from the frenzied activity occurring around the world. By now Horace was desperate for more information as he suspected the tide had turned in favour of the Allies. Each morning after their night-time rendezvous he happily relayed the second-hand information Rose had supplied to him. The men also wanted to hear about the gory details of his sexual encounter but Horace was ever the gentleman, refusing to disclose any information about his lusty performance and his lover's eagerness and willingness to please.

Horace made one concession. As he crept back through the window out of the freezing cold early morning mist towards the end of November, his good friend Freddie Rogers lay wide awake on his bunk. His soft voice startled Horace.

'Is she a pretty girl, Jim?'

Horace peered through the darkness, walked over and sat on the bottom of his friend's bunk.

'She is that, Fred... a real stunner, 20 years old and the body of a film star.'

'And you've been shagging her, right?'

Horace grinned; he said nothing but his face told the story.

'You lucky bastard. You don't want to swap places and give me a ride one night, do you?'

Horace laughed, slapped his friend's leg. 'You couldn't compete, Freddie boy. I'm the Leicesters' greatest lover,' he said as he set off to get some sleep before the seven o'clock roll call.

Fred Rogers took a hold of his trouser leg as he leaned from the bed. 'One thing, Jim.'

'What is it?'

'A little favour.'

'Go on.'

Freddie Rogers paused for a second.

'Let me smell your fingers.'

'What?' Horace recoiled in shock. 'I will not, you dirty bastard.' He laughed, sincerely believing his friend was joking. But Freddie was not laughing; he couldn't have been more serious.

'Please, Jim, just let me smell them. It's been three years since I've had my fingers in a fine English girl, three years, big man... please.'

Horace was caught between a rock and a hard place. His friend was invading his privacy; it was almost like him sleeping with Rose.

'Please, Jim, three long years since I smelled a fine English quim.'

Horace wanted to tell him to piss off right there and then, to let his friend feel the back of his hand. He didn't know what came over him. Something triggered in the inner reaches of his brain. Compassion? Pity? He didn't know, but he found himself standing over his friend wafting the two fingers of his right hand a couple of inches from his nose.

Despite the darkness of the hour Horace noticed a fine film of tears in the man's eyes. Memories of home, of normality, memories denied to the man for so long. Horace dropped his hand and his friend smiled and broke into a poem. It was a soft whisper, one the rest of the men couldn't hear. It was a private toast given by Freddie Rogers to his good friend Horace Greasley.

'Here's to the cut that never heals, the more you touch it the softer it feels. You can wash it with soap, you can scrub it with soda, but it never loses that Billingsgate odour.'

It was the funniest poem Horace had ever heard but neither man laughed. Freddie Rogers hadn't wanted to crack a joke; he could not have been more serious. As Horace walked away to catch a few hours' sleep he wondered what three years' captivity and being deprived of everything that was natural to a man was doing to these men's minds.

Over the coming months, if Freddie Rogers was awake when Horace returned from the forest (and normally he was), it would become a bizarre ritual, an expected practice. Each time Fred would thank him, tell him it gave him something to look forward to. And of course he never stopped reminding Horace that he was the luckiest prisoner of war in the country.

Even the encroaching winter weather didn't curtail Horace's eagerness to get out of the camp and meet with Rose. Horace couldn't help noticing that each time they entered the small inner sanctuary of the forest church it was obvious that a new candle had been placed, the pews had been dusted or one of the many Bibles re-arranged. Clearly this was a special place and well looked after by the villagers. Rose had hidden a thick woollen rug under one of the pews at the back of the church and she'd take it out and spread it in front of the altar. More often than not Rose would bring a few candles of her own and place them strategically around the church and turn off the lights. They'd make love totally naked, no matter how cold it was. Their natural exertions increased their body temperature and blocked out the cold. It would allow them to lie, still naked, sometimes for 20 minutes, gazing into each other's eyes or caressing their hair without saying a word as the light from the candles cast tantalising shadows over their bodies. They were special moments, very special indeed, even more special than the act they'd followed.

On one occasion Rose had managed to bring a bottle of wine and some Silesian cheese. They made love and afterwards, sitting by the light of the candles, they sipped gently from the bottle and took turns to nibble at the block of strong-smelling cheese. They sat, still naked, as they edged ever closer to each other so that their lips were only inches apart. Their legs were intertwined, their arms locked around each other the way a groom and bride hold a glass of champagne, and they barely moved as their eyes locked together. As they neared the end of the bottle Horace experienced the dizziness and light-headed feeling so long denied him. The wine was too sweet, too cold and the cheese was far from fresh but it could have been dinner at the Ritz, such was the feeling. The best *maître d'* in the world couldn't have improved on the ambience of that small room in the heart of a Silesian forest in the depths of winter with the woman he'd kill a thousand men for.

But Horace still couldn't control the urge to escape for good. Making his way back into the camp and through the window to rejoin his fellow prisoners grew ever harder. He took another sip from the bottle of wine, swirled it round his mouth and spoke.

'I must get out of there, Rose, I must escape.'

Rose remained silent.

'I need maps, compass and money, papers and civilian clothes.'

Tears were forming in her eyes, as they did every time Horace broached the subject. As he continued Rose began shaking her head, broke the eye contact. They'd had the discussion a hundred times and each time Rose would tell him how impossible it was. She'd get a map and some money and quite possibly some stolen Polish paperwork and a compass. But the only way to cover the 420 miles of German occupied land was by train. Roadblocks and patrols were set up every ten miles and making the journey through the dense pine forests of Silesia and Poland was simply impossible. Rose explained that even on the short, hour-long journey from her village to the camp, German guards would sweep through the train two or three times, inspecting each passenger's paperwork.

'You can't speak Polish, Jim,' she'd plead with him. 'The first time you are questioned you'll be caught. Can't you see how stupid it is?'

And she'd sit in front of him with those big, sad, doleful eyes and beg him to sit the war out in the camp. She had her own selfish reasons. He was safe, free from the guns and the bombs and the artillery the rest of his countrymen were facing. They met regularly and made love and she gave him extra food, and each night like the one they were sharing made the war bearable. And of course she couldn't wait to tell him of the Allied successes and of how the end of the war was in sight.

'Please, Jim,' she begged, 'stay here with me. I couldn't live if ...'

Her voice tapered off in a whisper as she kissed him. They parted and she pressed her cheek into his. He felt the wetness of her tears as they came, each one tugging at his heart strings, each one pleading with him to stay.

As always, he promised he would stay. But it was no good; the feelings were too strong. He simply had to break free for good.

On 12 December, in an operation called Winter Storm, the Germans attempted to break through to the troops trapped in Stalingrad. It failed abysmally, the only real winner being the winter weather. As the year came to an end things looked brighter for the Allies. Rommel was trapped in Tunisia and the German army was still stranded at Stalingrad. On the other side of the world the Japanese appeared ready to abandon Guadalcanal.

January 1943 was remembered in the wood wool camp at Freiwaldau for an escape attempt. A big, tall, gangly young lad from Newcastle upon Tyne had totally disobeyed the command of the prisoners' escape committee and fled under cover of darkness. Young Bruce Harwood was a compulsive escaper with 'form' from two previous camps. No one knew how he escaped and he never ever told anyone, despite being put under enormous pressure by his fellow prisoners. Horace wondered whether he'd discovered the secret of the cotter pins. He'd managed to last four days – a new record – and had walked a grand total of 60 kilometres before being picked up by a German patrol. He'd been beaten to within an inch of his life and returned the same day to the camp he'd come from.

By way of punishment Bruce Harwood spent the next ten days in 'the hole'. This was an underground, freezing cold coffin, six feet by six feet with a ceiling no more than five feet in height, restricting the prisoner from even being able to stand. The only food came from the other prisoners via a small barred trapdoor in the roof. There was no toilet and no running water. On the eighth day Horace drew one of the short straws and gave up part of his ration, a chocolate bar from his Red Cross parcel. Young Harwood barely had the strength to realise Horace was there when he dropped the chocolate through the trap door and prayed the quivering, shivering wreck would see out the next two days.

On the tenth day the Germans gave permission to the prisoners to open up the hole. Bruce Harwood had survived… barely. He couldn't speak, had frostbite in both hands and lay in his own stinking excrement. The Germans allowed the prisoner a few extra days in the sick bay and young Bruce made a recovery of sorts, losing four fingers to frostbite. Several days after he was able to walk again, he queued up for his ration of soup. Horace watched him closely. Harwood was twitchy and nervous, scanning the forest beyond through a three-metre-deep roll of barbed wire the Germans had placed in the gap between the two barrack room buildings. There was no escape, no way through, especially with six German guards looking on in broad daylight. Young Harwood didn't give it a thought. As the prisoners and the guards talked around the huge bubbling soup cauldron, he seized the moment. No one was looking; everyone was focused on the sweet-smelling pot. He sidled casually over to the impregnable barrier and somewhere deep in the recesses of his brain a signal told him there was a way through.

It was impossible. He was caught like a rabbit in a snare. Each turn, each movement of a limb or twist of his scrawny body tightened the razor-sharp wire. It cut into his body without mercy until he lay still, breathing hard, unable to move, resigned to the fact that his latest escape attempt had failed.

Freddie Rodgers was the first to spot him trussed up like a piece of meat. He ran over to help, calling out to a few of the prisoners who also ran over. Harwood was crying now; blood covered his face and body. The prisoners' task was a grim one as they too fell victim to the razor wire. The German guards looked on. After ten minutes they'd managed to separate and prise enough of the wire apart so that Horace and Jock could take a leg each and drag him free. Harwood lay on the ground, exhausted. Without warning a German guard stepped forward, cocked his rifle and fired a solitary round into the centre of his back. The prisoners were outraged and for a minute or two the mood turned ugly. The German camp commandant backed his man up, saying the POW had had chance after chance. He could not simply keep escaping. Perhaps the taste of a bullet would make him think again. Harwood was still conscious and groaned as his fellow prisoners lifted him onto a makeshift stretcher – an old door that had lain in the rubbish heap of the camp for some time. As Harwood reached the entrance of the sick bay he fell into unconsciousness. He never recovered and died 24 hours later.

The incident affected Horace deeply. He lay awake on his bunk night after night, thinking about escape and the men and their mental state, and how he too might crack the longer he stayed incarcerated, caged like a wild animal in a zoo. Nevertheless he intended on keeping his date with Rose a few days later. At their last meeting she had promised she'd bring a map.

By now the snow was lying thick on the ground outside the window. The sight unnerved him. The vegetable garden, although covered with snow, was a well-trodden area and footprints from the German guards as well as POWs littered the uneven ground. Horace felt sure he could disguise his tracks with a cane stick that had supported runner beans in late autumn and had been left there for the spring crop.

'Don't run off too quickly this time, Jim,' Flapper said. 'Take an extra 30 seconds to work those prints in.'

'I will, Flapper, I will.'

With a movement now familiar to them all, the men heaved and he shot from the window, tucking his head under his body and springing to his feet after the roll. He took a few seconds to compose himself, then looked up and started his run to the forest. He'd gone no more than ten yards when he saw the headlights in the distance. He hadn't heard the car, hadn't noticed it from the window, but he was in no doubt where it was heading. The one road that led to the camp was relatively straight and ran along the side of the forest. However, when it got directly in front of the camp, a sharp 90-degree turn brought it directly facing the gatehouse. The headlights were on full beam and Horace judged that within two or three seconds the car would hit the bend, straighten up, and light up the escaping prisoner like an actor on a stage.

It was too late to turn back and there was not enough time to get anywhere near the forest. His blood ran cold as he spied the fluttering illuminated swastika on the bonnet of the car and in a split second he instinctively flung himself into a four-foot snowdrift to his left. He gasped as the freezing snow found the gap between his neck and collar, and cursed as it came into contact with his hands and face as he attempted to conceal himself. He'd been just in time, as the car headlights cast a beam of light over the drift. It levelled up, slowed down and came to a halt outside the gatehouse, no more than 20 feet away. Horace was aware of car doors opening and closing and voices, then footsteps crunching thorough the snow. More voices – and then, to his dismay, the footsteps stopped. He'd picked up enough German to understand the conversation between the guards and the SS men. It was a routine call; they'd called by on the off chance. Five, ten minutes passed. The guards offered them a coffee but they politely declined.

Go for a fucking coffee, Horace wanted to call out, already beginning to shiver as the wet snow penetrated his clothing. But he dared not move. If he could have controlled his breathing he would have, acutely aware that one slight movement would mean death. The SS men didn't sit on the fence when it came to escapees. He remembered their brutality on the march to Holland then Luxembourg. They shot the prisoners dead for the slightest reason – exhaustion, answering back. On one occasion they had even shot a young fusilier for taking too long to empty his dysentery-ridden bowels at the side of the road. And he remembered with a pain that shot right through his heart the moment they shot the poor old French woman for daring to offer a bit of food to a starving man. They were bastards, utter bastards.

Still they talked... on and on. They talked about the war and the weather and the production of the camp, then they moved onto their wives and girlfriends and even what they'd had for supper.

Horace lay still in the snowdrift for nearly 30 minutes. He couldn't remember cold like it, not even at the first camp in the depths of winter. This was a different kind of cold, a wet, frostbiting, bone-penetrating type of cold, and he couldn't bear it any longer.

At last the car doors slammed shut and the engine started up. But still he had to lie for another agonising five minutes as the guards shared a cigarette before resuming their patrol. He pushed down on the snow with his numb hands and raised himself to his knees. A thousand white-hot needles tugged and ripped at every muscle, every sinew of his body as his freezing bones refused to operate. He forced one foot in front of the other, made back for the window then wondered how on earth he would climb through. No way could he climb through in his frozen condition and no way could he give a little shout and ask his mates to lend a hand. Time was running out; he had to make a decision – the guards would reappear any minute.

Rose would be waiting, panicking; she would be desperate. He wondered if she'd been watching the incident from the boundary of the forest. No, he remembered now. They'd agreed to meet at the church. He had to go.

The half-mile walk took him nearly 20 minutes but each step was less painful than the one before. He looked up at the dark sky through the gaps in the trees. It looked heavy, like a huge sack of potatoes waiting to burst, and he wondered if daylight would ever penetrate through.

By the time he crashed through the door of the church he was almost thawed out. Rose ran to him, immediately wrapping him in the rug that had been laid out before the altar. A small pewter flask of brandy she'd taken from her father's drinks cabinet helped the revival process. As she draped herself around him, the heat from her body warmed him better than he could have possibly imagined. He explained the story about the SS as she stroked his brow, occasionally kissing him on the lips or slipping his cold fingers deep into her mouth, sucking on them, warming them in an instant.

Horace looked into her eyes and smiled. 'I don't think I'm in any fit state to please you, Rose.'

Rose's expression never flickered. 'Whatever condition you are in, Jim Greasley, you will always please me.'

'Maybe so, Rose, but I swear the old fellow won't be making an appearance tonight.'

Rose grinned. 'Are you sure about that?' She slipped a hand between his legs and squeezed. 'He seems OK to me.'

Horace didn't have the energy to resist. He repositioned the rug and lay back with his hands behind his head. 'I swear, Rose, I don't think I'm up for the job. It's the cold and the diet. We need more meat in the winter to fight the cold. The food may be better than the previous camp, but in winter we need more.' He smiled. 'That's my excuse, Rose, and I'm sticking to it.'

Rose stood up and began loosening her coat. She played with the buttons, stretching the moment out. 'I won't accept excuses, prisoner,' she teased. 'I have spent three hours travelling here today and you will make love to me. It will do you good, warm you up a little more.'

She cast her coat over the pew and slowly and seductively she unbuttoned her thick woollen trousers and lowered them to the floor. Horace sat and marvelled at the private impromptu strip show unfolding before his eyes. She hooked her hands into her delicate white knickers and lowered them to the floor. As if commanded by an invisible force Horace repositioned himself on his knees as Rose stepped from her knickers and inched ever nearer.

He'd heard all the stories from the older men but had never had the inclination or desire to explore the female form further than he already had. Tonight was different; tonight Rose had the urge to push the boundaries that little bit further too. It was a mutual decision, one they hadn't ever discussed, but one that just happened there and then in the tiny chapel deep in the Silesian forest. Her tiny pubic triangle was only inches from his face and his hands instinctively found her buttocks. She parted her legs, leaned back ever so slightly and he pulled her towards him as his tongue located the dewy folds of her moist vagina. They made love again with an urgency they couldn't control and lay in each other's arms, wanting the moment to last forever.

'Tell me, Rose,' Horace was breathing hard.

'What is it?'

'The family way.'

'The what?'

'It's what we say in England if a woman is with child.'

'What about it?'

'It doesn't happen to us, why is that?'

Rose sat up. 'I do not know why, Jim. I really don't.'

'Aren't you concerned?'

Rose lifted her clothing from the floor and began to dress.

'Not really, Jim. In a few years I will be called up to the war, fighting on the wrong side.' She sighed. 'A baby gets me out of it. Mothers of the Fatherland are respected and adored by the Fuehrer. Another little child to immerse and indoctrinate into the ideals and philosophies of the Third Reich.'

'So pregnancy isn't a problem?'

'Not at all. But one thing's for sure: any child of mine will be born as far away from Germany as possible. My child will be brought up in a free home where he will be taught about rights and wrongs and the value of freedom.'

'He?'

'What?'

'You said "he", Rose. You would like a boy.'

Rose buttoned up her cardigan. 'Perhaps, Jim, perhaps. But on one condition.'

'What's that?'

'We call him Jim.'

As Horace walked back through the forest he suddenly remembered the map – the map hadn't arrived. He remembered Rose's promise, one that she would break again and again.

Back in his bunk Horace reflected on achieving a new level of sexual intensity in his growing relationship with Rose. He'd been late getting back; it must have been nearly four in the morning before his head hit the pillow but it had been worth every delicious second. He'd pay for it later on, generally late afternoon as the last of the prisoners wandered into the camp barbershop. Perhaps he'd have a word with them, feign a little illness and catch up on an hour or two. He'd agreed to meet Rose the following week and he wanted to boost his energy levels.

CHAPTER
FIFTEEN

The near miss with the SS didn't put Horace off. He still escaped on average two or three times a week for his rendezvous with Rose. He wasn't physically able to make love to Rose every time, the food had not improved and his lack of sleep and nocturnal activities were taking their toll. He wondered if the food or rather the lack of it contributed in some small way to his failure to make Rose pregnant.

Sometimes they would simply go for a long walk, three or four miles into the forest and make their way up onto the mountainside in darkness where they could see the camp illuminated below them. They were special moments. They would sit in silence for hours, wrapped in each other's arms, exchanging body heat while Rose's thick woollen coat hung draped around their shoulders, the biting wind tormenting their exposed flesh.

At times Horace was distressed as he looked out onto the camp below, knowing he had to return. He feared for Rose's safety too, knowing she had to make the long walk back to the station on her own in the darkness. There were German patrols in the forest, not unlike the Home Guard back in England. They were older men, 45 years plus, or younger men with a disability that prevented a front line posting, but they had guns and they were ruthless. There had been tales of rape and the occasional murder of some poor unfortunate out and about, clearly up to no good. They didn't ask questions; the victims were simply shot and buried deep within the forest.

Rose could not contain her excitement as Horace opened the door to the church. She ran forward into his arms. 'Jim! The Germans have surrendered at Stalingrad! It's true!'

The news was momentous. It rendered Horace speechless as he lowered himself into a pew with his hands resting on his knees. Rose had heard the titbits of information as she sat with her father tuning in to the airways of the world. The news had not come from German radio but from a high-frequency American station delivering every development of the war to anyone who tuned in. Rose had sat and delivered the perfect translation to her father.

Hitler had taken a huge gamble and it looked as if it had backfired. He had been beaten by the harsh Russian winter and the sheer volume of troops drafted in from every corner of the country. Still Hitler ordered Field Marshal Paulus to fight on even after the Russians had recaptured the last remaining airfield held by the Germans. Goering's aircraft of the Luftwaffe would no longer be able to supply the beleaguered German troops on the ground. They were starving and freezing to death.

'Can't you see, Jim, the war is nearly over?' Rose continued. 'We can be together at last! We can be married and have children.'

Horace took her in his arms and whispered softly. 'I hope so Rose, I hope so.'

Horace and Rose did not make love that night. Horace blamed the diet again but he was lying. Horace was thinking about the end of the war and for once daring to think realistically about an Allied victory. But he was also thinking about what sort of revenge the Russians, the Americans and his own countrymen would inflict. Rape, torture, ethnic cleansing? The Russians especially – by all accounts they had suffered terribly at the hands of the Nazis. They would seek their revenge on the German nation, soldiers and civilians, of that there was no doubt.

He held hands with Rose as they made their way through the forest and she was actually smiling. She was smiling, happy that the war seemed to be coming to an end, happy that an Allied victory seemed to be in sight. But despite what she had told him about Silesia and their independence and her family's fierce hatred of the Nazis, she would be a German in the eyes of the Russians. Didn't she realise the danger she was in? It was a thought Horace couldn't get out of his head. He wanted to take her in his arms and shake some sense into her. But for now he'd leave it – he didn't have it in his heart to tell her what might lie ahead.

Horace was back in the forest chapel the following week and this time they did make love. They didn't hang around and got dressed quickly. This venture into the forest would be a little different, though: Rose had promised to take him hunting to supplement his diet. She led the way to the village three kilometres from the camp. It was just after midnight, and the small village of Pasicka was in complete darkness. They were thankful for the light of a full moon. Rose pointed to the gardens that backed onto the forest.

'See, Jim, all the villagers keep a vegetable garden.' Horace peered out over the well-cultivated land. He could see the tops of turnips and winter swedes and a few bushes of sprouts.

'And Jim, some keep livestock.' She grinned as she pointed to several rabbit hutches and hen huts. 'We need to get some more meat into you, Jim Greasley.'

This wasn't the sort of hunting Horace had in mind but beggars couldn't be choosers.

Again Rose seemed to read his mind. 'Don't feel too bad about it, Jim – most of these villagers are German.'

That sealed it. At first they collected sprouts and a few carrots, then as many small swedes as Horace could squeeze into his pockets.

'Next time you should bring a bag, Rose. I'll be able to get a few turnips, too.'

'I will. But now, darling, it's time for meat.'

Horace pointed to a hen house ten yards from the nearest back wall of a small cottage. 'Over there. You keep watch and give me a little whistle if you notice a light going on or a curtain moving.'

He was just about to set off when she grabbed at him. 'Are you mad, Jim? Haven't you heard the noise a hen makes when it's in danger? Go for the rabbits – they are silent.'

Horace lifted his hand and stroked her cheek. 'You're right, Rose, not just a pretty face.'

'I have my uses, Jim.' She winked as Horace set off slowly on his hands and knees, taking care to keep his head down. The hutches weren't locked: the wire meshed gates were simply held together with twine. The rabbits reminded Horace of the prisoners back at the camp. Escape would have been easy for the rabbits by simply gnawing through the rope. But they weren't going anywhere – why should they? They had a warm bed and they were fed regularly. Why should they venture out into the great unknown?

As Horace reached in and grabbed the first rabbit he wondered whether this poor creature ever had any inclination of escape, ever thought for one moment to start chewing at the twine. He dispatched the rabbit with a familiar pull and twist at the back of its neck. The third and fourth vertebrae and the spinal column separated with little effort and life left the small creature immediately. His father had always told him not to hang back while teaching him the trick in the fields and forests of Ibstock.

Horace remembered the first few kills when he had delayed the inevitable, how he'd thought about the feelings of the rabbit and whether its offspring would miss its mother or father that night as he or she failed to return. Tonight was different. Tonight there was no remorse, nor feelings of guilt. He reached into the cage again, caught the hind legs of another rabbit and repeated the exercise. The creature fell limp but then twitched a three-second dance of death as the nerves of its body made a final protest. Horace remembered the first time this had happened to him as his father had killed a rabbit and handed it to him to hold. Reluctantly he'd held on tightly to the back legs and after a few seconds the nerve reaction had kicked in. Horace had squealed, convinced the rabbit had come back to life and instinctively threw it three feet into a ditch. His father had doubled up laughing at his son's reaction, while Horace had stood there feeling stupid and embarrassed.

He returned to Rose, all smiles.

'We'll be eating well tomorrow, Rose – rabbit stew.'

Rose kissed him passionately for two or three seconds by way of a token reward and just for a second he got the urge to make love to her right there in the forest. Jesus he thought, no woman had ever made him feel this way. He wished he could fight the feelings, wished he could just go one whole day without thinking about her and one whole night without imagining the beautiful sensual folds of her body, her pert breasts and the soft feel and taste of her vagina. Just one day and night he thought, just 24 hours...

As Horace tied a rabbit down each trouser leg he thanked

his lucky stars that the Russian officer's uniform he'd been given to wear belonged to a man far bigger than him. The trousers were held up by string and the dead creatures fitted quite comfortably down each leg with enough room to manoeuvre himself through the bars. He made an undignified entrance, the extra weight causing him to lose his balance and crash to the floor.

'Fucking hell, Jim!' It was Flapper. 'I don't mind you spending every sleeping hour shagging the arse off your little German bint, but some of us want some kip.'

'Aye, shut the fuck up,' shouted a Scottish voice.

Horace couldn't contain his excitement any longer as he started to loosen the string on his waist. 'Wait till you see what I've got, lads.'

Jock Strain struck a match and lit the candle underneath his bed.

'Jesus,' he exclaimed, 'he's getting that cock of his out again.'

'No wait, watch,' Horace said as he felt for the ears of the creature down his right leg. Then, like a magician at the London Palladium, he produced the rabbit right on cue, with perfect timing. 'Hey presto!'

Jock Strain, the prisoners' resident chef, was fully awake now, clearly interested in the additional supplies for the early evening recipe. 'Where the hell did you get that?'

Horace didn't answer and instead pulled out its mate from the other leg. He stood with the two animals held aloft in triumph. 'Once a hunter, always a hunter,' he exclaimed. He didn't have the heart to tell the men they were domesticated rabbits he'd simply lifted from a hutch.

'Holy mother of God!'

'Rabbit stew.'

'Meat.'

'Fucking hell!'

Most of the men were awake now, as Flapper Garwood tried to contain the noise and the men's excitement. He looked at his watch. 'I make it about another minute before Jerry walks past that window. If you don't shut the fuck up nobody will get anything except a night or two in the hole.'

The warning registered and silence fell through the room. Flapper gave Horace a congratulatory slap across the back as Jock got up from his bunk to examine the catch. 'Magic, Jim, bloody magic. What a stew we're going to have today! If only we had a few more vegetables to pack it out a bit.'

Suddenly Horace remembered the swedes and carrots and winter sprouts, and a big smile spread across his face.

'What? What is it now?' Jock asked.

Jock Strain cooked for just over 95 men. The Germans normally supplied the provisions early in the morning with the chef preparing the vegetables, meat and stock during the course of the day. They'd talked long and hard about saving one of the rabbits for another day but Horace had boasted there were plenty more where that had come from. He felt he owed the men something for helping him with his escape plan every time he broke out and he felt it was the least he could do. He vowed to bring a little something back each time, even if it was just a few extra vegetables.

So the men had voted for a feast and nothing had been wasted. Every single last morsel of flesh from the two rabbits went into the stew. Brains, heart, liver, kidney, lungs – even the genitals from the male rabbit. The carcasses had been left in the pot until the very last minute so that every ounce of goodness had soaked in to the stew.

The smell from the pot was different; the men noticed the extra meat and vegetables straight away. Suddenly the one-ladle ration had become two. Jock made a point of telling each man receiving the extra ladle that there would be more of the same if they kept their mouths shut. The German guards didn't seem to notice – they were too occupied discussing their fears about the way the war was progressing. Horace wasn't just imagining it; there was definitely an attitude change coming over the guards. Telltale signs: anxiety, a certain nervousness, an occasional smile in the direction of a prisoner. Were they preparing for the end of the conflict? Were they getting ready for defeat?

Late the following afternoon Horace was approached by one of the most senior prisoners in the camp. Sergeant Major Harris was with the regiment of the 10th Lancers. Almost to a man his comrades had been wiped out at Abbeville in France in the early days of the war.

Sergeant Major Harris asked Horace to take a walk as the rest of the men queued up for the evening ration. They walked slowly around the perimeter of the camp, Sergeant Major Harris half a step ahead of Horace with his hands behind his back.

The Sergeant Major stopped and looked around. Horace took that as his cue to stop too.

'Not too many Huns around here, Greasley, are there?'

'No, sir.'

'Good. What I want to talk to you about is rather sensitive.'

Horace felt he knew what was on the Sergeant Major's mind.

'I know all about you, Jim Greasley, and I know what you've been getting up to.'

Horace felt like a ten-year-old schoolboy waiting outside the headmaster's office. Horace was waiting for a lecture, for six of the best. But the tirade never came.

'I know how many times you've escaped and what it is you've been doing.' He gave a little grin and Horace had to concentrate hard to keep his face straight.

'And I know all about the rabbits too, and the extra bits and pieces you put in the pot for the chaps.'

The Sergeant Major placed a hand on Horace's shoulder and squeezed gently.

'Do you have any idea what you have done for the men's morale?'

Horace opened his mouth to deliver an apology, but the Sergeant Major continued.

'You're a hero, Greasley. You give a glimmer of hope to the poor wretched souls in here.' He smiled again. 'Me included. You're giving a stiff two fingers to Jerry every time you break out of here and the effect you are having on the men is magnificent.'

The Sergeant Major seemed to pause for a second or two, as if he was choosing his words carefully. 'You realise that it is the duty of every prisoner to try and escape and make it back to England, don't you?'

Horace wanted to say yes, wanted to tell Sergeant Major Harris that it was the first thought that crossed his mind as soon as he broke from the cover of the camp. He wanted to tell him how Rose would be bringing him a map and money too, and that a compass and clothing would follow soon. He wanted to tell Sergeant Major Harris how he'd begged the escape committee for help and that he wanted to get back to England, he really did. The next sentence from Sergeant Major Harris's lips stunned him.

'I don't want you to make it back to England, Greasley.'

'What, sir? I... I don't understand. I was...'

'I want you to stay put, continue what you're doing. The war is all but over; you'll be home quick enough.'

'But, sir...'

'That's an order, Greasley.'

CHAPTER
SIXTEEN

H orace continued his meetings with Rose. They made
love on a regular basis and continued with their forays
into the surrounding villages to supplement the prisoners'
soup pot. The map and money and the other items were
seldom mentioned and never materialised. Rose continued
supplying the details of the events of the war as they were
relayed over the airwaves. Horace lapped up the information
voraciously but felt a profound frustration that he couldn't
hear the information first hand, detail by detail.

It was summer of 1943, the fourth Horace had spent in
captivity. Deportation of Jews from the Warsaw ghetto
to Treblinka extermination camp had begun, even as
German civilians were being evacuated from Berlin.
Rome had been bombed by the Allies for the first time and
by the end of August Italy was drawing up plans to
surrender. It all seemed to be going well for the Allies but
the Germans showed no signs of letting up their offensive.
In a worrying development, scientist Wernher von Braun
briefed Hitler on the V2 rocket and the project was
approved as a top priority.

Horace and Rose lay completely naked on top of the rug

that had been stored for so long in the back of the small church. Rose lay with her head on Horace's chest, breathing lightly, slowly recovering from her exertions. Horace stroked her hair, trying to control his own breathing too. Both were bathed in perspiration from the unusually sultry evening. Horace studied the beautifully formed small of her back as it blended perfectly into her buttocks. He stretched down and caressed her backside. She purred with approval. In one swift movement, Horace reached under her hip bone and flipped Rose onto her back, then lay over her with his arms supporting his weight. Rose was taken by surprise as the wind was knocked from her lungs.

'That's a little rougher than I'm used to, Jim, but if you want to make love to me again then I submit.'

It was a pleasant thought, but the last thing on his mind.

'Can you get me a radio, Rose?'

'A what?'

'A radio.'

'I heard you, Jim. I heard you the first time.'

'Well, can you?'

Rose reached across for her underwear and began to dress herself. Horace followed suit as he pulled his trousers from the back of the pew. Rose was thinking; he didn't want to interrupt her thoughts. After a few minutes she spoke.

'Impossible, Jim.'

Horace's face fell. 'But why?'

Rose pulled her light cotton dress up over her thighs and began fastening the buttons. His eyes were drawn to her firm young breasts.

'The Germans confiscated every radio in the village nearly a year ago.'

'But your father has one, you listen, you bring me...'

'Yes. It's in the attic of our house, Jim, and it's the size of a small horse, built into an old dresser. It's not as if it will fit in my purse.'

Horace tried to hide his disappointment. He had seen the same radio sets in the upmarket furniture stores around Ibstock and in Leicester city centre. They were built into sideboards and desks, each one taking at least two men to load it into a furniture wagon for delivery to the wealthier families in the area. He wanted to push Rose further, ask if it were possible to get a smaller model, but he realised that the villages in Silesia were more backward when it came to technology than his home town in Leicestershire. Even if the radio was a more manageable size – one that Rose could carry on her own – it was simply too much of a risk to ask her to board a train in German-occupied Poland, on a train heading in the direction of Allied prisoner of war camps. Jesus... how could he be so stupid?

'Not to worry, Rose – it was just a thought. Let's go rabbit hunting.'

The two lovers dressed and walked into the forest hand in hand in the direction of the village. The roof of the forest gradually disappeared as they neared the village and the stars that hung high in the sky illuminated their way like tiny seeds of light.

They'd perfected their craft and targeted different villages at random. They had been lucky and hadn't been caught, but Horace felt that their luck would run out soon. They'd pillaged the surrounding villages for months now and the local rabbit population was dwindling rapidly. There had even been fights and arguments among the civilian workers in the camp suspicious of each other, wondering whether there was a thief in their midst. It was almost comical, and Horace had had to control his laughter on more than one occasion. The prisoners were above suspicion. How on earth could they be responsible? They were under lock and key every single night and there were no signs that any of them had escaped.

As they neared the edge of the wood the dim lights of a few cottages shone through the branches of the trees. Rose turned and faced him.

'I could smuggle the parts in for you.'

'What?'

'The radio parts. If you tell me what parts you need to build a radio I could try and get them for you.'

The following morning Horace had requested that Jimmy White – a sapper from the Isle of Wight – meet him in the barber's quarter. At first, Jimmy White had declined the offer but was told in no uncertain terms by a superior officer to report. A little after ten, Jimmy sauntered in, mumbling that he didn't need a damned haircut, he'd only seen Horace two weeks ago. He sat down in the chair, still moaning.

'I don't know what your fucking game is, Jim. I like a bit of length on my hair. Jesus, fuck! I went long enough when those bastards shaved it to the wood. Now it seems you want to do the same.' Jimmy White looked into the broken, makeshift mirror and caught a look in Horace's eyes that told him he hadn't been summonsed for a haircut.

Jimmy White smiled and waved his forefinger at the mirror. 'You're fucking up to something, Jim Greasley, aren't you? I might have known. I've been hearing rumours about you; it wouldn't surprise me if they were true.'

'Nice weather we're having lately, sir.'

'C'mon Greasley, stop pissing about.'

'Don't know what you're talking about, sir.' Horace grinned. 'Something for the weekend?'

Jimmy White sat in the chair and although Horace's scissors were poised at the ready, they were never called into action. Horace kept up the charade for a minute or two then decided he'd wound the man up enough.

'I hear you're a bit of a radio ham, Jimmy.'

'I knew it,' Jimmy White exclaimed. 'I knew you didn't bring me here for a haircut.'

Horace grinned. 'Absolutely right. I brought you here to build a radio.'

Jimmy White's mouth fell open. 'You're fucking mad. Build a radio? You're fucking crazy.'

Horace pulled at a strand of Jimmy White's hair and snipped at it with his scissors.

Jimmy pulled his head away. 'I've heard the stories; you escape from the camp at night and raid the villages, pinching rabbits and hens. You're a fucking nutter. And now you want to build a bloody radio?'

'That's right. I'll get you the parts.'

'So, it's true? It is you that escapes?'

'Correct.'

Jimmy White rose from the chair, began pacing the room.

'Impossible. It's just not possible, I'm afraid.'

'Anything's possible,' stated Horace. 'They said it was impossible to break out of here but I've managed it 57 times.'

Jimmy White whistled. 'Fuck me.'

'I'd rather not, thanks.'

Jimmy White shook his head. 'You don't understand, Jim. I'd need valves and a transistor, a capacitor and a resister, an amplifier and primary and secondary winding units and earphones. Then I'd need some solder and some wiring and if it were possible to get all that in here, where would we put it and more importantly, when and where would we listen to it?'

Horace spoke. 'Write me a list. You're to move into the prison staff quarters tomorrow night. Colin Jones has agreed to swap with you.'

'No, Jim, I won't. It's impossible, you'll get us all killed.' He was shaking his head in exasperation. 'And what about a power source? Ain't you forgotten Jerry turns our electric off at 11?'

Horace placed his scissors into their small wooden box and turned to face the stunned man. 'Get your list together and let me worry about the power source. All you need to worry about is brushing up on your radio skills.'

'Aren't you listening, Jim, you nutter? I ain't coming into your billet and I ain't building no fucking wireless.' Jimmy White threw the barber's protective gown to the floor and stormed towards the door, grabbing it and flinging it against the wall. As he left he turned around and pointed a stiff finger in the direction of Horace. 'And that's fucking final.'

CHAPTER
SEVENTEEN

'I must be bloody mad,' Jimmy White mumbled as he walked into the prisoner of war staff quarters towards a smiling, grinning Horace Greasley. 'I'm telling you, Jim, you won't be able to get a hold of those parts.'

'Welcome to the Grand Hotel Shanklin, James. Make yourself at home.'

'Stupid cunt.'

Horace pointed to the empty bunk. 'Your suite, sir. Please let me know if there's anything I can do to make your stay more comfortable.'

Jimmy White mumbled something indecipherable and threw his meagre possessions wrapped up in flannelette onto the bed.

'Breakfast is at 7.30 with maid service around ten.'

'Silly bastard.'

Although Horace didn't know it, Jimmy White was in awe of him. He now knew first hand that Jim Greasley was the prisoner responsible for bringing the meat and extra vegetables into the camp. He owed him a huge debt of gratitude as he'd managed to gain a little of the weight that had fallen from his bones over the past few years and like the other prisoners, he'd welcomed the news Jim had delivered about developments in the war.

Jim had refused to name his source but there was a rumour that he'd formed a relationship with a German girl in one of the villages. It was too preposterous for words and of course Jim had always denied it. Jimmy White supposed he'd heard the information about the war second hand, listening in to conversations as he'd cut the guards' hair.

And now here he was, Jim Greasley, claiming he could somehow get his hands on a selection of radio parts and he had the know-how to hide them and a power source to tap into. It wouldn't work... it just wouldn't work... an impossibility.

It took 14 visits to Rose before every part needed to assemble a radio had been neatly stacked behind a loose panel above the shelf that Horace slept under. The final component had been a capacitor that Rose had really struggled to get hold of. Rose never disclosed her source. Horace had asked her one evening, but she'd flatly refused to tell him. The average Silesian villager was right behind the Allies, she'd explained, and securing the parts hadn't been nearly as impossible as Jimmy White had imagined. Rose also explained the danger she was placing everybody in and the very real possibility that the Germans would find out about the radio. Horace and his partners in crime would be tortured to reveal their providers and Rose could not take the chance of placing her suppliers in danger if one of the prisoners were to crack.

Horace understood. He did not ask again.

The week before the capacitor came into the camp Horace had managed to rig up the power supply.

A huge black lead stove stood in the middle of the staff quarters. Although the Germans were sparing with the wood used to fuel the stove, it had occasionally been lit in the depths of winter, giving a little relief from the biting cold. A steel chimney ran to the ceiling, secured by a 12-inch cast iron plate that was held in place with a dozen bolts. Horace had wondered if there was some sort of false ceiling or void in the roof and during the hours of darkness, by candlelight, the prisoners had managed to take the bolts from the plate. When taken away and the chimney loosened and removed, there was just enough room for a man to squeeze through the hole.

Horace stood on Jock Strain's shoulders and eased himself through the gap in the ceiling. He had been right. The ceiling of the hut was false and the beams of the roof lay exposed. Jock pushed him up by the heels and he lay carefully on the thin wooden supports. He would need to be careful. He took the length of rubber covered wire from his pocket and gripped it in his teeth. The men down below extinguished their candles and Horace lay quietly for a full ten minutes until his eyes grew accustomed to the dark.

The prison staff quarters and the barrack room below were completely in darkness. However the beams of the roof above the German guards' quarters were clearly visible from the light shining through the gaps in the ceiling. Horace took a deep breath and began edging slowly towards the ceiling above the Germans' quarters.

It was only 15 feet from the hole to the main light fitting in the centre of the guards' ceiling hut but it took Horace the best part of an hour to reach it, crawling ever so carefully, a an inch or two at a time. The light fitting had been badly constructed and a small gap allowed Horace to see clearly into the room below. Four German guards sat smoking and playing cards and Horace fought a strong urge to unbutton his flies and piss on them through the gap. He had a job to do; revenge and retribution would come later.

The Germans were quiet, concentrating on their cards, and

if a pin dropped it could and would be heard. It was no good. He'd be caught. A simple rustle of clothing would be heard a mere few feet away. Horace cursed under his breath. At that moment a hand was decided on the lay of a card. To a man the Germans shouted and whooped and yelled, one in triumph, the others in frustration or disappointment.

Over the next 90 minutes Horace bided his time, waiting for each noisy reaction to the card game before carrying out a task, cutting the wires and connecting them to the exposed light fitting wires above the guards' quarters. It was painfully slow progress.

Nearly three hours after he'd eased himself into the roof void he dropped down to the floor of the prison staff quarters with a live wire and a huge grin. Only Jock Strain and Jimmy White had managed to stay awake.

Jimmy White had disconnected a bulb from the ceiling of the hut. Jock held his thick coat around the bulb, the three men creating a human light barrier as Horace brought the wires into contact with the base of the bulb. As the wire touched the points of the bulb the three men's smiles were illuminated in the darkness. Horace pulled the wire away immediately, fearful of a German patrol passing the window. It was another victory. However small, it was a victory and the three men couldn't quite believe it.

Jimmy White wanted to get on with the task there and then. Horace talked him out of it. It had been a long night. Horace taped up the exposed wiring with flannelette, climbed back into the roof void and carefully laid the wire a few inches from the edge of the hole. Then he sat on Jock's shoulders to bolt the cast iron plate back in place. The three men returned to their bunks, but although Horace was exhausted, his mind would not empty enough to let him sleep.

Tomorrow the last few components of the radio would be

connected up. The power source was in place. Would they be listening to the news from London in a little less than 24 hours? It was a tall order, and Horace prepared himself for disappointment. He tried not to think of the risk and danger he'd placed Rose in over the last few weeks. He only hoped it would be worth it.

As was usual, just after seven the next morning a German guard opened up the prison staff quarters. Jimmy White made a burst for the door. Horace found him in the toilet block with his trousers at his ankles.

'Fucking hell, Chalky, you don't look so clever.'

Jimmy White groaned as his bowels moved again. 'Jesus, Jim, I'm shitting through the eye of a needle. I don't know what it is I've eaten but I swear there can't be anything left in my body.'

'You look like shit.' Horace stated the obvious. 'And Jesus Christ, you stink to high heaven. You'd think something had crawled up your arse and died.'

Jimmy White looked up. 'I think it has, mate. Can you tell the MO to get me excused from duty today?'

When the MO and a German civilian medic eventually made it into the toilet block Jimmy White hadn't moved. One smell of the area was enough to convince the German to sign the paper confining Jimmy White to barracks for the day. Twenty minutes later Jimmy White lay on his bunk. Horace wondered for a second whether it was a ruse to work on the radio during the hours of daylight, but no, it was impossible to create an smell like that artificially. Jimmy White was genuinely in a bad way.

When Horace returned to the staff quarters after work detail that evening, Jimmy White hadn't moved from the position he'd left him in that morning.

'Still buggered, Jimmy?' he asked.

'Fucked, Jim. I'm as weak as a kitten.'

Horace was disappointed. They were so near to having the radio ready, maybe two or three parts to connect up. Never mind, he thought to himself, they'd waited long enough. What was another day? He looked at Jimmy White; he was a deathly grey and in no condition to concentrate on something so technical. Horace ruffled his hair. 'Never mind, Chalky boy, there's always tomorrow.'

As Horace walked over to his bunk he added, 'Just you make sure you're OK for tomorrow night, mate. We've a date with London.'

Horace didn't receive a reply, which made him look over towards his friend's bunk. Jimmy was lying on his side, still clutching at his stomach trying to relieve the cramp, but he was grinning despite the discomfort. No doubt about it – he was definitely grinning.

'What?' Horace asked. 'What is it?'

'What do you think?' Jimmy answered.

Horace's stomach started churning. He became aware of a dry sensation in his mouth and his throat seemed to almost close as he forced the words from his mouth.

'It's ready, Chalky, isn't it?'

Jimmy White grimaced as he forced a smile onto his face. 'You fucking bet it's ready, Greasley. Just what the hell do you think I've been doing all day?'

Horace would find out later that Jimmy White had found a death cap mushroom in the forest while on work detail. He'd eaten a tiny piece of it and induced cyclopeptide poisoning. He had gagged while he swallowed it, knowing exactly what the end result would be, and that eating too much of the fungus could kill him. Jimmy explained that he needed to work on the final components in daylight. It was simply impossible by the light of a flickering candle.

The effort had drained Jimmy White of all his energy. He explained that every part had been set in place, but of course he'd been unable to connect to the power and therefore couldn't check that the radio even worked, let alone search for a signal and a recognisable English-speaking news station. Only too aware that Horace's impatience would have the set powered up as soon as it was dark, he started offering his excuses.

'It's nearly four years since I rigged a set up, Jim. I'm a little rusty.'

Horace was focused on the stove's chimney and the cast iron plate in the ceiling.

'Maybe things have moved on?'

Horace looked at the shelf above his bunk and the loose wooden panel that hid the radio. Not only had Rose came up with every part Jimmy White had asked for, but she'd managed to get hold of each major component in the smallest possible dimensions available, in order that the radio would fit comfortably in the frame of the wooden hut. It had been a tight squeeze but they'd managed to fit it all in.

'Some of the parts looked a little old, Jim. They may not be compatible with the other bits.'

Horace tried not to think of the worst-case scenario – that the radio wouldn't work. Rose had risked life and limb to get those parts to him. Surely to God Jimmy White had the knowledge to piece them together and surely to God if he'd even suspected that some part wasn't quite right, he'd have said something?

Horace lay on his bunk looking out of the window, waiting for darkness to come. Jimmy White took a turn for the worse and begged Horace to wait until tomorrow night before attempting to connect the radio. Horace wouldn't have it. It wouldn't do any harm to at least try. As usual, the Germans cut the lights just after 11pm. Horace lay in the darkness for about 20 minutes before he heard Flapper strike the match. He turned over and caught the familiar sight of the big Londoner silhouetted against the candle.

'Jim,' Garwood whispered across the room. 'Are you awake?'

Horace rolled over and faced his pal. 'You bet, big man.'

'Are we gonna give it a try, then?'

Horace slipped from his bunk and crept over to Flapper's bunk. 'You bet we are, mate, you bet.'

They positioned themselves directly under the chimney of the black lead stove. Horace opened his legs as Flapper Garwood ducked down and slipped his head in between Horace's thighs, and with a surge of effort pushed himself to his full height. Horace placed two hands on Flapper's head for balance as he climbed up to stand on his shoulders. He reached inside his trouser pocket for the small spanner and as Flapper held him steady, proceeded to loosen off the bolts from the cast iron plate. It took three or four minutes before it could be detached from the ceiling and handed down to Flapper.

Flapper now held the chimney in place as Horace climbed down the body of his friend and dropped to the floor. Flapper carefully eased the chimney from the stove and laid it against the wall. He lifted Horace back into the roof void and Horace traced the live wire over the roof and down the hollow walls over to the shelf above his bed. Flapper brought over the candle and as he placed it on the shelf he prised the wooden panel from the wall. Horace dangled the wire down towards the shelf as Flapper reached up inside the hole, eagerly praying for contact with the dangling wire.

'Got it,' he said.

Horace eased himself back over the hole in the roof and

dropped quietly to the floor. He walked over to where his friend stood with a grin and a handful of rubber-coated wire. The two men stood in awe for a minute or two. Only the secondary winding unit, the amplifier and part of the capacitor were visible. Every other part had been strategically placed on the wooden frame that separated the interior and exterior walls of the hut. Jimmy White had done a fantastic job of concealment, making use of every square inch of space. Horace spoke.

'Impressive, isn't it?'

'I'll say,' said Flapper.

'Think it will work?'

'We'll soon find out.'

Horace didn't hang around and within a minute had connected the radio to the power surge. The tiny red light beside the winder sparked into life, emitting a faint glow. The two men smiled. As Horace reached for the headphones, Flapper placed a hand on his arm.

'Wait, Jim.'

'What is it?'

'It's not right... Jimmy should be here.'

Horace smiled in acknowledgement. 'You're, right mate. Go and wake him up.'

Under protest, Jimmy White shuffled over to Horace's bunk and collapsed in a heap, still complaining about his tender guts. 'Can't we wait until tomorrow, lads?'

Flapper and Horace shook their heads in unison. Jimmy could barely pick out the white of their teeth as they smiled under the dim light of the candles. 'Impatient cunts!' He rested his head on the mattress and placed his hands behind his head. 'Tell me what you hear.'

But before Horace had a chance to place the earphones on his head, Jimmy White leaned over onto his elbow with his backside pointing towards his pals and let fly with a fart so loud that Horace was sure it would be heard in the German quarters next door. It took barely three seconds before the stench kicked in. It wasn't a smell, it was a stench – the worst, foulest smell Flapper and Horace could remember in a long while.

'You dirty bastard!' Flapper squealed as he rolled over onto the floor desperately trying to escape the invisible noxious odour.

Horace's hand covered his mouth as he spoke through his fingers. 'You filthy, filthy, filthy bastard!'

Jimmy White lay clutching his stomach, but this time with mirth as he giggled like a schoolboy. 'Serves you right, for making an ill man get out of his bed,' he laughed. 'Serves you right, you bunch of bastards.'

As Jimmy's laughs and the foul smell eventually subsided, Horace removed his hand from his face. Jimmy White closed his eyes again, satisfied with his one-man protest. 'Just tell me what you hear,' he repeated.

Horace shook his head and reached inside the exposed hole for the primary and secondary winding units. He remembered the radio back home in the lounge at Ibstock. The Empiric portable 4v wireless receiver housed a very useful frequency dial so the operator would have an idea where to find his favourite stations. A white wooden needle could be viewed through the glass exterior. Dad could generally tune into his favourite channels within seconds.

That wasn't the case here. There was no dial and no needle, just two winders four inches apart. Horace knew it would be trial and error to find an English-speaking station but after an hour fiddling and pushing and pulling at the wheels he hadn't even managed to secure a local language station, German or Polish. As each minute passed he grew more disillusioned.

Jimmy White was still awake. Horace had urged him a

couple of times to give it a go but Jimmy had declined, claiming he would be in a better frame of mind the following evening. He had a point, thought Horace. He threw the earphones onto the bed in frustration.

'All I can hear is fucking static, Jimmy. I haven't heard one voice. Surely I should have heard a voice? I don't want to hear Churchill or the fucking Queen, I just want to hear a voice. Hitler would have been nice, for once. I wouldn't have minded if I'd heard Hitler speaking or even Musso-fucking-lini, but no, I've heard nothing.'

Jimmy rolled over onto his stomach. 'It might be wired up wrong. I'll take a look at it tomorrow.'

Flapper chipped in. 'Give me a go, Jim.'

Horace handed him the earphones. 'Be my guest.'

Despite his best intentions Flapper didn't have the delicate fingers or the patience to participate in such an exercise. After ten minutes he cast the earphones back onto the bed.

'I'm going to kip. Chalky's right – we can take a look at it tomorrow.'

Jimmy White eased himself from Horace's bunk and walked gingerly over to his bunk. Horace replaced the false wooden panel with a sigh and wandered over to help Garwood replace the chimney and the iron plate. At least they'd achieved something, he thought to himself. The radio was wired up and ready for a little fine-tuning tomorrow. It might take a day or two but they'd get there.

Sleep didn't come easy. He dozed but couldn't fall into a deep slumber.

Unbeknown to Horace, Jock Strain couldn't either. What the hell Jim Greasley was doing, removing the bloody panel above his shelf again? He eased himself from his bunk and crept over towards him. 'What the fuck are you up to?' he asked.

'I can't sleep, Jock. I thought I'd give it another go.'

So Horace sat on one end of the bunk and Jock sat on the other. They sat in silence for almost an hour while Horace tried every combination. Slowly, carefully, like a safe cracker on the combination wheel of a safe, he learned to sense when the winding units had come to the end of the line and changed direction. After about 20 minutes, when he was sure the winders had come to the end again, he would start all over again. Each time he tried to go slower and slower. He'd heard voices the last couple of times – or was that his imagination? He wanted to hear voices – was his mind playing tricks on him? No, he'd definitely heard something. He sighed and looked across at Jock. Miraculously he was still awake.

'One more go, Haggis, eh? Then we can turn in. Get Jimmy to take a look tomorrow.'

Jock Strain nodded, rubbing at his eyes.

Horace took a deep breath and started again. Five minutes into the repeat performance he paused. There was no mistaking it this time – he'd definitely heard something.

The Scot sensed it too, noticing a spark of interest in the face that had showed no emotion for nearly two hours. 'What is it, Jim?'

Horace held up a hand, lightened his grip on the winding wheel. 'I dunno, Jock. It's just that I thought I heard a drum beat.'

The hairs on Jock Strain's body rose. 'Describe it, Jim.'

Horace shrugged. 'What do you mean? It was a drum beat – how do you describe that? It just went boom… boom… boom. You know? Like a drum beat.'

'Drum radio,' Jock whispered. 'Drum radio,' he repeated a little louder.

'What, Jock? What did you say?'

Jock leapt to his feet. He positioned himself on his knees

next to the radio set. 'Just you keep that bloody winder where it is, Jim. You might have something.'

'Have something? What do you mean? Some bugger bashing away on a skin drum? Sorry, Jock, but that wasn't exactly what I had in mind when we rigged this little beauty up. I had more...'

'Drum radio, Jim!'

'What?'

'Drum radio, a BBC station brought out a few weeks after you were captured in France. You've never heard of it, have you?'

Horace shook his head.

'It's a news station. I caught a couple of broadcasts before I left for France. I came into the war a little after you.'

'A BBC station?'

Jock grinned. Horace repositioned his earphones as his fingers barely came into contact with the winder. Ever so delicately he eased the wheels to the right and left, taking care not to take them too far in either direction. All of a sudden he stopped breathing, his skin tingled and shivers ran the length of his spine. The unmistakable public school tones of a BBC newsreader burst into his eardrums.

Horace took his fingers from the wheel and breathed deeply. He held up a hand and then a thumb and a smile as wide as the mouth of the Thames burst across his face as he shouted to his friend kneeling on the floor. 'We've got the news, Jock! We've got the fucking BBC news!' Horace burst into tears and Jock quickly followed suit, all too aware of the effect a man crying had on him. Jimmy White heard the commotion and rose from his sick bed.

'Shut the fuck up, you two! You'll have Jerry in here.'

The sight of his two friends hugging each other with tears rolling down their cheeks astounded the radio ham. It could mean only one thing. 'It's working, isn't it?' Jimmy asked in disbelief.

Horace was still sobbing as he rose to greet him. 'We've got the BBC news, Chalky. You're a bloody genius, man!'

More men rose from their beds now. Freddie Rogers and Dave Crump came over too. By this time Horace was back on the earphones with the same, silly grin on his face listening to a report from Tunisia in North Africa. The Allies, it seemed, were heading for another victory and had full control of North Africa.

The smiling yet tearful faces of Flapper Garwood, Jock and now Jimmy White left the other men in the staff working quarters at Freiwaldau in German-occupied Silesia under no illusion as to what had been achieved. They slapped Horace on the back; some shook Jimmy White's hand and one even planted a big wet kiss on his cheek. They were heroes. Heroes in the same sense as a VC winner taking out a German machine-gun post, or a scheming general whose cunning plans swung the battle against all the odds. They were Montgomery, Churchill, General McArthur and Douglas Bader rolled into one.

Against all odds Joseph Horace Greasley and Jimmy White had smuggled in and built a radio capable of picking up a BBC news channel under the noses of their German captors. It was simply monumental – a triumph that ranked up there with anything Horace had achieved so far. It was another personal victory for him and at that very moment, his moment of conquest, he thought back to the woman who had made it all possible. The woman he loved with all his heart.

CHAPTER
EIGHTEEN

The Drum radio station was picked up with little effort the following evening. The 12 men of the staff quarters took it in turn to listen to the news reports. They kicked in on the hour, every hour for about 15 minutes, 24 hours a day. Horace only listened to about five minutes of the news that night. He heard with satisfaction that German and Italian troops had turned against each other in Rome and were fighting with themselves. Surely, he thought to himself, it's only a matter of months before this nightmare ends? Maybe weeks?

By the end of the following day every Allied prisoner of war in the camp at Freiwaldau was aware of the latest developments in the Second World War. In 24 hours the prisoners' morale had hit an all-time high. They were smiling, chatting and smoking cigarettes openly, without asking permission of the guards. They were thinking of victory and of their families back home. The German guards sensed the change in attitude, but were seemingly powerless to do anything about it. Horace sat on his bunk peering through the open window. He looked out onto the camp as the men lined up for their early evening meal and he absorbed their smiles, their contentment and felt an enormous sense of achievement and pride. He'd made the difference.

After he'd eaten he lay on his bunk waiting for darkness. He couldn't wait to share the good news with Rose. Horace got up and walked over to where Flapper lay as he quietly went over the details of his plan.

'If you think it'll work, Jim, I'm happy to give it a go.'

Flapper Garwood, Horace thought. Could a man wish for a better friend? He hadn't known this gentle giant before the war started, yet he'd been through thick and thin with him. In the camp outside Saubsdorf Garwood had lost over six stone and still he hadn't complained, actually managing to think of others. He had helped Horace through that hell of a march and saved his life on the death train. He'd always been around and Horace was one hundred per cent sure he'd spared the lives of many other prisoners by killing Big Stoop.

Horace dared to think about the end of the war. The medals and the awards would be handed out like confetti. Would anyone even think of the soldiers incarcerated in the camps? Would the likes of Flapper Garwood receive any recognition? He doubted it very much.

Flapper had begged to be allowed to escape into the forest too but Horace and the escape committee had forbidden it. Everyone agreed that Horace had good reason to risk his life each time. He had two good reasons actually, Rose and the extra food he brought to the camp. Even Garwood had to admit that real escape was nigh on impossible. And where would it stop? More men would want to go and each man attempting an escape would increase the chance of capture for everyone. They remembered young Bruce Harwood and what the Germans had done to him. But for once, Horace would need a little help and Flapper Garwood was the obvious choice.

Rose sat open-mouthed as Horace took her through the

events of the past 48 hours. She was sitting on a pew in the small church and leapt to her feet cheering as Horace told her about the first time he'd heard the voice from London. He laughed as she danced a jig around the small church, calling the Germans all the names under the sun. He was left in no doubt that this girl hated the Germans just as much as he did.

'My father will be so pleased.'

As soon as the words passed her lips she stopped dead in her tracks. It was slip of the tongue, a burst of emotion she should have contained.

Horace had guessed all along that her father must have known about his daughter's trips to the camp, her relationship with an Allied prisoner of war and perhaps even the radio. Horace wondered if he'd supplied the parts. Rose had quite naturally wanted to protect him. Horace stood up and walked over to her. Her bottom lip had begun to tremble and her eyes were glazed over with a film of tears as she refused to look him in the eyes.

'Don't get upset, Rose. Not on such a wonderful evening as this.'

She buried her head in his shoulder and the tears started.

'You knew all along?'

'I suspected.'

She looked up; the tears fell onto her cheeks. 'He hates them as much as you do. He'd spent 20 years building up that business and they just took it from him, took his Jewish workers away and stole his profits.'

Horace had forgotten about the rumours surrounding the Jews.

'Fathers are wise, Rose, when it comes to their daughters. It wouldn't surprise me if he suspected back in...'

'No Jim, surely not?'

Horace shrugged his shoulders. 'Let's get out of here,

Rose. We need to let the men celebrate. We need meat and vegetables for them.'

Rose wiped at her tears and managed to raise a smile.

'I have something for you to celebrate with.'

Rose produced two small bottles of Polish vodka from her bag. 'It's not much, but your men need to toast a victory.'

Horace took the two bottles and placed them on the floor. He pulled Rose towards him and kissed her for what seemed like an eternity. Afterwards they walked from the church and into the forest.

'Tonight, Rose, we are supplying the men with fresh chicken.'

Rose whistled. 'Are you sure?'

'Tonight it's a smash and grab exercise. You're not coming with me.'

'But Jim, I always...'

Horace placed a finger on her lips, leaned forward and kissed her gently. 'Not tonight, Rose. It's going to be noisy and dangerous. Tonight two soldiers of the British Army are going to stage a military exercise that will make the Duke of Wellington's exploits seem tame.'

Rose smiled. 'I do not know of the Duke and his wellingtons.'

Horace laughed. 'It doesn't matter, Rose. You just need to get yourself back home. It's a little risky. Remember, those hens are bloody noisy.'

Rose sighed, placed a hand on her heart and feigned a swoon. 'You are so brave, fighting those hens...'

Horace kissed her again and as he pulled back, her hand found the small of his back and she held him there. She pressed her hips into him. 'Jim, I have not told you, there is a price to pay for that vodka.' She smiled. 'Come with me into the forest and I will explain.'

Rose took his hand and led him back into the forest. Horace suspected he knew exactly what sort of currency Rose was talking about.

Flapper sat in the forest. He was breathing heavily. It had only been a 50-yard sprint from the hut but the adrenaline coursing through his body made the small run feel like a marathon. He had run in Jim Greasley's footsteps. He had escaped through the same barred window and now sat in the same forest where Jim had all his adventures – and he was envious. The feeling of freedom was incredible. He could run, he could hide, he could walk through the forest without the constant presence of a German uniform. Garwood took full advantage of the light of the full moon as he strolled slowly and quietly in between the trees. Every few paces he stopped, breathed deeply and drank in the silent, free atmosphere of Silesia.

He had escaped a little after midnight and been given instructions exactly where to meet his friend. The rendezvous would be at 1.30am. Flapper had an hour and a half to enjoy the ambience of a free environment, an unrestricted world.

Horace sat outside the small church chewing at his nails. Jesus, he thought, where is he? It had to be nearly two o'clock. Horace had left Rose just after 1.15 according to her watch, and it was only a ten-minute walk back to the church. He didn't have a watch himself but figured at least 25 minutes had passed.

Garwood was in torment. It was way past the time he'd arranged to meet Jim Greasley and he sat on the edge of the forest as the tears streamed down his face. He wondered just what sort of character Jim Greasley was. He knew now why his friend and the escape committee wanted to prevent the men from breaking out into the forest.

Garwood had thought himself so controlled as he'd made

that 50-yard dash, so focused on the planned operation ahead. He'd thought it would be just a matter of course that he'd turn round after the mission had been completed and simply slip back into the camp. It wasn't that easy.

He knew it was stupid, knew it amounted to signing his own death warrant, but still he felt the urge to run, run away from his captors, his incarceration. He had no maps, no provisions, no money and no extra clothing, yet still there was a feeling so strong it was tearing him apart. Surely he owed it to himself to at least try? He'd use the sun for direction, live off the land and raid the small villages en route as Jim Greasley was doing for meat and vegetables. He just needed to head north and make for the Baltic Sea. Once there he'd stow away on a ship to England. It wouldn't be easy but he'd make it.

Horace was pacing the ground outside the church. It was well after two o'clock. Something had happened. Had his mate been caught by the Germans? Would they have discovered that he was missing too? The camp would be in uproar, every German guard rallied and in position patrolling the perimeter. They would be out looking for him and he would have no chance of getting back in. All this to provide a little feast for the men. It was stupid. The committee was right: two men escaping doubled the chance of capture.

Why hadn't he kept to the normal routine – a couple of rabbits, a few potatoes and back into the camp? They had the radio set up; why risk such an achievement to provide a few extra bits of meat? Horace picked up his coat and started walking before he realised he didn't know where to walk to. The camp – he'd need to go to the camp to see if the alarm had been raised. Perhaps Flapper had just bottled it. Perhaps Flapper was still tucked up in his bed. Yes, that was it. He'd changed his mind.

Horace had gone no more than 20 yards when he heard his name being called behind him. Garwood stood in the shadows. He stepped forward, he was red-faced, his cheeks stained with grime. 'Jim, I'm...'

'Where the hell have you been, Flapper? One thirty, we said.'

'I'm sorry, Jim. I...'

At that moment Horace realised what had been going on in his friend's head. They were the same thoughts he'd had a hundred times. The guilt, the anguish, the sense of duty. Wondering if it were possible to make it back to England and thoughts of friends and family back home. 'You were going to head for Blighty, weren't you?'

Flapper stuttered, uncomfortable with the telepathic-like intrusion into his mind.

'You knew. You...'

'I've been there, Flapper. I've been there more times than you'd care to imagine.'

Garwood leaned against a tree and slumped to the floor. Horace knelt beside him as Flapper released his burden.

'I must have run over two miles before I turned back. I'd convinced myself it would be so easy. Then I realised I didn't know what direction I was heading in and I began thinking of you and the lads and the radio and the feast we'd planned and how I'd be letting everybody down because of my selfishness.'

Horace listened intently as his friend poured his heart out. 'Our place is in the camp, Flapper.'

Garwood looked up and wiped a tear from the side of his face.

Horace continued. 'We've done more for the bloody war effort than the average squaddie in the trenches of France taking out the Germans. We are needed in the camps, men like us. That's where the likes of you and I belong. I wouldn't be here, Flapper, if it wasn't for you. You saved my life on that train. I…'

'No, Jim, we…'

'Shut the fuck up and let me finish.'

Flapper smiled, took the hint. He wanted to hear what his friend was saying. He needed to hear it. He'd felt it many times, felt that he was contributing in no small part to the war effort. He was looking after his own, those that needed it, protecting and guiding them through their own personal hells. Everyone had a role.

'I know you killed Big Stoop.'

Horace gauged his friend's reaction to the statement. There was none.

'God knows how many men's lives you saved by taking that monster out. You've been my mate since camp one. I need you, Flapper. I need to talk to you every day, I need you at my right hand side when we plan our next ridiculous plan. I need you there to look after me and tell me what a silly bastard I am sometimes.'

Horace grinned. 'You're no good to me, mate, in fucking England. I need you here, the men need you here. Never mind the British fucking Army telling you your duty is to escape.' Horace leaned forward, gripped the big man firmly at the knee. 'Your duty is here. Your duty is to protect the men, help me get the BBC news to every prisoner within 50 miles of here.'

Flapper wanted to agree, to tell his friend that everything he was saying made sense and that it was the finest speech he'd ever heard. The feelings of guilt had drained away. Jim Greasley was right and amazingly, he wasn't angry. But then again, Jim Greasley had had those same feelings too. Flapper had always felt there was a reason he'd been captured and incarcerated in the camps that there was a purpose for being there. Jim had explained it with perfect clarity... he was the overseer, the protector.

And the man kneeling opposite him with a stupid, childlike grin on his face – who was this man? Jim Greasley was almost certainly one of the unsung heroes in the Second World War. He was the hunter, the gatherer, the engineer, the smuggler, the lover and the fighter, too. He was the most stubborn bastard he'd ever come across... and Flapper had been sent to watch over him.

The two friends sat crouched in the small Silesian allotment. They had filled a large bag with fresh vegetables and were now eying the chicken coop on the far side of the garden. The hens were nervous; they sensed danger. It was uncanny. Night after night Horace and Rose had raided the gardens, allotments, small holdings and farms in the area, taking their vegetables and rabbits. Not once had they attempted to take the hens, and the hens had sat silently while the rabbits had been killed in front of them. Now it was as if the hens knew. It was as if someone had told them tonight was their turn. Horace and Flapper were aware of the movement, the faint sound of clucking carried over on the evening breeze.

'The men must have chicken tomorrow, my friend.'

'Chicken and vodka,' Flapper replied

'Chicken and vodka,' Horace repeated.

Flapper looked a little nervous as he spoke. 'They're going to make some noise, mate. We must be quick – in and out like the fox. We must make it look like a fox has been in the sheds tonight, not two crazy prisoners from the camp down the road.'

Horace nodded. 'Then we must be as quick as the wind.'

Flapper looked across at his friend. 'Ready?'

'As ready as I'll ever be.'

'Let's go and feed our comrades.' Flapper punched Horace

playfully on the shoulder and the two men ran quickly over to their targets. Flapper Garwood reached the door to the hen house first and yanked hard on the handle. The twine holding the door in place snapped easily and he flung the door wide open. Horace leapt inside and feathers and sawdust flew all over the place as the poor hens tried desperately to evade capture. Horace picked a hen from the air in full flight and dislocated its neck with the action of an expert. Flapper caught another and tugged unsuccessfully at its neck four times, the poor bird squawking ever louder each time.

'Give it here, city boy,' Horace called to him. Horace killed it first time.

'One more,' he whispered. Three birds in the pot, a veritable banquet. The third bird was caught and killed within 20 seconds.

Just as they were leaving Flapper reached up; another hen flew through the air. He caught it by the leg and put its head in his mouth, clenched his teeth and pulled. The bird's head came away from its body with little effort as Flapper spat a mouthful of feathers into the air.

Horace was dumbfounded. 'What are you doing, for Christ's sake?'

Flapper spat the head into the corner and threw the still struggling body of the hen to the floor. His blood-splattered face grinned at Horace. 'The fox, mate. We must make it look as if our friend the fox has been in here.'

Horace smiled. 'The fox... right.' And he remembered on the odd occasion a fox had managed to break into his father's sheds in Ibstock and the sheer devastation and unnecessary killing he'd witnessed the next morning. Flapper was right; a fox would always leave at least one dead bird behind.

Horace and Flapper slept with the dead birds, vegetables and vodka under their bunks. The German guard made his regular seven o'clock appearance then disappeared. The men had been staggered at the booty now held in prison staff quarters and Jock made a list and a new recipe for that evening's meal. He had managed to steal a few spices from the German cook house and even persuaded the camp commandant to be a little more generous with the bread ration. And incredibly, he'd used all his powers of persuasion to beg the ingredients to make pastry. Against his better judgement the camp commandant had supplied just enough eggs and flour and milk to make a very thin pie crust for one hundred men.

It rained that evening and as was the procedure during inclement weather, the evening meal was cooked indoors on the stove of the prison staff quarters, out of the view of curious German eyes. It was perfect... a perfect evening.

Nearly one hundred prisoners crowded into the area where 12 prisoners normally slept. Each brought with them a container in which a carefully measured drop of vodka was poured. Some savoured the taste; others threw it back in one and a few kept it for the meal to follow.

The cook had wasted nothing; every bit of the chickens was used, in addition to the extra vegetables. Jock had created another culinary masterpiece. To start with - spiced potato skins. The men had been reluctant at first; no one had ever dreamt that the waste of the potato could be put to such good use. But Jock had softened the skins in boiling water before frying them up with the stolen spices and some chopped onions and the juice from tomatoes. The taste was exquisite.

And then, to follow – chicken pie.

The men had to be patient as the Germans had only supplied the cook with two medium-sized pie dishes. Each dish fed about ten men and the men waited around for hours before being given their own slice of heaven. No one seemed to mind. They sat around smoking tobacco from their Red Cross parcels and talking about the end of the war. Horace was one of the last to be served and savoured every delicious mouthful. Afterwards he raised his small glass of vodka in the direction of Jock and toasted his good health.

Everyone in the room knew just who it was that had provided the extras for the evening banquet but like every well-kept secret, nobody uttered a word. Nobody proposed a toast to the hunters. And that's exactly how Horace wanted it.

At around 10.30 with every last man still in the room, Horace stood with a sheet of paper. 'And now, gentlemen,' he said in a whisper. 'Here is yesterday's news from the BBC.'

CHAPTER
NINETEEN

I t was while he was watching the men rolling their tobacco the previous evening that the idea had come to him. In every tenth parcel the Red Cross had provided a cigarette-rolling machine that the men would share. The thin cigarette paper was placed lengthways into the machine and the tobacco distributed evenly inside. The gummed edge of the paper would then be moistened with saliva and snapped shut. A manual rolling movement would take place and when the machine was opened a neatly formed cigarette would result. Horace had discussed his idea with the other men in the hut but, they had flagged up several obstacles.

Horace owed it to Rose to make the radio work. It shouldn't just be viewed as an object of luxury, something to amuse a dozen prisoners. No. It was a morale booster; he'd already witnessed that and he was determined that as many prisoners as possible should be in a position to receive regular news updates. Uncensored updates, real news, not propaganda. It would make their last few months in the camp much more bearable. When the time came to escape the camps, a little knowledge of world events might even make the difference between life and death.

Within a month, the production unit of the camp was underway. Two former journalists with a knowledge of shorthand had been brought into the staff quarters, as had two extra pair of earphones, courtesy of Rosa Rauchbach.

A typewriter and thin typing paper had already been supplied to the prisoners. The Germans would normally give their own carefully selected version of war events in the form of a newsletter that would be typed up by two of the prisoners and distributed among the prisoners. It was seldom read, being too ridiculous for words. Reports in the past had told of Churchill's death, a Russian capitulation and among others, London, Edinburgh and New York being invaded by German storm troopers.

This time, the endless supply of typing paper stolen from the German offices would be put to better use. The journalists listened in to the midnight news, took notes in shorthand, then spent the next hour or so writing them up in longhand, condensing as they went. At 2am the typists were woken and spent an hour of darkness by the light of a candle typing the journalists' reports. At six o'clock another two-man shift commenced, rolling the typing paper into the middle of the cigarette paper with a quarter inch of tobacco at each end.

The cigarettes were swapped and handed round next morning at roll call, and continued throughout the day. Before the evening food was dished out every prisoner in the camp had been kept up to date with world events via the previous evening's BBC news.

And still Horace and his fellow prisoners in the staff quarters weren't content. They stepped up the shifts during the night and increased the cigarette news production. They started with the next camp down the road. The different work parties passed each other every day. They would generally stop and have a natter; the German guards were none too bothered now. The prisoners would hand an occasional cigarette to their fellow prisoners, always taking care to ask permission from their captors. What harm could it do? the Germans thought. The prisoners receiving the cigarettes would be told to nip them straight away. In time, those same prisoners would pass on real cigarettes to the working party from Freiwaldau, so that the production could be maintained.

The highly efficient news machine continued through the winter and into the spring of 1944. The recipients of the news were reading about the heavy bombings of German cities and that Japanese troops had retreated from Burma. However, they would also hear towards the end of March 1944 of the grievous losses the RAF suffered during a huge air raid on Nuremburg. The committee of the camp journal – as it was affectionately known – agreed that all news would be reported without exception, no matter how tragic it was and what effect it might have on the prisoners. They all agreed not to compromise the honesty of the operation.

Unknown to the prisoners of Freiwaldau, in May 1944 the Allies were preparing for D Day. Reports filtered across the airwaves of increased Allied bombing in France in preparation. The camp journal delivered the news but its team were unaware of the real reason behind the intensity of the bombing.

Occasionally a radio part would malfunction but Horace continued to escape and meet up with Rose, and she would always have a replacement within a few days. By the summer of 1944 the camp journal was being read by a staggering three thousand prisoners of war, every single day. That was too many men. It was only a matter of time before a slip of the tongue would be overheard by unfriendly ears. It happened as a camp civilian worker relieved himself behind a hedge adjacent to one of the working parties in the forest, four miles from Freiwaldau.

The news had been good the previous evening and the prisoners could not contain their excitement. Late August and early September 1944 had brought night after night of monumental news. The radio brought reports that Paris had been liberated and De Gaulle and the Free French had marched triumphantly down the Champs-Elysées. The Germans had also surrendered at Toulon and Marseilles in the south. Canadian troops had captured Dieppe and the Allies had entered Belgium. Brussels, Antwerp, Ghent, Liege and Ostend had all been liberated by the Allies. The Russians had also liberated the first concentration camp in Poland. It was the beginning of the end for Germany and the Third Reich.

Two prisoners of war were talking as they took a break at the side of the road. Rather carelessly and a little too loudly, one of them handed a cigarette to his friend from another camp and announced that the news was good. 'The radio was red hot last night by all accounts.'

'It was?'

Andrezj Netzer, a Silesian with Nazi-sympathetic views, was spilling a stream of hot urine into the hedgerow. He was hidden from view and nipped the end of his penis to slow the flow for fear of being heard. What a stroke of luck, he thought to himself as the conversation continued. His mind was already working overtime, wondering how this information, if passed on to the right people, would further his rise up the pecking order in the camp. Overseeing and supervising the outside working parties was certainly better than some of the jobs in the camp but as winter approached, he had his mind set on a nice warm office job, pushing paper and drinking hot coffee all day.

'The Allied troops have entered Germany, according to the reports from the BBC.'

'Get away.'

'They have, at a place called Aachen. And the Germans and the Japs are surrendering for fun.'

The second prisoner whistled as he fingered and stared at the cigarette containing the news. 'So it's true. This war really is coming to an end.'

'It looks that way, pal. It looks that way.'

Andrezj Netzer shook the last drops of urine from his penis and buttoned up his flies. He waited quietly as the prisoners bade each other farewell and moved away.

Horace and Rose began to make plans for the end of the war. They hadn't made love that evening; Rose was too full of excitement and planning. They lay in the church just talking. For once they were fully clothed.

'New Zealand.'

'What?' Horace replied.

'New Zealand,' Rose continued. 'We can go to New Zealand. My father said the government of New Zealand are making plans for the end of the war. It's a big country and they are encouraging farmers to work the land.'

Without realising, Horace was nodding. Rose was in full flow.

'You have farmed before, Horace. We could apply.'

Horace never heard the next few sentences; his mind was far away. He had dreams of a sheep farm and a wife and children and a beautiful climate, and peace. They'd discussed the end of the war many times. He wanted to be with Rose – he wanted to be with her forever – but he'd always wondered, where would they live? Taking a German Silesian girl back to England was impossible. For five years the Germans had brought terror to his country. They'd bombed and shot and slaughtered. How many families in Ibstock had lost sons, daughters, fathers and mothers, uncles and aunts? His fellow

243

countrymen wouldn't understand, especially in a small village the size of Ibstock.

He could not take Rose back to England.

What of Silesia? Could they make a home there? It was too uncertain. It was not clear what sort of retribution the Russians would demand from the German population, and would they class the Silesians as the same? Rose had worked in the camp; her father was the owner. As far as the Russians were concerned she was one of them. It didn't bear thinking about. Horace had heard the rumours on the grapevine about what the Russians were doing with the German population. Soldiers or civilians, there was no distinction. Stories were filtering through of mass slaughter, hangings, torture and gang rape. A shiver ran the length of Horace's spine.

'You're not listening to me, are you? Rose said angrily.

'I'm thinking about New Zealand, that's why.' Horace pulled her down on the rug and kissed her. He slipped his hand up her skirt, found the thin material of her panties and massaged her clitoris with his forefinger. She moaned for a split second then took his wrist and pulled it free.

She broke the kiss. 'You are truly thinking about New Zealand, Jim?'

'I am.'

'You want to live with me forever and give me lots of babies?'

'I do.'

Rose smiled. 'I love you so much, Jim Greasley.'

'I love you too, my English Rose.'

Andrezj Netzer could barely contain his excitement as he walked through the camp gates of Oflag VIII Oberlangendorf. Without hesitation he went straight to the commandant's office. A middle-aged sergeant looked up from the desk.

Netzer was aware of that look, the sort of look most Germans gave him. The sort of look that said he was a piece of shit they'd scraped off their shoe. After what he was about to disclose they would no longer look at him like that.

Horace lay on his bunk wide awake. He hadn't slept a wink and had watched the moon creep slowly across the sky. It was a cold clear evening; the constellations of the stars of Orion, the Plough, and the Great Bear were clearly visible. During his time in the camp he'd learned to read the sky well and calculated that it was around three in the morning. He'd listened to the news that evening and heard of the Russian advance through Prussia, Poland, Hungary and, yes, Silesia. It was good news, but his thoughts were with Rose. For some reason he couldn't quite put his finger on, he wished it were the Americans who were marching through Silesia.

He gazed out over the forest and sat up as he picked out a tiny beam of light three or four kilometres in the distance. The light came nearer. Despite the cold of the evening Horace became aware of perspiration on his forehead and a warm sticky feeling gluing his shirt to his back. The single beam of light turned into two… car headlights, then another, and another. Eight cars powered their way into the compound. Within minutes the German guards had run around to the front of the camp, unaware and unsure who was coming in at this unearthly hour. They feared the worst – Americans? Russians? Had that awful day had dawned at last?

No. There were no trucks full of soldiers, no tanks or heavy artillery. They were SS staff cars and Horace knew instinctively they were here to search for a radio. It was a well-executed and brutal exercise, designed to show the prisoners there was still plenty of fight left in the German war machine. The SS went into the barracks and the staff quarters heavy handed and noisily. Any prisoner a little slow in responding to the early morning alarm call would be kicked out of bed and receive several blows from the butt of a rifle. It took no more than three minutes before every prisoner in the camp stood outside in the cold October air of Silesia, some in little more than a vest and underpants.

A large, evil-looking SS officer with a dark moustache began speaking.

'Prisoners of the Fatherland, we are here tonight to right a few wrongs. We are not stupid and we know that a communications network has been set up in one of the camps in the area. We have reason to believe it is here at Freiwaldau.'

Horace glanced across at Jock Strain and next-in-line Jimmy White. Horace hoped that he was not looking as frightened as they were, though he suspected he was.

'Keep calm,' a voice whispered. It was Flapper. 'They know fuck all, they're only guessing.'

'Pretty good guess,' Horace retorted.

The officer continued. He pulled out a sheet of paper. 'First, we must tell you the way the war is going. You have been receiving nonsense from your country. They would have you believe that the army of the glorious German Fatherland is on the run.'

The officer let out a forced laugh. The minor ranks around him smiled on cue; one or two of them laughed along with the officer.

'Nothing could be further from the truth, you stupid English dogs.'

The officer pulled out a pair of glasses from his pocket and put them on. He peered over the top of the lenses at the assembled prisoners. 'This news comes from an intercepted American broadcast.' He looked up again and smiled. 'This is not German propaganda; it comes from your own side.

'Germany has put down the Warsaw uprising while the so-called glorious Russian Army stood by and watched.'

He read from a list. It was brief and succinct and gave a wholly different opinion from that which Horace had been hearing from the BBC over recent weeks. He tried hard to block out the officer's voice but the events he was relaying had happened; he'd heard them with his own ears but from a British perspective.

'We are winning the battle of Debrecan against your Russian allies.' He paused, looked up. 'You had better hope that you never ever meet a Russian soldier. They are worse than animals and kill and fuck anything that moves. They are truly devils sent from hell.' He went back to the paper. 'Our Japanese friends are winning the battle of Leyte Gulf and have gained control of the Pacific Ocean.'

The German officer spoke for ten minutes. He delivered his speech well and a few murmurs of discontent reverberated in the still, cool air.

It's all lies, Horace wanted to shout out, German propaganda. But then again, what if it really had come from the Americans? That would mean the BBC had been broadcasting lies and the war wasn't coming to an end. Horace's mind was in turmoil until he looked at the German guards. They weren't smiling, weren't sticking their chests out proudly. They had the same dejected look on their faces as they'd had for several weeks. Horace smiled, kicked Jock's ankle discreetly and nodded his head in the direction of two German guards.

'Look,' he whispered quietly. 'Look at those fuckers, they don't believe him either.' Jock looked over and Horace watched as a smile replaced the frown he'd worn earlier. In a bizarre relay game, prisoner upon prisoner was kicked, poked or prodded and made aware of the look on their captors' faces. At that moment Horace understood that the real news coming in each night from London simply had to continue finding its way to the 3000 Allied prisoners in the region.

The SS lined up outside the main sleeping barracks of Oflag VIII G Freiwaldau. The officer signalled and in they went. The prisoners could see them through the open windows, their uniforms lit up from the dim lights in the hut. They trashed the entire barracks. Bunks were broken, mattresses and pillows torn open and the personal belongings of the prisoners were brought out into the compound. Letters from home, photographs, books, magazines and rations from Red Cross parcels were all placed in a big pile before being doused in petrol and set alight.

Inside, the SS were still busy, ripping out shelves and punching in the panels above the prisoners' beds. One of the German guards was systematically destroying sections of the false ceiling with the butt of his rifle.

Horace feared the worst.

Someone whispered, 'Stay calm, Jim.'

Horace was aware that the eyes of a hundred prisoners were trained on him. Everyone in the camp knew that the radio was housed in a panel above his bed. Everyone knew he'd got the parts into the camp, it was his responsibility and he'd insisted the radio was to be built into his section of the wall.

The SS and the camp guards made their way back into the compound. They'd found nothing.

The officer held a two-minute meeting with one of his underlings then nodded in the direction of the prison staff quarters. His troops and the guards moved quickly towards the open door. Horace swore his legs were about to give up the fight. The SS officer placed his hands behind his back, smiled at the prisoners and followed his troops into the hut.

Horace closed his eyes. The noise of the staff quarters being systematically torn apart was bad enough as he envisaged the scene inside. He heard the bunks being turned upside down and the mattresses being split with a knife. Worse still was the splinter of wood coming from the panels and the ceiling. The total destruction lasted no more than five minutes and then an eerie silence ensued. As the guards and the SS made their way out in to the darkness, Horace noticed one or two had smiles on their faces.

They had found something.

Last out was the German SS officer. He stood in the doorway and looked along the line of the assembled prisoners. He looked angry. Taking a deep breath, he bellowed at the top of his voice: 'Bring me the barber!'

Horace swayed one way then the other, on the point of collapse. This was it – his number was up. Two German guards took him by the arms and frogmarched him towards the entrance of the hut. The radio had been found, found above his bed. He would be shot, but what about the others? Incredibly, right at this moment he was thinking of others. He thought about his roommates. What would happen to them? Would they be implicated too? He thought of Rose. They'd want to know his supplier.

Right there and then he made a suicidal decision. He couldn't take the chance of interrogation; he loved Rose too much for that. He was strong, a stubborn bastard, Flapper and Jock and the rest of the lads would always say, but just how strong and how stubborn was he? He couldn't take the chance of breaking under interrogation and revealing Rosa's name. On his way out of the hut he'd break free and make a run for the forest. He'd be cut down in a hail of bullets and Rose would be safe. His English Rose... safe.

Horace was physically dragged to his bunk and ordered to

stand to attention. The SS officer had lost his temper and stood no more than three or four inches from his face, shouting and cursing. Horace looked over his shoulder.

The shelf and the panelling were intact.

'You filthy fucking English *Scheißer!*'

Horace looked at the overfilled tin can of cigarettes and the ash and discarded butts on the shelf. There were chocolate papers and a mouldy tin of bully beef. He watched as a fly made its way over a crumb of stale bread. A sticky patch of some unknown dried liquid covered the far end next to the window.

'*Hurensohn* – son of a whore – never in my life have I seen such a filthy bastard as you!'

The shelf remained untouched, the German officer refusing to let his men come into contact with such filth, such grime. The SS man cuffed Horace across the cheek and he fell to the floor. Never had he been so pleased to receive such a blow to the face.

His plan had worked. He looked around at the sheer wanton vandalism that had been carried out on his colleagues' beds and their surrounding area. His bunk remained untouched. The shelf hadn't been moved an inch and the panels that hid the equipment necessary to produce the camp journal remained in place. What tickled him more than anything was watching the SS officer standing just inches from what it was he was looking for.

The SS officer proceeded to kick and punch Horace back outside and into line, and the prisoners were made to stand in the cold for another hour. No one could quite understand why Jim Greasley stood the whole time with a smile on his face while his teeth chattered.

The radio had survived. It was business as usual.

Several weeks later in the camp at Oberlangendorf the commandant sent for his next in command. 'I have a job for you, Brecken.'

'Yes, sir.'

'I want you to accompany Andrezj Netzer and the work party into the forest today.'

'Yes, Commandant.'

'When you get a moment take Netzer deep into the forest.' The commandant paused, stroking his chin. 'Tell him you have a special job for him, make him feel important...' He smiled. 'He likes that.'

'Yes, Commandant.'

'And Brecken...'

'Commandant?'

'Put a bullet into the back of his head and leave him to the wolves.'

CHAPTER
TWENTY

H orace lay on his bunk. He was having one of those reflective moments, the sort of moment that all prisoners go through. He had been imprisoned for four and a half years... years that should have been the best of his life.

He'd been on the verge of manhood when he'd been sent to war without being consulted all those years ago. He'd established a successful career, discovered the fairer sex and enjoyed the weekend dances and the times with his father and mother and his siblings. He'd played football and cricket and boxed in Leicester as a youngster. He'd had so much to give, so much to see and do. Yet with the flutter of a white handkerchief it had all been taken away from him.

He'd missed four Christmases. They were always notified when it was Christmas Day and some of the prisoners kept note of the date and carried a calendar of sorts through the year. But normally in the camps one day just rolled into another. As Christmas Day was his birthday, he'd missed four birthday celebrations too. He remembered the cup of tea with whisky his father gave him every year and pictured the scene in the kitchen as his dad toasted his good health. Christmas Day in the camp was the worst day of the year for Horace Greasley.

But this year could be different. He was contemplating the craziest invitation he'd ever received: to escape and have Christmas dinner at Rosa's family home in Klimontow, a village in Silesia. It all seemed so easy as it was explained to him. Rose and her father had planned it well. The roads would be quiet on Christmas morning, she'd explained, and it was the only day of the year that the Germans didn't insist on an early morning roll call at the camp. They gave the prisoners the day off and left them very much to their own devices. Rose was right... he wouldn't be missed.

Herr Rauchbach would be waiting at the crossroads five miles from the camp. The journey to the family home would take a little over an hour and awaiting him would be a goose with all the trimmings and the finest bottle of Silesian wine. They'd start with a traditional fish salad and finish with Christmas pudding and chocolates.

A family Christmas, thought Horace, more than likely a fire in the hearth and perhaps even a drop of whisky. He'd need to try and think of a gift for Rose. Nothing to think of really: he had six squares of chocolate left from his last Red Cross parcel – that was it.

But other thoughts also crossed his mind. Why go back to the camp after the day's festivities? The war was all but over, or so they'd been told by the BBC. Even the British Home Guard had been told to stand down, such was the lack of threat from the now toothless German war machine, and the Japanese were increasingly turning to kamikaze tactics, a sure sign of desperation.

Worse was wondering what the reaction of the German commandant and his command would be when they finally received the news that they'd been dreading, that the war was lost. Why spare the prisoners' lives? Why hand them over to the Russians or Americans or the Red Cross? Surely such an exercise was fraught with danger? Taking the prisoners out into the forest and disposing of them would be the easiest course of action.

Horace thought back to the night of the radio search and the Germans burning all the prisoners' personal effects. Head it simply been forward planning, denying that the prisoners had even been there? Had Horace's many letters even arrived home?

The more he thought about it the more the Rauchbach household appealed. Why not hide there for a month or two?

It was 7am on 23 December 1944. Horace called a private meeting with his closest friends prior to the morning's roll call. Jock Strain, Flapper, Freddie Rogers and David Crump sat on the floor of the staff quarters, all suspecting what Horace was about to announce.

The men sat in resigned silence as Horace made clear his intentions. In one way it was another sign that the war was without a doubt coming to an end. The prisoners knew it, as did the family of Horace's girlfriend, and every one of the prisoners had witnessed the change in the guards. After Horace had made the announcement his friends said very little. The men went out onto parade and afterwards resumed their usual work roles. Horace walked over to the makeshift barbershop with lead in his boots and a heavy heart.

The cigarettes containing the previous evening's news were distributed as normal. Freddie Rogers and David Crump were on an outside party four kilometres from the camp. They had talked little of their good friend's imminent departure and eased the moment by handing out more cigarettes than was normal. It had come to the attention of two German guards.

'They hand cigarettes out like presents, Brecken.'

Sergeant Brecken stood watching the two prisoners. 'Yes,

they are feeling generous. They know they do not have many days left. But if you notice they receive cigarettes from the same men a few days later.'

The guard, Froud, furrowed his brow. 'And what does that mean, exactly?'

Brecken shrugged his shoulders. 'It means they are playing at being home when cigarettes were in plentiful supply. They are trying to re-enact their Friday and Saturday nights in their towns and cities in England. They are giving Christmas presents. They are not giving them away, Froud, they are simply playing give and take... happy friends. It's an act, a charade.'

'Herr Feldwebel, I would...'

The senior man from the camp held up a hand. 'Silence. I have more important things to deal with than worrying about Englishmen giving out cigarettes.'

Brecken slung his rifle onto his shoulder and walked over to Freddie Rogers and David Crump. A Silesian man was begging for a cigarette but Rogers and Crump were flatly refusing.

'Why do you not give this man the gift of tobacco, prisoner?' Brecken asked Freddie Rogers.

'He is not my friend, sir,' Rogers replied without thinking for a second. 'I have not seen him before. I only give cigarettes to my friends.'

The German's theory that the prisoners were playing out a game was confirmed. He turned to the Silesian.

'Come, Netzer, come with me into the forest. I have a special assignment for you.'

'A special job?' Andrezj Netzer stuttered. A smile crept across his face. 'Yes, sir. Straight away, sir.'

The German walked away into the forest and the Silesian scuttled after him. Brecken stroked the butt of his rifle as if it were a small puppy. His finger momentarily located the trigger before checking that the safety lock had been disengaged.

Christmas morning 1944. After another flawless escape Horace lay shivering in the fringe of the forest looking back at the camp. He studied the barrack room and the staff quarters and the window he'd used to such good effect in the past two years.

Everything seemed so quiet. Flapper had already replaced the bars. Horace watched as two cold, bored and hungry-looking guards passed the window without even looking up. He thought about the good and not so good times he'd shared with Flapper and Jock and the rest of the lads sleeping soundly in their beds, looking forward perhaps to their last Christmas morning under German control.

He had left the escape till later than usual, just after 5.30, giving plenty of cover of darkness before the sun came up. The meeting with Rose would take place at 6.30, two kilometres from the camp on the main road out.

Rose stood silhouetted in the darkness, a solitary figure stamping her feet occasionally, trying desperately to ward off the cold. He watched her for a couple of minutes as she peered down the road in the direction of the camp. He crept up on her from the forest and threw his arms around her. She gave out a little squeal as he turned her around and kissed her. She broke the embrace quickly.

'Come quickly, Father is waiting.' She took his hand and began to walk away.

Horace made no attempt to move; she was aware of the resistance immediately. She looked deep into his sad eyes and knew. Her own tears started before she spoke.

'What is it, Jim? Talk to me.'

Horace shook his head. 'I cannot come, Rose, you know that.'

'But why, Jim? Please, we...'

He held a finger to her lips as a tear fell to the ground.

'You know why.'

'No, I don't... tell me.'

Horace sighed, took her hand and walked slowly up the road. 'I must see your father and thank him, but I won't place you at risk any more than I've already done.'

'No, Jim. I... We...'

Horace interrupted. 'You've loved me more than any woman could ever love a man and every time we've met or made love I've placed you under a death sentence.'

Rose was shaking her head, sobbing loudly now as the realisation sank in that they would not be spending their first normal day together.

'Our love has survived the impossible and one day I will tell the world about it.' He stopped and turned her to face him, took her two hands in his. He watched as a tear trickled down her cheek and he leaned forward to kiss her. She turned her face away in an attempt to show her disapproval.

Horace waited.

She looked back at him. 'I love you, Jim... I want to be with you today of all days.'

'I know you do and I want to be with you too,' Horace continued, 'but I won't place your family in danger. One day I will tell the world all about my English Rose. I will tell them how pretty she is and how kind and generous she is and how special it was each time we made love. I will tell them about the little church in the forest and the rabbits and the hens and I will tell them how my English Rose fed my friends and supplied radio parts that kept three thousand men happy.'

'We are reaching three thousand prisoners?' she asked with a puzzled look on her face.

'We are,' Horace replied proudly with a beaming smile. 'We worked the numbers out last night.'

Rose shook her head. Horace pulled her to him and her arms wrapped around his back. She buried her face in his chest as he stroked at her hair.

'In my book I will tell the world how she made a difference. And I will tell anyone that will listen to me that she did all that because she loved me.'

She looked up into his eyes. 'And how to you propose to tell the world all that, you damned stupid stubborn Englishman?'

Horace looked up. Dawn had painted the sky a dusty winter pink and for once he felt real freedom. At first he couldn't put his finger on it and then it came to him.

'Listen.'

Rose looked up. 'What is it?'

'Can't you hear?'

'Hear what?'

Horace smiled and pointed. 'Look...'

A tiny red-breasted robin sat on the road sign barely four feet away as if taking in the whole scene. It chirped and sang and cocked its head from one side to another and made no attempt to fly off.

Rose smiled. 'It's beautiful.'

'It's free,' Horace replied.

Horace and Rose stood in silence for two minutes while the tiny creature continued with its early morning chorus. Eventually it flew off into the forest. Rose punched him playfully in the stomach. 'You haven't answered my question.'

'What?'

'How do you propose to tell the world our story?'

Horace thought for a moment.

'I will write a book. It will be the greatest love story ever written.'

Rose laughed. 'You're a dreamer, Jim Greasley... a bloody dreamer.'

Horace took her hand again and started to walk. He had the idea of a book firmly in his head; the images and memories were so clear. The only thing that was missing was the ending.

Rauchbach understood. It was a surreal meeting, a prisoner, the owner of a German prisoner of war camp and his daughter, who'd been having a three-year sexual affair with that same prisoner. Only once did Rauchbach ask Horace to reconsider. The man and ultimately his daughter would come to respect the decision.

Horace made the long journey back to the camp. The landscape seemed to dissolve out of the dawn. He watched his boots and the road in front of him, not even bothering to hide in the forest any more. Each step placed a greater distance between him and Rose, between him and a normal family Christmas dinner. Horace and normality. With each footfall that crunched on the thin film of snow, he regretted the decision to return to captivity.

CHAPTER
TWENTY-ONE

Each night Ivan went to bed with the images of Auschwitz as fresh in his head as if it were yesterday. The job of liberating each camp was supposed to have been an honour.

General-leytenant Karpov, in charge of the 322nd Rifle Division, had stood proudly, four miles from the camp in Silesia. He had warned his troops of the atrocities committed in the camp but said they would cope and that the prisoners would welcome them like heroes. Ivan watched the faces of his comrades. They were smiling, some looked proud, others relieved that this damn war was ending. Was he the only one not smiling? Even General-leytenant Karpov, a man who never smiled, had what could loosely be described as a slight grin on his face.

Sergei wasn't smiling. Sergei was in pain. The shrapnel wound in his leg was beyond repair and the medical men had all but given up. Sergei would not be liberating the next camp at Freiwaldau; he would be on a wagon heading for the hospital in Prague. Ivan wiped at the sweat on Sergei's brow. He was concerned: it was freezing cold and Sergei shouldn't be sweating.

Sergei had been his close comrade right through the war and had held him like a son when they'd encountered the horrors of Auschwitz and he'd broken down and cried like a small boy. It had all seemed so innocuous as they'd walked through the gates. A sign hung above the camp that read *Arbeit Macht Frei* – work makes (one) free.

The SS had massacred most of the prisoners before the Red Army had come into the camp, and 20,000 more had been sent on a death march. The 7,500 prisoners left were the most pathetic, wretched souls Ivan had ever seen, their sunken, shallow eyes devoid of any hope. They had simply been left behind to die. The SS thought it unnecessary to waste a bullet on them. Some were so weak they were unable to speak. The Red Army would find upwards of a million items of clothing, evidence of the scale of the Nazi massacre in Auschwitz alone. Most victims were killed in the gas chambers but many were also killed by systematic starvation, lack of disease control, forced labour, and individual executions for little or no reason. A Jewish prisoner told of one SS officer who executed two or three prisoners each day as target practice from an office high above the camp.

The Russians would also find documents buried in the grounds, detailing the mass extermination of Jews, Poles and Romany gypsies. Worse still, the papers would name and shame the so-called doctors in the camp. The Nazi doctors at Auschwitz had performed a wide variety of experiments on the helpless, defenceless prisoners.

General-leytenant Karpov, a man fluent in several languages, would read the letters to his disbelieving troops. He would tell them how SS doctors tested the efficiency of X-rays as a sterilisation device by administering large doses to the female prisoners. Dr Carl Clauberg was accused of injecting chemicals into women's uteruses in an effort to glue them shut. They used prisoners routinely as guinea pigs for testing new drugs.

The worst was yet to come. An emaciated Pole, in a voice

barely above a whisper, told Karpov the story of a doctor called Mengele, the 'angel of death'. Karpov translated his account word by word. Mengele was particularly interested in research on identical twins. He induced diseases in one twin and killed the other when the first died. He was simply curious to examine the different autopsies. He took a special interest in dwarves and the mentally handicapped. The Pole told how he had worked in Mengele's office and that his paperwork detailed how he injected the prisoners with gangrene simply to study the effects. It was at this point that Karpov announced there would be no quarter given to any German they found, military or otherwise, and they were to be beaten then shot on the spot. He finished by telling his comrades that shooting an SS stormtrooper would be too good for them. The men in black would be spared the bullet: much worse lay in store for them.

Sergei spoke. 'My leg, Ivan.' He lifted the dirty material, exposing a gaping wound. 'It stinks like the fucking arsehole of a dog.'

Ivan gagged as the aroma hit the back of his throat. 'It isn't too bad, Sergei,' he lied. 'I have smelled worse, and tomorrow you will be in a hospital bed in Prague with a pretty Czech nurse washing your cock.'

Sergei smiled. 'I hope so, comrade... I hope so.'

Ivan recalled how Sergei had suffered his injury. The sight of children's clothing had brought Ivan to tears. As they'd searched the camp for survivors, the skeletons and mass graves were discovered. The small bones of the boys and girls had rendered him hopeless. Sergei had approached General-leytenant Karpov and was given permission to take him out of the camp. Ivan blamed himself when their convoy was attacked by long-range German artillery and Sergei had been injured. It was a guilt he would carry with him for the rest of his life.

CHAPTER
TWENTY-TWO

The news filtering over the airwaves was welcomed by the prisoners, as it told of the liberation of the extermination and concentration camps at Auschwitz and Plaszow and many POW camps such as Sagan and Gross Tychow. The men in Freiwaldau wondered when their turn would come.

Horace listened carefully as the news hinted at the revenge being carried out by Russian soldiers. It seemed nobody was spared and a mass exodus of German civilians was on the run from the bitter Red Army. Incredible as it seemed, they were running to the Americans.

On 20 March 1945 Horace met Rose. Their after-war plans were not discussed; New Zealand and sheep farms and babies were not on the agenda. Horace was persuading Rose to run for her life. He had been trying to make her see sense for weeks. This evening was different. Horace was adamant he wouldn't break out of the camp again. He knew she would not join the exodus as long as he continued to meet her. This was their last meeting and Rose knew it.

'I will go,' she announced, just a few minutes into their meeting. 'I will run to the Americans, but only if you come with me.'

'No, Rose, no!' he cried. 'It's too dangerous. The place is teeming with German soldiers on the run making their way back to Berlin, Hamburg and Dusseldorf. If we are caught together we'll be shot on the spot. You must take your chance alone. You can...'

She was crying again as she interrupted. 'But we can help each other, we can...'

'No, Rose. As soon as a German hears me speak he'll know I'm an escapee and he'll think nothing of putting a bullet into me. Is that what you want?'

It was a cruel but necessary blow, anything that would make her see sense. Horace knew that if they were caught together it would mean a bullet for the escapee and one for the collaborator – after the Germans had had their fun with her. He wanted so much to take his chance with her, felt sure between them they'd probably make it. But probably wasn't good enough. On their own they'd stand a better chance.

He held her shoulders, tried to make eye contact. 'Look at me, Rose. I won't meet you again, do you hear? You must go to the Americans. Please... tell me you'll go the Americans.'

It was barely a nod – hard to distinguish between the trembling and the sobbing – nevertheless it was a slight nod of the head.

Horace lifted her forcibly from the ground as he wrapped his arms tightly around her. He was so relieved. They kissed and hugged and sobbed as the two of them broke down and the tears fell to the forest floor. The decision had been made. There was no going back.

'It's for the best,' he explained as he handed her a note with his address in Ibstock. 'As soon as you can you must write and tell me where you are.'

'We can be together, Jim?'

'Yes, of course we can. The war will be over in weeks and I'll come for you.'

'But you do not know where I will be.'

'You'll tell me.'

'Yes, I will tell you where I am.'

Rose hesitated. 'You will come, Jim, won't you?'

Horace leaned forward and kissed her gently on the forehead. 'I will come for you, my English Rose. Wherever you are I will come, even if I have to walk there barefoot over broken glass.'

'My mother and father are staying in Silesia to take their chances with the Russians.'

'No... no! Surely not, Rose?'

'They are too long in the tooth. My mother was born in the village, my grandmother is nearly 70 and barely able to walk, she lives only three doors away.'

'But your father, he was in charge of...'

'The camp, yes I know. It is hoped the Russians do not find out. He will tell them we are Silesians, not Germans. They will survive.'

Horace and Rose sat and talked for most of the night, and made love as the dawn tugged at the top of the forest trees. His orgasm seemed to last for an eternity. Rose noticed too as she felt his ejaculation explode inside her again and again.

'Where did all that come from?' she asked with a smile. Horace grinned and said it was down to the extra rations.

They watched the sun come up. Horace was in no hurry to get back to the camp. The security had been scaled down dramatically; it was as if the Germans were no longer concerned whether men escaped or not. The night patrols had become sporadic to say the least and the roll calls that had been part of daily life for nearly five years had stopped altogether.

Rose looked at her watch. 'It's nearly 7.30. You must be going.'

She spoke gently in German. Horace didn't stop her. '*Ich moechte mein ganzes Leben mit dir verbringen, so gerne mit dir alt werden.*' Horace picked up the words, understood the meaning. She wanted to spend her whole life with him, wanted them to grow old together and in her fragile, desperate state had drifted into the language she'd known from childhood, the language the Germans had forced her ancestors to speak.

Horace nodded silently, aware of the tears forming in his eyes. He had known this moment would come eventually but it didn't make it any easier. What a crazy turn of events. The war was won and the Allies victorious, he would be a free man any day and yet the woman he loved, the woman who had achieved so much, the woman who had made the difference, was running in the opposite direction in fear of her life.

March 1945
The Soviet army marches towards Berlin.
Patton's troops capture Mainz in Germany.
US and British forces cross the Rhine at Oppenheim.
Montgomery's troops cross the Rhine at Wesel
The Red Army enters Austria.
The Allies capture Frankfurt.
It is clear the German Army is under attack from all sides; the soldiers are in general retreat.

April 1945
Ohrdruf death camp is liberated by the Allies.
Heavy bombing at Kiel by the RAF destroys the last two major German warships.

Bergen-Belsen is liberated by the British Army. One of the first on the scene is the BBC reporter Richard Dimbleby. He wrote:

> *Here over an acre of ground lay dead and dying people. You could not see which was which ... The living lay with their heads against the corpses and around them moved the awful, ghostly procession of emaciated, aimless people, with nothing to do and with no hope of life, unable to move out of your way, unable to look at the terrible sights around them ... Babies had been born here, tiny wizened things that could not live ... A mother, driven mad, screamed at a British sentry to give her milk for her child, and thrust the tiny mite into his arms, then ran off, crying terribly. He opened the bundle and found the baby had been dead for days.*
>
> *This day at Belsen was the most horrible of my life.*

The Soviet Army reaches the suburbs of Berlin.

Still the prisoners of war at Freiwaldau wait for their liberation.

Hitler swears an oath to stay in Berlin and head up the defence of the city.

Himmler, ignoring the orders of Hitler, makes a secret surrender offer to the Allies.

The 1st Belorussian front and the 1st Ukrainian front of the Russian Red Army encircle Berlin.

30 April 1945

Hitler and his wife of 24 hours, Eva Braun, commit suicide.

Goebbels and his wife kill their six children then take poison in the same bunker.

CHAPTER
TWENTY-THREE

The German guards roused the prisoners just after three in the morning. They were ordered to prepare to evacuate the camp. Thirty minutes later they had left the compound and were walking up the road alongside the forest that Horace was so familiar with. They passed the spot where he had stood with Rose on Christmas morning. He looked for the robin but it was nowhere to be seen.

The men were unusually subdued; they were in unknown territory as the march snaked silently along the twisting road. Horace had noticed some of the guards had gone; they were not with them on the march. The officers had disappeared and the sergeants too, and the camp commandant was nowhere to be seen either. He wondered what it all meant. The longer they marched the more reassured he felt that they were walking to freedom. If the guards had wanted to shoot them they would have taken them into the forest beside the camp and massacred them there. There was simply no reason to march them mile after mile for no reason.

One or two of the men were posing the question to the guards. This would have been unheard of a few months ago. Even so, the guards were giving nothing away. Horace got the distinct feeling they were just as much in the dark as the prisoners were. After an hour or so they reached the crossroads where Horace had spoken with Herr Rauchbach. The German guards told them to rest for a while as they took on water and had a smoke. The prisoners' mouths remained dry; no provision had been made for the prisoners, such was their haste to leave.

They marched hour after hour, mostly on the roads but occasionally the guards forced them into a forest or across a field. They marched past breakfast time and lunchtime too, but still no food and water came from their captors. A few of the prisoners had saved a few squares of chocolate from their Red Cross parcels or a biscuit or two which they tried as best they could to share with their colleagues. Flapper munched on an onion like an apple. He had taken what little was left from the vegetable patch and shared it out among the prisoners. Horace ate dandelion leaves once more and passed the news along the line about the goodness and nutrition in each leaf.

The German guards didn't fare much better as they nibbled on ration packs of biscuits and chocolate. Occasionally they would brew up a coffee and hand out packs of wrapped sandwiches. Not once did they make any attempt to offer any to the prisoners. Early that afternoon the roar of an aeroplane overhead forced the entire march onto its stomach. Horace swore it flew just a few feet over his head as he looked up and saw the Russian pilot take stock of the situation. The plane banked and swooped down again, this time peeling off about half a mile from the stranded men. He'd heard the stories of friendly fire, particularly where the Americans were concerned. This time he needn't have worried.

The plane flew past them, banked steeply and the roar of its engines filled the sky. Horace figured it was about three miles to the east as it swooped into a steep dive. It was then that they all noticed the focus of its attention. A German train laden with troops, tanks and an array of vehicles, too far away to be heard or even noticed by the prisoners and guards, crept slowly along the track on the long retreating road to Berlin. The Ilyushin 2 Shturmovik attacked the train with a faint roar from its 7.62mm machine guns and 30mm cannons. Another roar this time as the prisoners voiced their approval. The guards stood back and watched the spectacle unfold. They did nothing.

Time and time again the Ilyushin 2 Shturmovik banked away and returned. The crew were accurate and sparing with each round as the German troops on board tried in vain to bring the plane down. Four or five separate plumes of smoke rose from the stricken train. It had come to a halt. The Russian pilot turned away, happy with the result. He flew directly above the line of prisoners, most of whom were now on their feet waving and cheering the plane. As the Russian pilot approached the assembled group of prisoners he performed a victory roll and disappeared from view over the forest that lined the road. It was the last they'd see of him. A few of the German guards cursed and swore but made no attempt to remonstrate with their captives. The other guards were visibly sullen, quiet... resigned to defeat and acutely aware they were in the last few days of the conflict.

By nightfall the men were exhausted. That awful empty feeling inside that Horace remembered so well was with him again. It was with him again at breakfast time and at lunchtime the following day. The prisoners were getting restless and several talked openly about overpowering the guards and making their own way to the Russian lines. The German guards looked decidedly uncomfortable and their fingers hovered and twitched nervously oh, so close to the triggers of their rifles. It was only a matter of time before someone cracked.

The makings of a mutiny were put on hold later that afternoon as the Germans made an announcement. They had decided to make camp near a small farmhouse by the side of the road. It looked deserted, as if the occupants had decided to leave in a hurry. The Germans said the prisoners were free to roam the farmhouse to search for food. They posted seven or eight guards on the perimeter of the farm with rifles cocked. Feldwebel, the German sergeant, gave notice that the guards on duty had been given clear instructions to shoot to kill any man who attempted escape. Horace was aware of the desperation in his voice. The situation had turned, and at that very moment Horace knew their captors would not hold them much longer. He feared the desperation of the situation; the tension in the air could be cut with a knife. The prisoners made a point of smiling and joking when in earshot of the guards. It all added to the strained atmosphere.

Jock Strain walked up to Horace with a big smile on his face.

'You used tae bide on a farm, Jim, didn't ye?'

'I did that, Jock. Why? What's up?'

'The lads have found a pig with a litter of wee piglets and they're ravenous.'

'What, the piglets?'

'No the men, they...'

'I know it's the lads, you silly Scotch bugger,' Horace laughed. He climbed to his feet, the idea of pork already playing with his sense of smell. 'You get the fire prepared and I'll find a knife.'

Horace found an old boning knife in what looked like a makeshift repair shop at the back of the farmhouse. The memories of his father's instruction to him as a 14-year-old had faded but quickly returned as he sent four of the piglets to meet their maker and went to work on preparing the small bodies for the fire. Another butcher from Derbyshire took great pleasure in helping him and within the hour the piglets were being spit-roasted on an open fire. The smell was like heaven on earth. He closed his eyes. The smell took Horace back into the small kitchen of 101 Pretoria Road, Ibstock. He was with Mum and Dad, Sybil and Daisy... he opened his eyes, smiled at Jock Strain holding a makeshift plate and a fork he'd found in a kitchen drawer in the farmhouse.

'It'll be another hour or so yet, Jock. Can you wait? Don't want you to be getting food poisoning now, do we?'

Jock grinned. 'Sure, Jim. I can wait, though I doubt with the shite I've eaten over the last five years that a bit of raw meat would dae me any harm.'

'Maybe not, Jock, but best to wait.'

Jock's smile disappeared as a German corporal seemed to appear mysteriously through the smoke of the fire. His rifle hung menacingly across his shoulder and he smiled as he spoke in broken English.

'Smells good, *ja?*'

Horace spoke in his best German. '*Es riecht wunderbar*' – It smells wonderful.

The corporal pawed nervously at the butt of his rifle as he broke into his native tongue. '*Ich habe Anweisung von dem Feldwebel, ein Schweinchen fuer unser Essen mitzunehmen*' – the sergeant has instructed me to take one piglet for us to eat.

Horace stood and took a step forward. The flames licked menacingly at his boots as he peered through the smoke. He gritted his teeth, held the bloody knife up in front of his face and roared at the startled man.

'*Sag dem Hurensohn, er bekommt nichts*' – Tell the son of a whore he gets nothing.

Flapper took a step forward and positioned himself to the left hand side of Horace. Jock came from the other side with his fork held out in front of him as the German started trembling. He tried to regain his composure but it was hopeless. His facial muscles twitched. He tried to control them but the little operating levers and pulleys disobeyed the commands from the brain. He wanted to stand firm but was hardly battle-hardened and strong, having spent the whole of the war patrolling prisoner of war camps two or three miles from his home village. He took a step back and pointed his finger at Flapper. 'You will all be shot, *Arschloecher*!' – arseholes!

As he turned around and hurried away Horace called after him. '*Wichser*!'

Jock looked at him.

'What does that mean, Jim?'

Horace grinned. 'I told him he's a wanker.'

'Your German is very good, Jim.' It was Freddie Rogers. 'But I'm afraid you might just have upset them a little. We'd better be careful, find a few more weapons around here and prepare a little welcoming committee if we are to hold onto the ham.

'Upset them? I haven't even fucking started,' Horace replied. He looked over to Jimmy White, Flapper and Jock Strain and grinned. It was a schoolboy grin, an apple-scrumping grin, a look that said 'let's see how far we can push them'.

'Jock, Jimmy, let's get the bloody radio set up and let the Germans see us do it.'

'You stupid *Arschloch*, Ernst! The Englanders will think we are scared.'

'Yes, Ernst, and we are hungry. Where is the pig?'

Corporal Ernst Bickelbacher suddenly felt very afraid. He'd expected a sympathetic ear when he returned from his confrontation with the prisoners, at least a little support. He'd expected his fellow soldiers to be angry, ready to teach the English dogs a lesson they wouldn't forget. Now it was his fault and nobody seemed in any great hurry to get off their arses. And he'd heard on the prisoners' radio that a million Russians were in Silesia liberating dozens of camps. There was no mention of what was happening to the guards of those camps but Ernst Bickelbacher could guess.

Karl Schneid spoke. 'What do you expect, sending the fucking country boys in? You should have sent a Berlin boy in.'

Karl Schneid considered himself tougher than most of these bloody backwater inbreds. At least he had seen a bit of front line action before a bullet through a kneecap forced his posting to eastern Silesia. These soft bastards would bow to anyone, he thought to himself as the hunger pains gnawed at the lining of his stomach.

Suddenly it was all too apparent to Ernst Bickelbacher. The war was lost. German against Englishman, German against Russian, and now German against German.

'You are from Berlin, Karl?'

'*Ja*! And proud of it.'

Ernst Bickelbacher smiled, stared at his one-time colleague and spoke slowly but with dramatic effect. 'Then I suggest you get back there quickly.'

Karl Schneid pulled himself to his feet. 'And why is that?'

Bickelbacher could smell Schneid's breath, stale... like he would imagine poison to smell.

'Tell me why,' Schneid demanded.

'Because the Russians are there right now, Karl, and they are having the time of their lives avenging the deaths of their countrymen.'

'No! I don't believe you.'

'It's true; I heard it on the prisoners' radio.'

'The prisoners have a radio?'

Ernst Bickelbacher nodded slowly. 'The Russians will be fucking your wife in the street as their comrades wait their turn.'

Karl Schneid lunged forward and grabbed Bickelbacher by the throat. Bickelbacher made no attempt to resist or fight back. Far better to be throttled here and now than wait for the Russians, he thought to himself as several of his fellow guards joined the mêlée.

Karl Schneid panted hard as two powerfully built colleagues held him by the arms. He stood in front of Bickelbacher and cursed and swore. Bickelbacher stood in the shadows and made no attempt to respond. He hadn't resisted, hadn't swung a punch in anger. No one seemed to notice as Bickelbacher unbuttoned the clip from the holster of his Luger. He placed the barrel in his mouth and squeezed the trigger.

Jimmy White, Jock, Flapper and Horace had managed to dismantle the radio in the few short minutes they'd been given to vacate the camp, concealing the parts around their bodies. It took no more than 15 minutes to reassemble the radio at the farm and another two minutes to tune it in. A power source and wiring had been found in a farm workshop. They didn't bother with the headphones this time. Now the radio was on loudspeaker and the reports could be heard by just about every prisoner.

There were almost three hundred Allied prisoners in and around the farmhouse that night. There were no more than 20 German guards. The prisoners found an array of various weapons: pitchforks, knives, an axe, a sledgehammer and clubs of various shapes and sizes. One of the prisoners found a box of six-inch nails and some of the men had hammered them through lumps of wood so that four inches of the nail protruded from the other end. Then the prisoners heard a shot in the distance and prepared for a German assault.

False alarm.

The prisoners took it in turns to patrol and eat, ready to call out to the others at the first sign of a German guard. The German delegation arrived after about an hour. As they walked cautiously towards the fire Horace turned the volume up to full. The diaphragm of the speaker vibrated, distorting the well-spoken tones of the presenter from London. Horace turned it down a notch or two so his voice could be heard with perfect clarity. There were eight German guards, rifles slung across their chests, held menacingly in front of them.

Horace remained seated as he chewed casually on a piece of pork. He looked up at the nervous-looking men.

'*Guten Abend, meine Herren. Das Essen ist gut heute Abend*' – Good evening, gentlemen. The food is good tonight.

'The radio is good too,' added Jimmy White, holding a rusty pitchfork. 'The Russians are all over Silesia, it says.'

Horace stood and took a few steps forward. Slowly he raised his knife to the face of the German officer. The smell of slightly overcooked meat permeated the cool night air and lingered tantalisingly on the breeze. 'Care for a piece of pork, my friend?'

Horace almost felt sorry for the man. Almost, but not quite. His position was hopeless, a few German rifles against the wrath and fury of a crudely armed mob. Unknown to him, his personal protection unit was slowly retreating behind him, leaving him exposed and vulnerable. He almost sensed it as he spoke, desperately trying to retrieve an ounce of dignity from the situation.

'My men have eaten, there is no need.' He took a step back,

tried but failed miserably to raise a smile, a last shred of dignity. 'We will leave at first light. Eat well, gentlemen. We have a long day ahead.'

As the Germans retreated, the men began a slow handclap and shouted and screamed every insult their basic German vocabulary could muster:

'*Drecksau!*' – Dirty pig!

'*Hundesohn!*' – Son of a dog!

'*Arschloch… Hurensohn… Wichser!*'

One English insult rang out. 'Bunch of cunts!' It was Flapper. He beamed, his teeth glistening in the light of the flames. 'Sorry, Jim, the old German is still a little rusty.'

'I'm sure they get the drift, Flapper,' said Horace. 'I think they'll understand.'

It was evident at first light that the Germans had already left. Freddie Rogers came back with the news. 'I've seen where they camped last night and they've scarpered, no doubt about it. We're on our own, lads.'

So what now? The prisoners simply marched along the road in the direction their German captors had been leading them the day before. The march was somewhat subdued and it unsettled Horace. It didn't make sense. They were marching on a full stomach. Bacon and eggs, the first Horace had tasted in five years. The war was undoubtedly won – the swift exit of the German guards bore testimony to that. So why weren't the men singing? Why weren't they smiling? Why wasn't Horace singing and smiling?

The crux of the matter was the great uncertainty. Were there still pockets of German resistance or aircraft in the area that wanted to take out the prisoners of the camps? Had their German captors joined forces with other regiments and units and were they simply waiting in ambush further up the road? And the Russians… What of the Russians? What were they really like? Were they the barbarians and madmen the Germans had made them out to be? Horace and his fellow prisoners were about to find out.

Three hundred yards up the road a convoy of trucks rumbled towards the line of weary Allied prisoners. A large red star could clearly be seen on the bonnet of the first truck. The Russian officer spoke good English. Sergeant Major Harris took over proceedings and introduced himself with a handshake. The Russian officer was smiling, made a point of shaking a few hands and ushered his men towards the prisoners. Only now they were prisoners no more. A few of the Russian troops offered the Allies vodka from plain glass bottles and some of the men drank freely. Horace abstained. The atmosphere was all very pleasant, not what Horace had expected at all.

Sergeant Major Harris addressed the troops, informed them they were now officially repatriated and on their way to Prague in Czechoslovakia. He said they would be split up and put in different camps depending on whether they lived in the north or the south of England, Scotland, Ireland or Wales. From there they would be put on planes and taken to the RAF base nearest to home. It was over. They were free men.

CHAPTER
TWENTY-FOUR

Horace hugged his great friends, Jock and Flapper, Freddie Rogers and Chalky White. Some of the Russian troops joined in; it was all quite bizarre and too much to bear for the majority of the men who shed tears openly. Men who'd been incarcerated for more years than they cared to remember suddenly realised their days with each other were now numbered. Men who had been sick of the sight of each other fought back the tears and clung to their last remnants of friendship. For the first time they exchanged addresses and made plans for get-togethers and reunions. Freddie Rogers invited anyone who was listening to a weekend on the Isle of Man and promised the biggest party Douglas had ever seen. Horace pledged he'd be there.

Horace was wiping the tears from his face too. But they weren't shed for his fellow sufferers; they were for his English Rose. He wondered where the hell she was and whether she was even alive.

It was a good six hours before the convoy of ten four-ton Russian lorries reached the patient men. They had waited so long for this moment. Time was no longer an issue. They'd smoked the last of their cigarettes as they sat in the early evening sunshine, eaten the last of their chocolate and biscuits from the now almost exhausted Red Cross parcels. The men were assured that food, drink and cigarettes were in abundance in Prague. As they climbed aboard the lorries, more vodka was handed out and more handshakes were forthcoming from their Russian allies.

The date was 24 May 1944. Horace had been in captivity for four years and 364 days. Five years less one day.

It would take nearly four hours to reach Prague. Several of the men got steadily drunk. It seemed that despite the rationing of cigarettes, bread and even bullets and vodka were always in plentiful supply. A few Russian soldiers had joined the Allies in the back of the four-ton truck and one led the singing. They sang for hours. One slightly built Russian sang just about every folk song in the entire history of his country. The ex-POWs interspersed his songs with their own renditions of 'I Belong to Glasgow', 'The Northern Lights of Old Aberdeen', and Flapper sang a terrible croaky version of 'Maybe It's Because I'm a Londoner'. The Welshmen sang about the hills and the valleys and a lone Irishman lamented about lonely prison walls and a young girl calling to him. He sang about the fields far away and about how nothing matters when you are free. He sang like a nightingale. Horace listened to the lyrics; the song told of a nation downtrodden, of a man sent a million miles from the only place he had ever known, away from his family, away from his home for little reason. Horace was aware of a solemn young Russian soldier with tears rolling down his cheeks as the Irishman sang to a hushed and respectful audience. As he finished, the troops broke out into a spontaneous round of applause and begged him to sing again. He declined.

It was all too much for Horace. For him there was no celebration, no songs he could draw on that told of the futility of war, of the wickedness of mankind and of humiliation, genocide and desperation. No one had penned those words; no one had composed such a song. No one sang the lyrics of a forbidden love in impossible circumstances; no words... no words.

As they approached the outer districts of Prague, half the truck wallowed in a drunken sleepy stupor while the rest seemed to struggle just to focus on the man sitting opposite. Everyone except the lone silent Russian. Horace couldn't blame the men, couldn't and wouldn't deprive them of this moment, yet it seemed he was one of very few sober persons on board.

As Horace climbed from the back of the lorry the scene that unfolded before him was like something from a horror film. Every Russian soldier appeared to be drunk – even the driver that climbed from the cab clung to a bottle of vodka. As he bounced into a lamppost Horace wondered how they'd ever made it to Prague in one piece. The streets of Prague were littered with dead or dying bodies, dead German soldiers hung from lampposts burnt to a cinder, and the smell of petrol and burning flesh lingered in the still evening air. Horace watched the tattered, blackened corpse of an SS soldier swinging eerily from a protruding metal shop sign.

'There are many Germans hiding in the city, comrade.'

It was the English-speaking Russian officer who had liberated them and who had conversed with Sergeant Major Harris.

'I will not stop them. They must have their revenge. The Germans have slaughtered my countrymen by the million.'

A group of Russian soldiers had found a young German girl cowering in a coal bunker underneath an ironmonger's shop. The name on the shop had been a giveaway: Herbert Rosch. Herbert was her father, German by birth, his wife Ingrid a native of Prague, a proud Czech. Herbert detested the Nazi regime as much as his wife did. They had fallen in love and married in 1928. Both had been burned alive from a lamppost an hour earlier as their only daughter had watched in horror from a small slit window below ground. She'd covered herself in coal trying to escape the mob but a young Russian soldier had spotted a piece of exposed flesh. Her face was blackened from the dust. She was no older than 16. The Russians threw her to her knees.

'What does she know?' cried Horace. 'She was a child when the war started. Please, make them stop!'

The Russian officer turned away as one of his sergeants began unbuttoning his trousers. His comrades cheered as he waved his large erection in front of the girl's face, his comrades ripped and clawed at the girl's clothes until she was naked. She was unceremoniously thrown across the sidecar of a motorcycle combination and two of the men forced her legs apart. As the sergeant moved in behind the screaming girl and inserted his fingers roughly into her vagina, Horace lunged towards her in a vain effort to offer some protection. From nowhere the all too familiar feeling of a rifle butt connected with his temple and he was aware of the ground rushing towards him at a speed difficult to comprehend.

When he came round an hour later, Flapper relayed the story. The sickening spectacle had sobered him up rapidly. At least 20 Russians had vented their sexual frustration and fury on the poor girl as they'd taken turns to rape her. A Russian general had eventually put her out of her misery with a bullet through the back of the skull. The onlooking crowd had cheered the execution.

'They're as bad as the Germans, Jim. You didn't see the worst of it.'

Tears streaked Garwood's face. The muck and grime from the march ran in tiny rivers down the big man's face.

'At first I thought it was just the German girls they were raping. In a strange way I could understand that. But it didn't make any difference Jim. Anything went. They raped the Germans and the Czechs, the Poles and the Slavs – and their commanders just looked on. Young and old, it didn't matter, Jim. They raped them on the pavements and in the doorways of shops and any poor bitch even suspected of having a pint of German blood in her was executed right there on the spot when she'd served her purpose.'

Garwood was crying now, sobbing like a baby.

'It wasn't supposed to be like this, Jim. It shouldn't have ended this way.'

Horace held him as his tears flowed too.

They arrived at the holding camp on the outskirts of Prague shortly after midnight. Despite fears that they'd be split up, Horace and Garwood, Jock Strain, Dave Crump and Freddie Rogers had managed to stay together. They'd be separated in a few days, they were told, so make the most of it. A Russian soldier was assigned to their billet and slept in their dormitory. It was the young man who had sat in tears on the truck that had brought them to Prague. Horace studied him as he sat on a bunk and stared into space. His eyes were sunken and hollow; they told of horror and suffering. He carried the worries of the world on his shoulders.

Horace approached him. 'You speak English, my friend.' It was a statement, not a question.

The Russian nodded. 'How did you know?'

Horace placed a hand on the man's shoulder. 'The song of the Irishman on the truck, it moved you to tears.'

The Russian stood. 'It did, comrade, it did. He sang of the free birds singing. It was beautiful... he sang like the bird in the song.'

Tears welled up in his eyes once more.

'And why does that sadden you so much?'

The Russian sighed as he paced the wooden floor. 'I have been to a place where the birds do not sing. I have been to a place called hell.'

'What is your name, soldier?

The young Russian looked up. 'Ivan... my name is Ivan.'

Things resembled normality the next morning. The Russians were sober, most nursing hangovers, and many Allied men complained about the worst headaches they could ever remember. Flapper Garwood had spent his hours of slumber in a nightmare hell reliving the events from the night before. Horace had managed to snatch just a few hours' sleep, his dreams drifting between the heavenly vision of Rose and the all too real picture of a battered, bruised and murdered teenage girl. How on earth could the exact same female form appear so different, arouse such different emotions in a man?

Then he heard it: a roll call. Would you believe it? A bloody roll call, Horace thought to himself as he stood on parade and shouted his name, regiment, rank and number to the English-speaking Russian corporal. It was to be expected, he supposed. The Russians would need to split the men into regiments or even counties in order to arrange the required number of planes to Britain.

After a huge breakfast of scrambled eggs, sausages and toast they were told they were free to roam the city but warned there might still be pockets of German resistance holed up in the suburbs. They were given a generous amount of money and told to be back in the camp by nightfall. Ivan accompanied them.

The streets were strangely quiet and there was little to do. They managed to find a few cafés with a supply of overpriced

Czech beer and a few of the men managed to seek out the numerous Czech prostitutes still doing the rounds.

Horace sat in café Milena with Freddie, Ivan, Jock, Ernie and Flapper, and nursed a small glass of beer for three hours. Jock and Freddie had upped the pace a little and Flapper was drinking like there was no tomorrow, trying to block out the memories from the night before. Ivan stuck to coffee. It was just after noon when they heard the commotion from outside. A Czech burst into the café; the barmaid relayed the gist of the conversation in broken English. Two German SS men had commandeered a Russian T34 tank. It would be their swansong, their last, suicide mission, and they were determined to kill as many Allied soldiers and destroy as much of Prague's historic architecture as possible as they blasted at anything and everything with the 85mm guns.

Russian tanks had surrounded the SS men and blocked off their avenue of retreat, but the Germans were putting up a good fight. The tank rumbled and roared towards café Milena. Horace and his friends took a step back as a frenzied mob seemed to crawl over the tank like ants on a dead fly. Incredibly, inexplicably the tank seemed to slow down.

'He's out of fuel,' Freddie Rogers offered by way of an explanation.

Sure enough, as Rogers uttered the words the tank seemed to splutter, a plume of black smoke puffed from the rear exhaust and the tank came to a halt 20 yards from the doorway of the café. The friends watched as the crowd battered and prised and jemmied at the turret of the tank, using anything and everything that would let them get to the enemy inside. Horace could only imagine the fear the SS men inside the tank would be feeling.

A cheer rang out from the crowd as the escape hatch suddenly broke free. The hands of Russian soldiers and

Czech nationals clawing at the cover peeled it back like a can of tomatoes. Three or four attackers seemed to reach inside and physically pull a man from within. As soon as his body was exposed to daylight the crowd attacked him with fists and clubs. One man used a wheel jack, blow after blow raining down on the German's skull and shoulders. He was nearly unconscious as the main body of the mob joined in with their boots.

Oberfeldwebel Lorenz Mayr was in no condition to know the horror of being burned alive. He was stripped of his SS uniform and strung from a lamppost with a rope in an undignified state of undress. As the crowd cheered, he was hauled 15 feet in the air. Blood rushed to his brain and escaped from the fractures and holes in his skull. It was all too much for him and he lapsed into an unconscious state from which he would never recover. He knew nothing of the petrol that doused his body and even less as the flames licked around it.

Then the crowd turned their attention to the other SS man cowering in the depths of the tank. Their patience was exhausted; this time they turned to the power of petrol as they poured gallon upon gallon into the small space. The crowd whooped and cheered as the terrified SS officer, soaked to the skin in combustible fuel, emerged with his hands held high in a pathetic demonstration of surrender.

Horace closed his eyes as the first match hit the German's sodden clothing. He screamed as an uncontrollable fireball erupted around him and he ran down the street. As he screamed, the mob cheered. Within ten seconds he had fallen to the pavement. He was silent. It was all over. At first Horace thought the crowd were stamping at him to put the flames out. But even after the fire had subsided they still stamped at the man, still kicked at his face and body long after he'd breathed his last breath on earth.

Ivan stood in the doorway and watched in horror. '*Мы хуже Нациста*,' – we are worse than the Nazis – he muttered to himself.

A week had passed, and most of the pockets of German resistance – the tail-enders, the desperate men who had been left behind for whatever reason – had been flushed out and murdered. The ex-POWs were getting restless now, a little agitated that the planes had still not been sent to take them home. The Russians explained that hundreds of thousands of Allied prisoners were waiting to be sent back home and they would need to be patient. There required number of aeroplanes simply wasn't available.

It was a lie. Although they didn't know it, the prisoners were being used as bargaining tools, pawns in a bizarre negotiating game. Stalin had insisted that 1.5 million Soviet prisoners of war were to be sent back to Russia. These POWs had surrendered voluntarily to the Germans; thousands had even joined the German war effort; others were simply anti-communist. Repatriation to Russia would mean certain death in the gulags, and both Churchill and Harry S Truman – the new president of the United States – had flatly refused Stalin's request. Stalin was simply biding his time as the people of Britain and America demanded to know when their men would return home.

It was 6 June 1945, the day the Allies agreed to divide Germany into four areas of control. The Russian army sent to rid Prague of the Nazis had stood down. Many were on their way to Berlin. Those remaining in the city had seemingly calmed down after three weeks of violence, rape and mass murder; some played football in the parks and streets. For the first time Horace noticed the normal people of Prague trying to rebuild their lives, going about their daily business. For the first time, the girls and women of the city ventured out onto the streets.

Ivan and Horace, Jock Strain and Flapper were walking along the banks of the Vltava river in the shadow of Hradcany Castle. It was a stiflingly hot summer day but the sun had not yet made an appearance. The river mirrored the dark grey, sinister-looking sky, and reflected the mood of the men. They were free to walk the city, to talk and eat where and when they liked, and free to come and go from their camp on the outskirts of the city at any time, as long as they were available for a roll call at nine each morning. But all the men wanted was to get back home.

Horace suspected that Ivan had his orders to watch over the men, make sure they didn't run off or attempt anything stupid. He carried his rifle at all times. The men questioned him from dawn till dusk, but it was clear to Horace he knew nothing about when exactly the Allied planes would take them back. Horace and Ivan sat down on a bench by the river and gazed out over the troubled waters that had witnessed so much death and destruction during the past few weeks.

Ivan spoke. 'I have been here since early May, in this beautiful city that the Germans have occupied for many years. I have heard the tales and the stories of the uprising and how the citizens of Prague fought the Nazis with bare hands and stolen small arms.' He paused and looked at Horace. 'And still my comrades raped and murdered them for fun.'

'It's not your fault Ivan, you mustn't blame...'

'It is my fault. It's my fault Sergei died,' he snapped, 'my fault that I did not lift a hand to stop them raping and killing, my fault... all my fault.' Ivan buried his head in his hands and the tears flowed. 'Always my fault.' He spluttered through steepled hands as his body heaved up and down through the sobs. Horace took his hand.

'It isn't your fault, Ivan, it's the fault of the playmakers, the politicians and leaders who allow normal men to commit such

288

acts. It's the fault of the captains and generals who do nothing to stop it.'

Ivan looked up. His eyes were bloodshot, the tears streaked his face and he raised a false smile. 'You are right, comrade.' His bottom lip trembled as he wiped the tears from his face. 'It isn't my fault; I didn't ask to be sent to the war.'

'Me neither,' Horace smiled, 'me neither.'

As the group of men walked away from the river, Horace asked the question.

'Tell me who Sergei was, Ivan.'

CHAPTER
TWENTY-FIVE

Two days later the same group of men found themselves on the same bench overlooking the river. It was Ivan who heard the commotion. A dozen Czech citizens were screaming and pointing across the street. 'Come quickly!' he commanded the men. 'They have spotted a Nazi in that furniture shop.'

By the time the group arrived, a large crowd of civilians had gathered at the doorway of the old store. Horace looked up at the imposing, boarded-up three-storey building as Ivan spoke to one of the citizens. The district below Hradcany Castle was in one of the more elegant parts of the city and Horace imagined the store in another, pre-war era, the successful owner reaping the rewards of a lifetime's labour – a pleasant house in a smart suburb of the city, a pretty wife and several children. What had become of the owner? he wondered, as he dragged his finger through the dust on the brass hinges and fingered a bullet hole two inches from the opening.

Ivan interrupted his thoughts. He pointed to an old lady. 'This woman spotted an SS man at the window on the top floor.'

'She's sure?' Jock asked.

Ivan nodded. 'They have no weapons. They are too scared to go in.'

Flapper took a step back. 'It looks like it's up to us, then.' He ran at the door with his shoulder and the rotten wood frame splintered on impact. Flapper took another two running kicks at the door and eased himself through the gap he had made. Ivan and the rest followed.

'Here,' Ivan unclipped his holster and handed his Russian-made Nagant revolver to Horace. 'Be careful, comrade. I have a nasty feeling that the old lady may be right.'

The four men heard the noise at the same time.

'What was that?'

'Sounded like a child crying.'

The sound came from the basement. Flapper walked towards the door he'd just broken down. 'I'll guard the door, you three check it out.'

Horace handed the pistol to Flapper and they made their way down a darkened stairway that led to some sort of cellar. A door was slightly ajar and this time there was no mistaking the sound of a child. But she was not crying: the child was wailing, a girl's cry, screaming as if her life depended on it. When the three men reached the girl she cowered away. Her arms and legs were twisted at a grotesque angle. They were broken. Ivan knelt down and spoke in Czech. He talked slowly, he soothed the child, and after a few seconds she spoke. The girl groaned, raised her broken limb barely an inch and pointed to the corner. The tiny crumpled body of her small brother lay in a heap.

Jock rushed over. 'He's still alive – barely. He's unconscious. Jesus fucking Christ, his little arms and legs are snapped in two.' Jock fought back the tears. 'What sort of bastards could do this?'

Ivan spoke. 'The SS.'

The little girl spoke in her native tongue between the tears and through the pain barrier as Ivan listened and relayed her words to Horace and Jock.

'The girl and boy found an opening at the back of the store. It was a playground to them; they thought they were the only people that shared a secret. They played among the boxes and bounced on an old sofa to see who could jump the highest.'

Ivan put his hand over his eyes and shook his head.

'And then the SS came in two days ago.' He spoke through gritted teeth. 'They demanded money and maps and food and water and held onto the little girl while her brother ran home to fetch what he could.'

Ivan bit into his bottom lip, drawing a thin trickle of blood. He trembled with rage as he fought for dignity, trying so hard not to break down in front of the tiny child. 'The little boy brought back nothing. This... this... was their punishment.'

Still the little girl rambled on, almost delirious with pain. She spoke in a slur. Ivan fell back against the wall, his legs unable to support his weight.

'My God... oh, my God.'

'What is it?' Horace asked

'I don't believe it.'

'What?'

The little girl was pointing at some old tea chests.

Ivan spoke between the inevitable tears. 'One of the soldiers held each limb against the box while the other bastard snapped them like sticks in a forest.'

The three men stood speechless as the horror of the torture sank in. Horace couldn't quite contemplate the evil that had been dished out on two innocent children.

Ivan broke the silence. 'The little girl says they are still here.'

Jock Strain carried the little boy over to his sister and tried to reassure the girl – in an accent and a language she'd never heard before – that they were safe. She seemed to understand. Jock stayed with the children as Horace and Ivan climbed the stairs to where Flapper stood on guard. Horace relayed the story quickly as Flapper seethed with rage. Handing the pistol back to Horace, he took the stairs two at a time, such was his determination to root out these monsters masquerading as human beings.

They found them on the third floor, cowering behind some shelving. They held their hands up immediately and handed over their weapons. Horace inspected the Lugers. They were out of ammunition.

Flapper's self-control broke. He flew at the first SS officer, fists flailing, punching him around the head and body in an uncontrollable fit of rage. As the man fell to the floor he continued with his boot, screaming out obscenities. Horace gave him two minutes then dragged him away. Flapper stood panting, looking down at the bloodied mess moaning on the floor. Ivan walked over to Horace and held out a hand. He gave the pistol to the Russian. The German SS officer started crying and begging for mercy.

'*Bitte nein, Gnade! Erbarmen!*' – Please no, be merciful!

Ivan turned and walked slowly towards the other trembling officer. He stood for a few seconds, stared, then spat in his face. The German begged even harder as the spit hung from his eyebrow and nose. It shook and trembled in time with the movement of the petrified man's body.

'*Gott, nein... Gott, nein... bitte... bitte!*'

Ivan lowered the pistol and looked out from the third-floor window. He shouted something to the crowd below through a broken pane of glass and Horace watched as the people parted slightly. He walked over to the German again.

'Shoot the bastard!' shouted Flapper from the far side of the room.

Ivan raised the gun and squeezed the trigger.

The 7.62 bullet shattered the SS man's kneecap and he squealed like a stricken dog. Another bullet to the other knee and he collapsed in a hysterical heap, shouting and screaming for mercy.

Horace and Flapper then witnessed the impossible. Ivan Gregatov was a slightly built soldier, no more than five foot eight inches tall. The SS officer he'd just crippled once stood six feet tall and weighed at least twenty pounds more. But young Ivan found strength from his anger. He took hold of the crying man's throat and with one hand lifted him up against the back wall. The German's useless legs hung limply as he struggled for breath. The Russian's other hand sought the man's testicles and with a scream and a surge of adrenaline, he took the full body weight of the German and held him above his head for a second or two in a bizarre show of anger and strength. As he shuffled his feet, he turned towards the window and the pavement below. He took two unsteady short steps and propelled the whimpering German into the panes of glass. The man screamed for the two seconds it took him to hit the ground. He was barely conscious but still alive as the mob took over. In less than a minute they had kicked him to death.

A groan from the floor reminded the men that one SS officer still remained. The half-stunned German was unceremoniously kicked down every step from the third floor to the ground and into the street. There the children lay on makeshift wooden stretchers, attended by several women. A doctor injected the little boy's arm with a clear substance. He was conscious and even managed to raise a half-hearted smile as Jock stroked at his hair. Jock waved as the children were ushered quickly away.

Now the baying mob turned their attention to the SS man, who lay whimpering on the pavement. Jock and Horace,

Flapper and Ivan looked on as a rope was tied around the German's ankles. The other end was thrown over the street lamp and four or five men hauled him upwards as he swung like a pendulum, his terrified eyes scanning the crowd, awaiting the next move.

A can of petrol appeared and the German shouted and screamed, '*Nein... Nein!*'

But the proud can-holder took great pleasure in slowly pouring its contents onto the black Waffen SS uniform. The petrol poured into his face, stinging his eyes and burning his mouth. To prolong the agony and the torture just a little longer, the holder drew a ten-foot line of petrol across the ground and stood back with a satisfied grin. Then he reached into his pocket and struck a match as the German twisted and thrashed like a trout in a fishing net. He held the match up as it burned and after a few seconds he knelt to the ground.

As the flames exploded the crowd cheered and a few of the men kicked out at the head of the dying man. The cries and screams of the SS man would stay with Horace for many years to come and nightmares of the burning, swinging man would return night after night.

The men returned to the camp with barely a word spoken. Ivan mumbled something quietly in his native tongue. The next morning Horace found a barely legible note on his bed. It read simply, '*Я хуже чем они* ' – I am worse than them – and it was signed 'Ivan'.

Jock Strain found the young Russian hanging in the toilet block with an electric cord around his neck. He'd been dead for some time.

CHAPTER
TWENTY-SIX

Rose sat apprehensively on the train as it approached Karlovarsky, a small station 30 miles east of Prague. She pressed her face against the window to get a better view of the platform. The train slowed; she heard the screech of the brakes as they ground against the wheels. As the platform came into view the train gave a jerk and the sudden motion threw her forward. She sat back in her seat, picked her bag up from the carriage floor and looked out of the window again.

The station was a swarming mass of boisterous, menacing-looking troops. A small lorry sat on the platform, its rear tarpaulin rolled up to the bars of the roof. Two soldiers sat either side of a machine gun loaded with a belt of ammunition. It was pointed directly at the train. A small flagpole jutted out from the side of the truck. The red star of the Soviet Union fluttered on the early evening breeze.

CHAPTER
TWENTY-SEVEN

I t was another six long weeks before the men were told they were on their way home. In that time some had been moved to other camps in the city. Ernie Mountain had been one of them. Horace promised to look him up as soon as they got back to Ibstock.

The release order had been signed for the 1.5 million Soviet prisoners of war held by the Allies. Stalin in turn gave the order to hand over the remaining Allied prisoners to the Americans. The men were loaded onto Russian trucks and driven towards the outskirts of the city. They were heading to the Soviet US embarkation line, where they would be handed over and taken to a nearby airbase. Horace was the last man on the back of the tarpaulin-covered lorry. As they left the city limits on the main road to the west, Horace watched the elegant but battered skyline of Prague disappear into the distance.

The men were told to disembark and prepare for a march.

'Why the fuck can't they drive us there?' responded Jock. 'Haven't we walked enough lately?'

Horace was curious too as he looked up the long, straight road ahead. He was about to find out why the Russian truck was unable to make the 30-mile trip west. After a mile or two Horace noticed a line of Russian guns pointing south. He tapped Jock on the shoulder. 'Jesus, Jock, what do you think they're pointing at?'

Jock shrugged his shoulders. 'Fuck knows, Jim.'

T34 tanks sat alongside long-barrelled field guns and O34 tanks sat behind the 76mm guns and B35s that Horace recalled seeing on the road to Prague all those weeks ago. Each gun, each tank was daubed with the red star of Soviet Russia.

'I thought the fucking war was over,' laughed Jock.

'Never mind,' Horace replied, 'at least the buggers are on our side.'

Jock pointed to the opposite side of the road. 'Aye, and so are they.'

Horace's heart sank in fear. Two hundred yards in the distance another line of tanks and guns was facing in the opposite direction, pointing menacingly towards the Russians. Only this time there was no red star to be seen, only the silver star of the US. As they came nearer they could see GIs sitting on top of trucks, in jeeps, smoking, talking, and milling around with no real purpose other than to keep a very watchful eye on their Russian allies. The Russian troops were doing likewise.

By now every man on the march was aware of the two lines of heavy artillery and tanks, the full fire power of the Russian and American ground forces – every barrel, every rifle trained on each other. The most worrying aspect was that they were slap bang in the middle of the thin road that separated them. Mile after mile it seemed, gun upon gun, tank upon tank, full regiments of men on parade, troop carriers and jeeps – all accompanied by the constant sound of aircraft droning overhead. The men walked on slowly, unable to comprehend what was going on. It looked as if another war was about to break out.

Jock shook his head. 'Just ma fucking luck. World War Two finishes and here I am in the middle of fucking World War Three.'

'It could kick off at any minute, mate,' whispered Horace. 'I just can't figure it out.'

The two lines of weaponry and troops continued for the entire length of the road. The men walked in silence and those who believed in a God prayed. Eventually the massive show of strength petered out and the guns disappeared from view. Horace heard on the radio that evening that the prize they were considering fighting over was Germany. They were so close to another war; all it would have taken was one stray bullet, one itchy trigger finger or a loose mortar shell fired by accident and all hell would have broken loose.

Eventually the travel-weary, hungry men – some nursing yet more blisters – walked through the gates of the American air base just outside Karlovarsky. Within the hour they were showered and fed and had been issued with fresh British uniforms and clean underwear. Each man was given one hundred cigarettes, a bar of chocolate and two bottles of freezing cold American beer.

A source of amusement among the men was that German prisoners of war were working there as cleaners and cooks. Trust the Americans, thought Horace as a German in pale green fatigues picked up pieces of rubbish around the camp entrance. The Germans, of course, were only too pleased to be under the charge of the Americans when the Russians were just a few miles down the road.

As he drifted off to sleep in the dormitory of block number four on the western fringe of the American camp with a soft feather pillow under his head for the first time in five years, Horace dreamed of Rose and peace and green fields and home…

'Another bloody roll call!' Horace cursed as he left the mess tent with Flapper. 'Five fucking years we've had roll calls. Wouldn't you think these Yanks would give us a bloody break?'

'Take it easy, Jim. They might be telling us when we're going home.'

Horace stopped suddenly. 'Shit!'

'What is it, Jim?'

Horace threw a thumb over his shoulder and pointed back at the dormitories. 'I've left my bloody fags, haven't I? You go on ahead; I'll only be a minute.'

Flapper checked his watch. 'But Jim, they said we needed to be…'

'Calm down, Flapper. I've waited five years for freedom – surely they can wait five minutes for me?'

'Suit yourself. I'll tell them where you are if they call your name.'

Horace broke into a steady jog. He'd left his cigarettes under his pillow. It would only take a minute, and he'd probably catch Flapper up before he even made the roll call.

Horace walked through the door of the dormitory and couldn't quite believe his eyes. He wasn't the only man in the room as he'd expected. Everyone should have been at roll call but there was one other person in the dormitory. That one other man was a German prisoner of war, a captured soldier judging by his age and well fed appearance. As Horace looked on silently, the man put his hand under the pillow of Horace's bed and began stuffing his entire cigarette ration into the pockets of his uniform. Horace hadn't really lost his temper during his five years of captivity. He'd come close to it on a number of occasions and his self-control had probably saved his life. He'd remained controlled in the barbershop in Saubsdorf when the SS man had beaten him to a pulp. Not even when he'd challenged Willie McLachlan to the fight in Lamsdorf could he really say that he'd lost his temper.

But now as he watched a thief at work, a thief whose countrymen had killed and tortured and maimed and had tried everything to break the hearts and souls of his friends for five years, something just snapped. He thought of the break this man had been given, of the trust placed in him by the Americans, and the previous evening he'd watched the German prisoners in the mess tent as they ate the very same food from the very same table as them. As he watched the German creep silently to each bed, lifting each pillow in turn, Horace simmered and shook as the pressure cooker inside his head eventually exploded.

'You thieving bastard!' he bellowed at the top of his voice as he covered the short distance between the door and the bed the prisoner was rifling.

The German barely had time to register the movement as Horace's fist hit him squarely in the mouth. As the two men tumbled through the gap in the bunk Horace aimed punch after punch at the German's face and body. The startled man scrambled to his feet and made a desperate break for freedom, but Horace dived and caught the heel of his boot as he reached the door. Flipping him over, Horace powered another fist into his face, then bundled him through the door. The German lay face down in the dirt. Horace stood over him as he raised himself to his knees. He attempted to stand up straight but Horace hammered his boot into the seat of his pants. The terrified man sprawled back into the muck face first.

'Move, you fucking thief!'

It was a hundred yards to the American chief in command's

HQ and Horace repeated the exercise over and over again. He kicked the German every step of the way. By the time he reached the office of General Dirk Parker his right foot was aching but still he didn't relent. The general's door was slightly ajar; he was glad of the early evening breeze. Finally Horace allowed the German to stand up straight and made him stand to attention. As the bloodied man eased himself up, Horace hit him one last time and he flew through the door of the startled general's office.

As the groggy German groaned on the floor, General Parker took stock of the situation and noted the British uniform. 'Private, what is the meaning of this outrage? We are Americans, not Barbarians. We do not treat our prisoners in this way.'

Horace should have calmed down and explained the circumstances that brought him to the general's office. Instead, he hit the German again.

'Stop now, Private, or I'll have you on a goddamn charge. I won't have this violence brought into my office.'

Horace was breathing heavily now. 'He's the bastard you should be charging – he's a fucking thief.' He leaned over and reached into the prisoner's pockets, emptying handfuls of cigarettes onto the general's desk.

'Five years these cunts have battered and tortured and degraded me.' He kicked the prisoner again. This time the general made no attempt to stop him as Horace poured his heart out. 'The bastards treated us worse than rabid dogs; they killed and tortured my pals and when we win the war they run from the Russians as fast as their legs will carry them.' Horace hauled the prisoner from the floor by the collar. 'We treat them well, feed and clothe them and allow them their dignity – the same dignity they tore from a million prisoners' hearts.' He looked into the bloodied swollen eyes of the German, who averted his gaze. 'And this... *this* is how they repay us.' He reached into the German's breast pocket and pulled out yet another full pack of American-issue cigarettes.

General Dirk Parker sank slowly into his chair. Horace released his grip on the prisoner, who crumpled into a heap on the ground.

Horace's composure returned in an instant. He had exercised his demons at last. It had taken no more than four minutes to rid himself of the bitterness of five years, but he felt calm and relaxed. He stood to attention and saluted the general. 'My apologies, sir. I lost my temper.'

The General made a quick phone call and two burly black GIs burst through the office door. The dazed German was dragged unceremoniously through the opening.

'Take a seat, Private...'

'Greasley, Sir.'

'Private Greasley.'

General Parker reached behind him and pulled a bottle of Kentucky Bourbon from his drinks cabinet and two glasses.

'I can assure you, Private Greasley, that the ungrateful German thief will be dealt with most severely.'

'Thank you, sir.'

'Meanwhile will you join me in a small token of my appreciation in apprehending this criminal?'

'Certainly, sir, don't mind if I do.'

As the whiskey hit the back of Horace's throat his mind went back to Ibstock, to Pretoria Road and those special Christmas mornings. The taste of whisky would always remind Horace of Christmas mornings, of birthdays and open log fires. He drained the glass in two large gulps and slid the glass forward as his eyes pleaded for a refill.

General Parker complied with his wishes and filled the glass.

Horace allowed himself the luxury of dreaming of the future as he drifted away on the effects of the strong alcohol. He wondered if it was too much to ask, too much to dream that the next Christmas Day would be spent with the woman he loved.

Freddie Rogers and Dave Crump left at dawn the next day, 2 July, and Flapper Garwood and Jock Strain the day after. There were emotional goodbyes. Horace loved every one of them like a brother. They'd stuck together through thick and thin and the hell of a war that nobody wanted. As Horace lay on his bunk he thought of the men who hadn't made it. Although he'd spent five years undergoing every torturous emotion a man could handle, he reminded himself that he was one of the lucky ones. He, Jimmy White and Sergeant Major Harris dozed on their bunks in the empty dormitory. There was nothing else to do.

Suddenly the door opened and Jimmy White was told to report to the airstrip on the far side of the camp within 20 minutes. It was as quick as that. The goodbyes were even quicker as neither man wanted to linger in the past. Now it was time for the future. What they had achieved between them was simply monumental. Strangely, none of them even mentioned it.

Two hours later Sergeant Major Harris and Horace received their instructions too. They were flying to RAF Royston in Hertfordshire. From there they would be sent on a train to their nearest home town stations.

The Dakota had been crudely redesigned and altered to accommodate 30 troops. Fifteen strangers sat on either side of the plane, a loose rope resting on their laps, the only thing that resembled any sort of safety belt. It was all rather nerve-wracking for Horace, as it was the first time he'd ever set foot on a plane. Sergeant Major Harris sat opposite, but the noise of the two Pratt & Whitney radial piston engines drowned out any meaningful conversation.

An hour and 20 minutes into the flight the pilot's voice crackled through the intercom. His voice could just be heard. He informed the passengers they were approaching English soil and a spontaneous yet muted round of applause broke out among the men.

'And now,' announced the captain, 'the white cliffs of Dover.'

The plane went into a steep dive as the engines seemed to lose power. Horace was aware of his last meal pressing at the top of his stomach. The Dakota levelled out and they heard the pilot's voice once more.

'Here goes.'

With a grinding sound and a chunky clunk the huge bomb doors in the bottom of the plane simply fell open. There was nothing between Horace and the white cliffs of Dover but a hundred feet of fresh air. Horace clung to the thin piece of rope for dear life. It was a nice gesture and a great view of the chalky deposits of the southern coast of England. But on reflection, Horace would have preferred to focus on the balding pate of Sergeant Major Harris.

The plane touched down at Royston aerodrome just before nightfall. The men underwent a 50-minute welcome speech from one of the officers, who filled them in on all the latest developments of the war and in particular, the momentous Victory in Europe day. They were billeted for the evening, given as much free beer as they could drink, and sent to bed after a fish and chip supper.

At noon the next day a convoy of Land Rovers took them to the train station at Stevenage and eventually, after more bureaucracy and roll calls, the men were placed on trains to

Northampton and Coventry, Ipswich and Oxford, Birmingham and yes, Leicester.

Leicester station hadn't changed. Miraculously, it seemed to have escaped the Luftwaffe bombs. Horace was the only man to alight there. He stopped on the platform and took in the ambience of the station. Holding his head high, he breathed in the air of Leicestershire as a solitary tear trickled down his cheek.

The civilian sent to collect Horace didn't have a difficult job to spot him.

'Are you Joseph Greasley?'

Horace nearly said no – he hadn't heard that name since it at had been used in the recruitment office in King's Street.

'Jim... er, Horace Greasley.'

The civilian looked down at his clipboard. 'It says Joseph here.'

'It's Horace.'

The man looked up and smiled. 'Horace it is, then.' He held out a hand by way of a greeting and Horace reached out and took it.

'Horace. I'm Bert, and I've come to take you home.'

CHAPTER
TWENTY-EIGHT

I t had been a long day: the long wait at Stevenage station and the stop-start, never-ending journey up to Leicester on the train. By the time the car pulled into Pretoria Road it was dark.

Mum and Dad, Sybil and Daisy just sat and stared. They stared at Horace for an eternity, just glad to have him back. He was thinner than when he'd left for France, maybe three or four stones thinner, but that was to be expected. The prisoner of war camps were never mentioned that evening, as if the family sensed the returning prisoner would talk in his own good time. Horace climbed the stairs to look at baby Derick in his bed. Baby Derick was now a seven-year-old boy and even though Horace stroked his hair, he slept on.

Back in the kitchen they talked about the war and the future and work and the farm, and they talked about Harold who was still in Africa tending the sick and wounded. He'd been made a sergeant, his mother announced. He had done really well in his role as a medic, and the higher rate of pay she received from the War Office had been more than welcome. He was due back home any time. He had applied for compassionate leave when he'd heard Horace was on his way home and it had been granted by the Regimental Sergeant Major. Good old Harold, thought Horace. Despite the war he had done really well for himself.

They talked. They talked and Horace listened.

He decided to wait until the morning to tell his parents about the girl who had helped him make it through the war.

'She's still a bloody German, Horace!' his father bellowed as they sat at the breakfast table. His mother sat with a white linen handkerchief and dabbed at the tears rolling freely down her cheeks.

The day had started so well. A cup of tea with a drop of whisky in it. Dad's way. Then bacon and eggs and hot buttered toast. Horace had told them all about the young German girl and about the food she'd supplied and the radio parts too. He said she was a heroine and if it hadn't been for Rose he doubted whether he would have made it back in one piece. The family had sat and listened. He'd been convinced his parents would understand. Why did he have to tell them he'd fallen in love with her? Why did he have to tell them he wanted to start a new life with her?

Still his father ranted on. 'The bastards have stolen five years of my sons' lives and bombed the hell out of our country and you take up with one of them.'

Horace wanted to tell his parents more, that she wasn't a German, she was a Silesian. But he didn't have the energy. The last thing he wanted to do was argue with his family on the first morning he'd taken breakfast with them for five years.

Father wasn't finished. He went on to say that if ever Horace brought that Hun back to Ibstock, his son would be out in the street with a suitcase looking for a new place to live.

Horace was shattered. But strangely enough, he understood.

His mother woke him just after 7.30. The warm summer sun

had filtered through the thin cotton curtains and already the east-facing bedroom was hot. 'There's a cup of tea in the pot, Horace. You might want to take a look at this before you come downstairs.' His mother handed him the letter. 'Dad doesn't know it's here. Best if we keep it our little secret.'

Dear Jim

I made it. I just hope that you did too and that it is your handsome eyes reading this letter and no one else. My journey was not without danger and some day I might find the courage to tell you about it.

I am tired but alive and I made it through to the Americans who have treated us well. I was picked up in Czechoslovakia and taken to Germany by truck. I am living in an American air base in a small dormitory with five German ladies. I have been here one week now and yesterday I was given some writing paper and told I could send a letter to my family. The American man in the posting office thought it strange that a German girl was writing to an Englishman. I told him I was a Silesian not a German.

It is strange, I have so much to tell you but when my pen touches the paper the words will not come. I want to tell you so much, so many things that are important to me – important to us both. Perhaps I will find the courage next time.

My feelings for you are as strong as ever, I believe you English have a saying that absence makes the heart even fonder. This I can now understand.

I will close now.

I love you more than ever. Please write back and tell me the same.

Your English Rose.

At the bottom of the letter was written the address of an American airbase near Leipzig, together with a seven-digit number. Horace's reply was in the postbox at the end of Pretoria Road by noon. He had to wait an agonising three weeks before the next letter arrived. The postman came between 6.30 and 7.00 each morning, seven days a week. Horace was always at the garden gate to greet him.

My Darling Jim
My heart is bursting with pleasure and relief. I am so happy to have received your letter and your words made me cry with joy.

I swear I am the happiest girl in the whole of the world and cannot wait to begin our life together. I understand why we cannot live in England. Germany too is in a mess with soldiers of many nations everywhere. On our way to the American camp we travelled through Berlin. The city is in ruins and it seems that the Russians have taken their revenge on many people, I do not like the Russians, Jim, and I feel it will be many years before it will be safe again. I will write for more information on New Zealand. We must be patient as travel at the moment is still impossible. Perhaps in a few months things may return to normal and we can meet once again, though it matters not, I will wait forever. I am writing this from my bed at the moment as I have been a little ill this week. I do not know what is wrong with me but I feel a little better today. Perhaps tomorrow I will get up and take some fresh air.

I miss you more than you can imagine. As always I send you much love.
Rose.

Two weeks later a different letter arrived, this time from the War Office in London. Horace was asked if he could confirm that a certain Rosa Rauchbach, a Silesian citizen, had helped the prisoners in the camps by supplying food and radio parts as she was claiming. Horace was only too happy to write back and tell the War Office that it was all true.

Four weeks later another letter from Leipzig arrived. Rose was ecstatic. The War Office in London had replied to the Americans' request and stated that Private J H Greasley of the 2nd/5th Battalion Leicesters had confirmed that her extraordinary tales of assisting the Allied prisoners in Poland were true. Rose had been rewarded with a well-paid job on an American airbase near Hamburg.

By this time Horace had opened his own barber's shop with the money his parents had put away during the war. The money was rolling in; between the two of them they were saving nearly ten pounds each week. Nothing could now stand in the way of their plans to emigrate to New Zealand.

Rose and Horace corresponded right up to Christmas 1945. And then the letters from Rose stopped. Horace sent more than a dozen letters to the airbase in north-eastern Germany, but they were never answered. He tried and failed to get to the airbase in Germany. He was told again and again that civilian trains and aeroplanes were not yet up and running so soon after the war. In desperation he even hitchhiked to Dover and stood for three days begging to be let aboard one of the few boats and ships making their way across the English Channel. In the end he was forcibly removed from the port under threat of arrest and had to make his way back to Leicester the same way he'd come. It had all been to no avail.

EPILOGUE

In December 1946 Horace received an envelope postmarked Hamburg, Germany. His hands trembled as he slid a kitchen knife under the flap and slit it open. But even before he noticed the unfamiliar style of the handwriting, something in his heart told him it was not from Rose. The letter was brief and to the point. There was no return address.

Dear Mr Greasley,

I regret to inform you that my dear friend Rosa Rauchbach passed away in December of 1945, nearly a year to the day of writing this letter. Rosa died two hours after childbirth, and her baby boy, who she named Jakub, died soon after. I received a box containing Rosa's personal possessions two months ago in which I found some of your letters.

I could not help but read them, please forgive me for intruding into your privacy but it was clear you loved her a great deal. I realise that the news of her death and that of her son must come as a great shock. I am sorry that I have had to be the one to break the tragic news.

Margit Rosch

It had been a year since Horace had received anything from Rose. He thought the time that had elapsed would have lessened the pain a little. It hadn't. There were so many unanswered questions. He thought about the last time they'd made love, the last time he'd gazed into her eyes and the last time he'd held her close. He thought about New Zealand and their plans and the irony of making it through five years of hell, of the dangers they'd faced day in day out, and then this...

He read the letter again and again until eventually a tear fell onto the parchment, causing the ink to run a little. He wiped at his eyes with the cuff of his sleeve, stood and took one last look at the letter before casting it into the open fire. It was over. Closure. Rose was gone forever. As he opened the door and walked outside, he fought against every emotion in his body. He would remain calm, dignified. He would rebuild his life with the same determination he'd shown each and every day for six years. Even now, even after this. As he turned and headed towards the open farm land, the thought that filled his head was this: Jakub... where the hell did she get that name from?

Silesian first names: Jakub (Jacob, James – Jim)